A Taste from the Past

GOOD OLD FOOD

*IRENA CHALMERS
AND FRIENDS*

A percentage of the royalties from this book
is being donated to benefit Meals on Wheels,
an organization that brings hot meals to
elderly people who are homebound.

BARRON'S
New York • London • Toronto • Sydney

Acknowledgments

I am humbled and delighted by the generosity with which many loved friends shared their treasured recipes and their wonderfully evocative memories, and thank them with all my heart.

STAFF

Managing Editor: Mary Goodbody
Assistant Editor: Mary Dauman
Copy Editors: Margaret Trejo; Maurice Goodbody III; Kathy Knapp
Contributors: Leticia Alexander; Pamela Anderson; Anna Brandenburger; Mary Dauman; Melanie Falick; Leopold Froehlich; Cathy Garvey; Gaynor Grant; Mindy Heifferling; Betsy Jordan; Kathy Knapp; Pamela Mitchell; Lisa Napell; Jane Stacey; Margaret Trejo; Suzanne Waugh; Elizabeth Wheeler

CREDITS

James II Galleries, New York:	China
Pratesi, New York:	Linen
Baccarat, New York:	Crystal
Buccelati, New York:	Silver

Cameo from the painting TEA LEAVES by William Paxton

Photographer:	Matthew Klein
Designer:	Milton Glaser, Inc.
Prop stylists:	Julie Gong, Linda Cheverton
Food stylists:	Ann Disrude

Photos courtesy of: American Heritage Magazine, The Bettmann Archive, Culver Pictures, Inc., De Wys Inc., Free Lance Photographers Guild, H. Armstrong Roberts, New York Historical Society, State Historical Society of Wisconsin.

All inquiries should be addressed to:
Barron's Educational Series, Inc.
250 Wireless Blvd.
Hauppauge, New York 11788

Library of Congress Catalog Card No. 88-3473
International Standard Book No. 0-8120-5841-0

Library of Congress Cataloging-in-Publication Data

Chalmers, Irena.
  Good Old Food

  Includes Index
    1. Cookery, International. I. Title.
TX725.A1C48 1988   641.5   88-3473
ISBN 0-8120-5841-0

PRINTED IN THE UNITED STATES OF AMERICA

890 880 98765432

≋ TABLE OF CONTENTS ≋

≋ INTRODUCTION ≋

Food memories are gloriously evocative. In our mind's eye, we conjure up our own time-enhanced reminiscences of our grandmothers' kitchens in a place and time when the spring was eternally greener, the summer sun shone more brightly, the autumn was golden and abundant and the soft snow was as white as the linen on the table. How well we remember the foods of our childhood, the freshness of the just picked vegetables, the smell of the newly dug, tiny potatoes, and the sweetness of the fruits gathered in the fullness of their time. Whether we yearn for clam chowder or chlodnick, egg drop soup, moussaka or manicotti, we all share the same early awakening to the joys of eating at a shared family table.

We eat very differently today. Instead of selecting only what is locally grown and harvested in its appointed season, we bring to our tables dishes from a dozen or more countries. We think nothing of offering the foods of three or four or more nations at a single meal. In our current quest for originality, we are borrowing Chinese, Thai and Japanese techniques and using them to reinterpret the dishes of France, Italy, and Mexico.

For those of us who cook at home, there is an enduring pleasure and comfort in preparing the food that is familiar to us. We go on loving the same music no matter how often we hear it. We go on loving the same food no matter how often we eat it. Indeed, the repetition is part of the joy of renewal.

The hallowing of tradition is seen perhaps most clearly in our food heritage. Every time we prepare and share the food of our immigrant inheritance, we forge a strong link both with our ancestral past and with future generations. For some, this may be a long-simmered sauerbraten while for others the casserole becomes carbonnade Flamande, a pot roast or an Irish stew. A once-a-year feast for one culture must include tsouriki, the traditional Greek Easter bread, while for those who grew up in another country it will be lebkuchen, rogelach or mincemeat pie. Almost everything around us has changed since our grandparents' day, but the soups and stews, the roasts and the abundance of each season, and of the food associated with national and religious holidays have remained the same in reality as in memory.

Our pleasure, as we re-create our grandparents' food, is just one part of the melody and harmony of long-ago meals. We can recall the vitality of their kitchens, the sounds, the smells, the bustle of relatives and friends, the excitement of all the dishes being brought from the kitchen to the dining table, the gathering together for Sunday lunch, or to celebrate a birth or birthday.

The recipes in this book have been carefully chosen to reflect the foods of many cultures that have joined together to make an even larger family than our own. Each preparation has been meticulously tested so that you will be able to confidently re-create the foods of your own country and of many others too.

The gathering of the reminiscences, so generously shared by friends everywhere, brought me great pleasure and I hope they will evoke many memories of your own.

Irena Chalmers
New York July 1988

SOUPS AND FIRST COURSES

≋ CLAM CHOWDER ≋

Serves 6

36 *chowder clams or 3 10-ounce cans minced clams*
1 *tablespoon oil*
3 *slices bacon, cut into small pieces*
1 *medium-size onion, finely chopped*
2 *cups milk*
2 *cups half-and-half*
3 *cups diced, peeled potatoes*
2 *tablespoons butter*
1/2 *teaspoon salt*
freshly ground black pepper

Scrub the fresh clams with a stiff brush and soak them in at least 3 changes of cold water to remove all traces of sand. Put the clams in a saucepan holding 1 inch of boiling water and steam them, covered, over high heat for a few minutes until the shells open. Strain the liquid through several layers of cheesecloth and set it aside. Pull or cut the clams from their shells, remove the necks if necessary, and cut the clam bellies into small pieces.

Heat the oil in a deep 4-quart pot. Cook the bacon until golden brown but not crisp. Remove the bacon with a slotted spoon and drain on paper towels.

Pour all but 1 tablespoon of fat from the pot. Add the onion and cook over moderate heat for 4 to 5 minutes, until softened but not browned. Add the reserved clam liquid or the liquid from the cans, if you are using canned clams), the milk, half-and-half, potatoes, and butter to the pot. Bring to the boil and simmer for 10 to 12 minutes until the potatoes are tender.

Add the clams and season the soup to taste with salt and pepper. Cook just until the clams are heated through, but do not allow the soup to boil or the clams will be tough. Check seasoning and serve immediately.

*"My grandparents had a house on the Oregon coast. It was a lovely old adventure of rising at the crack of dawn to go clamming with my grandfather. We would set out with our boots, pails and shovels and I would promise to dig so fast that not one clam would get away. I learned how to touch the sand with my toe to see how it reacted, or how to spot those little holes that might betray a temporarily lazy clam. My grandfather always encouraged me to have a go at the clam and I would dig furiously as the clam burrowed desperately, trying to escape— usually in vain. Triumphant and tired, we would trudge back with our spoils. I wasn't obliged to do the dirty work of cleaning the clams, but I did get to stir my grandmother's big pot set on the stove filled with clams and the other necessary ingredients to make a chowder I'll never forget."—
Susy Davidson,
Portland, Oregon*

 # GUMBO

Serves 6

½- to 3-pound chicken, cut up
Salt and freshly ground black pepper
¾ cup all-purpose flour
6 tablespoons vegetable oil
1 pound okra, chopped
2 onions, chopped
2 large carrots, chopped
2 cloves garlic, crushed
4 tablespoons shortening, bacon drippings or oil
3 quarts (12 cups) chicken broth
Tabasco sauce, to taste
1 pound medium-size shrimp, peeled and deveined
1 cup shucked fresh oysters

Rub the chicken pieces generously with salt and pepper and dredge with 1/2 cup of the flour. Heat the oil in a large heavy skillet and cook the chicken for about 10 minutes, turning the pieces so that they brown on all sides. Remove the chicken and set aside.

Add the okra, onions, carrots and garlic to the skillet and cook over medium-high heat for about 5 minutes, stirring, until the onion is softened and translucent. Remove the vegetables from the heat and set aside until ready to add to the soup.

Put the shortening or oil in a deep heavy pan and heat over moderate heat. Reduce the heat to medium-low, add the remaining 4 tablespoons of flour and cook for about 20 minutes to make a roux, stirring, until the flour turns dark brown. Be sure not to let the roux burn.

Add the chicken pieces and the vegetables to the roux and gradually stir in the chicken broth. Season with salt, pepper and Tabasco to taste. Bring to the boil, reduce the heat to low and simmer for 1 hour, skimming off any fat from the surface.

Take the chicken pieces from the gumbo, discard the bones and cut the chicken meat into smallish pieces. Return these to the pot, add the shrimp and simmer for 10 minutes. Add the oysters and simmer for another 5 minutes. Serve the gumbo in heated bowls over steamed or boiled rice.

*"I grew up right down the street from where I live today in New Orleans. In those days we didn't have gas and so most of the cooking was done in a big old iron pot set on a charcoal furnace in the yard. My mother made gumbo with shrimp, crab and oysters. Just those three ingredients. We have the best oysters in the world here, nice and salty. Some folks add chicken to the gumbo, too. In those days you cooked with what you had. Nothing else. And it was all so delicious."—
Audrey Baquet, New Orleans, Louisiana*

≋ Nanny's Turkey ≋ Soup

Serves 6

10 pounds leftover turkey bones
(from a turkey that was not overcooked)
4 large onions, coarsely chopped
3 stalks celery, coarsely chopped
3 large carrots, coarsely chopped
1 teaspoon dried thyme
4 bay leaves
2 handfuls parsley stems
2 teaspoons white peppercorns
2 cups diced celery
2 cups diced carrots
2 cups diced onion
1 cup uncooked white rice or 2 cups short fettucini
2 tablespoons chopped parsley
Salt and freshly ground white pepper

Put the bones in a heavy stock pot, large enough to hold all the ingredients. Cover the bones with water and bring to a simmer, skimming off the foam.

Put the the coarsely chopped onions, celery and carrots in a saucepan and and cook over moderate heat, stirring, for 5 minutes. Add the thyme, bay leaves, parsley stems and white peppercorns and cook for another 10 minutes. Add the vegetables to the turkey bones, scraping any leftover juices from the bottom of the pan.

Simmer the soup for 3 hours. Taste for flavor. If it needs more flavor, cook for 30 minutes more. If not, strain the soup into a clean saucepan. Skim the fat from the top and add the diced vegetables. Bring the soup back to a simmer and add the rice. If you are adding pasta, wait until the vegetables are cooked. When the rice or pasta are cooked, add the parsley and salt and pepper to taste.

"My family still likes to tell the story of how my grandmother's turkey soup rose like a phoenix from leftover holiday bones. Whenever she made it, it had that terrific homemade pizzazz and I recall one year in particular when my grandmother, who was then 80, 'reminded' my father for several weeks straight to 'bring home some bones' from the restaurant we operated in Chicago. When he finally brought about 10 gallons of bones home, my grandmother set about making soup. All day she simmered the pot of bones and water on the stove, adding peeled carrots, celery and onions. The fragrances of thyme, parsley, bay leaves and peppercorns floated through the kitchen and anyone who passed the stove during the day was asked to spoon a little liquid out so that Nanny could check on the quality. After hours of family vigil, one spoon finally produced the desired result. None of

Tomato Soup

Serves 4

1 tablespoon butter
1 onion, coarsely chopped
1 stalk celery, coarsely chopped
1 clove garlic, finely chopped
2 tablespoons tomato paste
1½ pounds (about 4 medium-size)
   fresh tomatoes, peeled and coarsely chopped
1 quart (4 cups) chicken broth
1 tablespoon fresh thyme leaves, chopped, or 1 teaspoon dried
Salt and pepper
Croutons:
3 tablespoons butter
8 thick slices French bread

Heat the butter in a large saucepan over moderate heat. Add the onion, celery and garlic and cook for about 5 minutes, until softened. Stir in the tomato paste. Add the tomatoes, chicken broth and thyme, and season with salt and pepper to taste.

Increase the heat to high and bring the mixture to the boil. Lower the temperature and simmer until the vegetables are tender and the flavors are blended, about 20 minutes.

Pour the soup into a food processor or blender and process until pureed. If using a blender, you will have to puree the soup in several batches. Strain the puree through a sieve to remove the tomato seeds, then return the soup to the saucepan and keep it warm while you make the croutons.

Heat the oven to 425 degrees.

Heat the butter in a small pan and brush it on both sides of the bread slices. Arrange these on a baking tray and bake until golden brown, about 6 minutes. Serve immediately with the hot soup, either on the side or floating on the surface.

us could figure out what the big deal about the soup was, until years later, after we had sampled other recipes. Nanny was very proud of her turkey soup— and rightly so." — Michael Foley, Chicago, Illinois

"One summer during the War when my father was still overseas, I remember being sent to my great aunt's place in Manchester, Vermont, for a few weeks. She had the biggest vegetable garden I had ever seen and I recall one rainy summer afternoon helping her peel tomatoes so she could make soup for supper that night. I particularly remember this for two reasons. One, it was the best tomato soup I have ever tasted, and two, I remember how much fun I had picking the tomatoes in the rain— barefoot and completely soaked through." — Amy Ayers, Harrisburg, Pennsylvania

FRENCH ONION SOUP

Serves 6

6 tablespoons butter
8 medium-size onions, sliced (about 8 cups)
8 cups beef broth
¼ cup Madeira (optional)
Salt and freshly ground black pepper
Long loaf French bread, sliced into 24 ½-inch-thick rounds
1½ cups grated Gruyère cheese

Heat the butter in a large saucepan over medium-low heat, add the onions and stir to coat them with the butter. Reduce the heat to low and cook gently for 30 minutes until the onions are soft, stirring occasionally.

Increase the heat to high and cook the onions for about 5 minutes, stirring continuously, to brown them. Add the broth and the Madeira, if you are using it, and season to taste with salt and pepper. Cover and simmer very slowly for 30 minutes, or even longer. (The longer it cooks, the greater becomes the depth of flavor; keep checking, though, to make sure the broth is not disappearing.) Meanwhile, lightly toast the bread slices.

Heat the broiler until very hot. Pour the soup into a large tureen or individual soup bowls. Float the toasted bread slices on the surface and top them with the grated cheese. Broil until the cheese has melted and is lightly browned. Serve immediately.

If your broiler is not deep enough to hold the tureen or soup bowls, you can use a very hot oven to melt the cheese, but watch carefully to prevent burning.

I have almost always seen it called "French" on menus, but I know very well that onion soup is familiar in a dozen languages and at home on the tables of rich, poor and in-between on six continents. It can vary, depending on the quality of the ingredients and the amount of devotion to the enterprise. Those who are true disciples will start with a serious soup bone and simmer it into a profound stock, before even starting to make the soup. After the broth becomes worthy, you will need the sweetest of butter for the onions, the finest cheeses to grate over the top and, of course, the French bread must have been baked by a master baker to achieve the right balance between the smoothness of bubbling, browning cheese and the crispness of the crust of the bread and the rich mellowness of the broth. Quite a simple soup really.

WHITE BEAN SOUP

Serves 4 to 6

1 pound dried navy beans or Great Northern beans
1 tablespoon vegetable oil
2 medium-size carrots, coarsely chopped
1 medium-size onion, chopped
3 cloves garlic, finely chopped
2 tablespoons chopped parsley
1 meaty lamb bone (about 2 pounds)
2 bay leaves
5 cups water
Salt and freshly ground black pepper

Rinse the beans and pick them over, discarding any pebbles or imperfect beans. Put the beans in a large pot and add enough cold water to cover. Let the beans soak overnight or for 8 hours. Drain the beans and rinse them.

Heat the oil in a large soup pot and add the carrots and onion. Cook for about 5 minutes until the onion softens. Add the garlic, parsley, lamb bone, bay leaves, beans and water. Season with salt and pepper. Cook over high heat until boiling. Reduce the heat and skim off any fat that rises to the surface.

Gently simmer the soup, partially covered, for 2 to 2 1/2 hours, until the beans are tender. Lift the lamb bone from the soup, cut off any meat into chunks and return the meat to the pot. Discard the bay leaves, adjust the seasoning and serve.

"If the Senate could have its version of navy bean soup, so could our family. That's what my dad always said when we'd sit down to a supper of this hearty soup. As a kid, I'd groan and roll my eyes when he'd say it. Now, it's one of my fondest memories of him.

"Mom made the soup from roast bone left from Sunday dinner. Often it would be lamb because we were all very partial to roast lamb. I love the richness of it and I didn't know that some people didn't like lamb until I left home. I'd never had it overcooked and ruined like so many people do. Mother just knew how to cook it. In fact, she knew how to cook the simple things and make them taste like thay were from the finest of chefs. Her instinct for seasoning was uncanny. It made eating at home a constant treat and surprise."— Kassie Belford, St. Louis, Missouri

DUTCH GREEN PEA SOUP

Serves 6

2 tablespoons butter
½ cup coarsely chopped onion
1 small clove garlic, finely chopped
1 ¾ cups quick-cooking split green peas
6 cups water
2-pound cooked ham shank, bone in
2 tablespoons finely chopped parsley
1 bay leaf
½ teaspoon sugar
Salt and freshly ground black pepper
1½ cups chicken broth

I once had the real thing; pea soup in Holland, on a small boat, on a terribly cold day. Pea soup is as Dutch as anything could be. It completes the landscape in the mysterious way some things do when you taste them on their native soil and it's as though you are having something entirely new.

Look closely next time you are standing in front of one of those splendid 17th-century Dutch paintings. Behind a pillar in a dark, gloomy church, in a small farmhouse beneath lowering clouds and windswept trees, on the table set before rollicking, rosy-cheeked peasants, you will sense the tantalizing nearby presence of a caldron of rich pea soup.

Heat the butter in a large pot over moderate heat. Add the onion and garlic and cook for about 5 minutes, stirring occasionally, until softened and translucent. Add the split peas to the pot and cook, stirring, for 5 minutes.

Pour the water into the pot. Add the ham shank, herbs, sugar, salt and pepper to taste, and the chicken broth. Raise the heat and bring to the boil. Reduce the heat to low, cover the soup and simmer for 2 hours.

Remove the ham shank from the soup. Cut the meat from the bone and discard the bone. Chop the meat into small pieces and reserve. Remove and discard the bay leaf.

Pour the soup into the blender and process until smooth. (You will have to do this in several batches.) Return the soup to the pot, add the reserved ham meat and heat through before serving.

Pasta e Fagioli

Serves 6

2 cups dried navy beans
¼ cup olive oil
¼ pound pancetta, chopped
2 cloves garlic, crushed
1 large onion, chopped
2 cups beef broth
2 teaspoons salt
Freshly ground black pepper
1½ cups canned Italian plum tomatoes, pureed
1 tablespoon tomato paste
2 cups tubettini or other short pasta
3 tablespoons finely chopped parsley

Rinse the beans and pick them over, discarding any pebbles or imperfect beans. Put the beans in a large pan, cover with cold water and soak overnight or for 8 hours.

Heat the oil in a small skillet. Add the pancetta and cook for about 3 minutes. Add the garlic and onion and cook over moderate heat until the onion is softened but not browned.

Drain the beans and return them to the pan. Add the beef broth and enough cold water to cover the beans. Bring to the boil. Add the pancetta-onion mixture. Cover the pan and simmer over low heat for 1 hour.

Add the salt, pepper, pureed tomatoes and tomato paste to the pan. Simmer, covered, for about 45 minutes or until the beans are tender. If the soup becomes too thick during the cooking time, add more water.

Just before the end of the cooking time, cook the pasta in boiling salted water until it is al dente. Drain well and add to the soup just before serving. Stir in the chopped parsley and check the seasoning.

"I've always thought it was lovely how certain ultra-humble foods can mean so much more, and have so much richer associations, than the luxury items we get accustomed to in this prosperous country. When my parents emigrated to America from Calabria in 1935, they were as poor as could be, and my mother often reminisces about trying to make ends meet during those first hard years in Chicago. Pasta e Fagioli was a staple on my folks' table then, and even after they became successful my mother served the dish often as a reminder of our 'roots.' Today I'd rather eat pasta and beans than any of those nuova cucina pastas that taste great, but that have no sentimental attachments for me."— Nick Clemente, Staten Island, New York

ITALIAN MINESTRONE

Serves 6 to 8

1 cup dried white navy beans
4 tablespoons olive oil
1 cup coarsely chopped onion
1 large clove garlic, finely chopped
10 cups chicken broth
2 tablespoons tomato paste
1½ cups coarsely shredded cabbage
4 ripe medium-size tomatoes, peeled, seeded and chopped
1 tablespoon fresh oregano leaves or ½ teaspoon dried
Small handful of fresh basil leaves, chopped, or ½ teaspoon dried
Salt and freshly ground black pepper
2 carrots, thinly sliced
1 cup broken uncooked vermicelli
2 small zucchini, thinly sliced
½ cup freshly grated Parmesan cheese

Put the navy beans in a bowl, cover with boiling water and allow to rest for 1 hour. Drain the beans.

Heat the olive oil in an 8-quart pan. Add the onion and garlic and cook over moderate heat until golden. Add the drained beans and the chicken broth, cover the pan and simmer for about an hour, or even a little longer, until the beans are tender.

Add a few tablespoons of the hot broth to the tomato paste, stirring until the paste has dissolved, then add the mixture to the pot along with the cabbage, tomatoes, herbs and salt and pepper to taste. Simmer for 15 minutes.

Add the carrots and vermicelli and simmer for another 15 minutes. Check the seasoning. Add the zucchini and simmer for barely 5 minutes. Serve immediately, passing the grated Parmesan separately.

GAZPACHO

Serves 6

8 plum tomatoes, coarsely chopped (about 3 cups)
2 green peppers, coarsely chopped (about 2 cups)
2 red peppers, coarsely chopped (about 2 cups)
2 cucumbers, peeled, seeded and coarsely chopped (about 3 cups)
2 medium-size red onions, coarsely chopped (about 2 cups)
2 cloves garlic, finely chopped
⅓ cup olive oil
2 tablespoons lemon juice
2 tablespoons white vinegar
4 cups tomato juice
1 to 2 teaspoons Tabasco sauce
1 tablespoon Worcestershire sauce
½ teaspoon salt
½ teaspoon pepper

  Put half the chopped tomatoes in a food processor and pulse 6 times, for 3 seconds at a time, until the tomatoes have released their juice and are finely chopped but not pureed. Transfer them to a large mixing bowl and repeat the procedure with the remaining tomatoes.

  Process the green and red peppers, the cucumbers and the onions in the same way, transferring each batch to the mixing bowl before processing the next. Add the garlic to the bowl and mix well.

  Stir in the oil, lemon juice, vinegar and tomato juice. Add the Tabasco, Worcestershire sauce, salt and pepper. Stir well and check the seasoning. Refrigerate and let the soup mellow for at least 2 hours before serving.

"Every few years I pay a visit to my Aunt Ines and Uncle Roberto, who live in Andalucia, that beautiful southern corner of Spain. Between visits, I think often and longingly of the region's white stucco houses, small and ancient, surrounded by a rainbow of carnations… of rising very early in the morning and drinking foamy, fresh milk with bread, of picking daisies in the garden. "I miss these things very much when I have to return home, but, most of all, I miss my Aunt and Uncle. Well, all right, I have to confess that I also miss Aunt Ines' wonderful spicy Gazpacho, which was always served with a glass of iced sherry— I have never tasted anything so refreshing and so vividly flavored. I hope to squeeze in another visit to Spain next year and share it with them again."— Cecila Gremingi, Los Angeles, California

LENTIL SOUP

Serves 6

1 pound lentils
2 tablespoons olive oil
1 medium-size onion, finely chopped
1 medium-size carrot, finely chopped
1 stalk celery, finely chopped
6 cups water
2 ham hocks (about 1 pound) or 1 ham bone
3 sprigs parsley
1 tablespoon fresh thyme leaves, finely chopped, or 1 teaspoon dried
1 tablespoon salt
1 teaspoon pepper

Rinse the lentils and pick them over carefully. Put them in a bowl, cover with cold water and let them soak for 4 to 6 hours or overnight. (Or follow the soaking directions on the package.)

Heat the oil in a large saucepan over moderate heat. Add the onion, carrot and celery and cook for about 5 minutes, until softened. Drain the lentils and add them to the saucepan with the 6 cups of water. Add the ham hocks or ham bone, the parsley, thyme, salt and pepper. Bring the soup to the boil over high heat, then lower the heat, cover and simmer for 1 hour or until the lentils are tender.

Remove the ham hocks or ham bone from the saucepan. If you are using ham hocks, take the meat from the bone and cut it into bite-sized pieces. Discard the bone and return the ham pieces to the saucepan. If the soup has cooled, heat it through and serve immediately.

Opposite: Gurken in Tomatensossen (page 38)
Page following: Chicken Soup with Matzoh Balls (page 22)

BORSCHT

Serves 6 to 8

1 pound beef brisket
2 pounds fresh beets
2 tablespoons butter
½ cup finely chopped onion
16-ounce can tomatoes, including juice
¼ cup red wine vinegar
1 teaspoon sugar
1 teaspoon salt
Freshly ground black pepper
8 cups beef broth
4 cups coarsely shredded cabbage
½ pound thick-sliced ham, cut into small pieces
2 bay leaves
5 to 6 sprigs parsley
2 tablespoons chopped fresh dill
1 cup sour cream

Put the brisket in a pan of boiling water and cook over moderate heat for 15 minutes. Lower the heat and simmer for 1 1/4 hours, partially covered. Remove the beef from the water, allow it to cool and cut it into small pieces.

Wash the beets but do not peel them; trim away the leaves carefully, leaving 1 inch of stem attached. (This will prevent the beets from "bleeding" into the water.) Put them in a large saucepan with enough salted water to cover and simmer slowly for 35 to 45 minutes, or until tender. Remove the beets from the saucepan with a slotted spoon and allow them to cool slightly. Remove the skins (it is easiest to rub them away with your fingertips rather than try to peel them with a knife or vegetable peeler) and grate the beets coarsely.

Heat the butter in an 8-quart saucepan, add the onion and cook, stirring frequently, until softened but not brown. Add the

"My mother, from the Russian part of Poland, made very good meat borscht. She used plate flanken sometimes, instead of brisket. She put it in a pot with water and boiled it for a while, skimming off the foam that came to the top. She added cut-up beets, salt and pepper and garlic to taste, as well as the sugar and vinegar, which you have to keep tasting to keep the balance of sweet and sour flavors. When I was a child we would put a clove of garlic and some coarse salt in the bottom of the bowl and crush them before adding the hot soup. Was it good on cold winter days!"—
Florence Jurgrau,
Boca Raton, Florida

Opposite: Empanadas (page 90)
Page preceding: Blini (page 46)

17

beets, tomatoes, vinegar, sugar, salt and pepper to taste. Stir in 1 cup of the beef broth, cover the pan and simmer for 50 minutes.

Add the remaining broth to the pan. Stir in the shredded cabbage, the ham and the beef and return the mixture to the boil. Tie the bay leaves and parsley sprigs together and add them to the soup. Simmer, partly covered, for 25 to 35 minutes.

Just before serving, discard the parsley and bay leaves, and pour the soup into a tureen. Garnish with chopped dill and pass the sour cream separately, to be spooned on top of each serving.

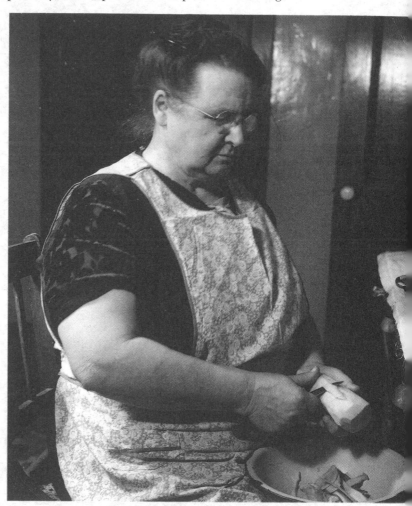

SHCHAV

Serves 4

1 quart vegetable broth
1 small bunch watercress, washed and coarsely chopped
½ pound sorrel, washed and coarsely chopped
½ cup chopped celery
2 tablespoons lemon juice
1 tablespoon freshly grated lemon rind
4 teaspoons sugar
Salt and white pepper
1 cup sour cream

Put the broth, watercress, sorrel and celery in a large pan and bring to the boil. Lower the heat and simmer for 40 to 45 minutes until the watercress and sorrel leaves have just about dissolved in the liquid.

Add the lemon juice, lemon rind and sugar. Season to taste with salt and pepper. Stir the soup well and simmer for about 5 minutes to give the flavors time to blend. Transfer the soup to a glass or porcelain bowl. Cover with transparent wrap and chill the soup for at least 4 hours, or until cold. Serve with sour cream.

"On hot summer evenings, my mother often prepared 'dairy meals,' consisting of cold borscht or cold shchav, chopped fresh vegetables with sour cream, fresh black bread and sweet butter.
"My younger sister, Belle, loved borscht, but I preferred the slightly sour, refreshing taste of shchav. If Mother prepared borscht, I would complain that Belle was the favorite child because Mother made her favorite dish. Of course, if she made shchav, Belle said the same thing about me!"—
Ann Greenberg,
Chicago, Illinois

19

CHLODNIK

Serves 6

1 pound young beets, including tops
6 cups cold water
3 tablespoons cider vinegar
3 teaspoons salt
1 teaspoon sugar
1½ cups sour cream
1 pound shrimp, cooked, shelled and deveined
2 tablespoons chopped fresh dill
3 tablespoons lemon juice
2 medium-size cucumbers, peeled, seeded and diced, for garnish
4 scallions, including tops, thinly sliced, for garnish
3 hard-cooked eggs, finely chopped, for garnish

Peel the beets and grate them coarsely. Wash and dry the tops and chop finely. Put the grated beets and tops in a large stainless steel or enamel pan. Add the water, bring to the boil and simmer, uncovered, for 10 minutes. Add the vinegar, salt and sugar and simmer, partly covered, for 20 minutes more. Drain the beets and set the cooking liquid aside to cool.

When the cooking liquid has cooled completely, add the sour cream and whisk until blended. Stir in the beets, shrimp, dill and lemon juice. Pour the soup into a large glass serving bowl, cover with transparent wrap and chill thoroughly for at least 3 hours.

Serve the soup in individual bowls and pass the cucumbers, scallions and eggs in separate dishes.

CALDO VERDE

Serves 6 to 8

6 ounces chorizo or linguica sausage, sliced
4 cups water
2 cloves garlic, finely chopped
⅓ cup olive oil
5 cups kale, cut into thin ribbons
3 cups chicken broth
6 medium-size potatoes, cut into ½-inch pieces (about 5 cups)
⅛ teaspoon pepper

Put the sausage in a large saucepan over moderately high heat. As the sausage begins to brown, add 1 cup of water along with the garlic. Cook for 5 to 10 minutes, until the sausage is cooked through. Remove the sausage from the pan with a slotted spoon and set aside.

Add the olive oil to the saucepan. Add the kale and cook for several minutes, until wilted. Remove the kale with a slotted spoon and set it aside.

Add the remaining water and the chicken broth to the pan. Bring to the boil. Add the potatoes and simmer for 15 to 20 minutes until tender. Return the kale and sausage to the pan and season with pepper. Cook for 2 to 3 minutes more and serve at once.

many restaurants there, laden with linguicas (Portuguese sausages) and kale. I always knew when we were in for a pot of this famous soup when my dad would start chopping early in the day and go marketing for the sausages. But the real telltale sign was the run to the bakery for the Portuguese bread, an essential part of the meal, in his view. I'll always remember the aromas on soup day … and I'll always remember my father doing what he loved best— cooking."—
Laurie Burrows Grad, Los Angeles, California

≋ CHICKEN SOUP WITH ≋ MATZOH BALLS

It's odd how you can have the same thing time and again and it's almost as if it didn't register until that one rarefied moment when all other memories of that particular food are banished. This one time, it is in such sharp focus, engraved forever, and even becoming more intense as you savor it on the palate of the mind. This is how it was for me with chicken soup with matzoh balls. I was suffering intensely at the time, with the gusting depth of pain you can only experience when you have finally accepted the awfulness that "he" won't ever call again. But then, my then-truest love, albeit in the surrogate form of a delivery boy, sent me a plastic, wide-necked bowl of … yes, that's what it was … and I sat in bed and smiled my way to the last drop. And I knew I was loved.

Serves 6 to 8

Broth:
3 ½-pound chicken
3 quarts (12 cups) water
1 unpeeled onion, halved
2 stalks celery, coarsely chopped
1 carrot, coarsely chopped
2 bay leaves
5 black peppercorns
Matzoh Balls:
2 eggs
1½ tablespoons chicken fat
⅔ cup matzoh meal
⅛ teaspoon salt
1 tablespoon chopped parsley (optional)
2 tablespoons chicken broth or water

Remove the giblets from the chicken and rinse them thoroughly. Rinse the chicken inside and out. Put the chicken and the giblets in a large pan and add the water. Add the onion, celery, carrot, bay leaves and peppercorns. Bring to the boil, lower the heat and simmer for 2 1/2 to 3 hours, skimming off the foam and fat that rises to the surface. Chill for 4 hours until a semisoft layer of fat has formed. Reserve 1 1/2 tablespoons of the fat for the matzoh balls.

Reheat the broth and strain it through a colander into a large saucepan. Discard the chicken bones and skin, the vegetables, bay leaves and peppercorns. Reserve the cooked chicken meat for another use.

To make the matzoh balls, combine the eggs and chicken fat in a small bowl and stir until well blended. Stir in the matzoh meal, salt and parsley. Add the 2 tablespoons broth and stir until just combined. Chill the mixture for at least 30 minutes.

Put about 6 cups of water into a saucepan and bring to the boil. Put the chicken broth over low heat and bring to a gentle simmer. Form the chilled matzoh mixture into 12 balls by rolling between the palms of the hands. Drop the balls into the boiling water, four at a time, and cook for about 2 minutes or until they rise to the surface. Remove the balls from the water with a slotted spoon and add them to the hot chicken broth. Cook the remaining matzoh balls in the same way. Serve at once.

CLEAR CHICKEN WING SOUP WITH SPINACH

Serves 4 to 6

3 pounds chicken wings
2 quarts (8 cups) water
3 1/8-inch-thick slices fresh ginger
2 whole scallions
1 pound spinach, washed, stemmed and torn into large pieces
1 to 2 teaspoons salt
Dipping sauce:
3/4 cup soy sauce
2 tablespoons sesame oil

Rinse the chicken wings well in cold water. Bring the 2 quarts water, ginger and scallions to the boil over high heat. Add the chicken and skim the foam as it rises to the surface. When the liquid returns to the boil, reduce the heat and simmer, partially covered, for about 1 hour until the wings are tender. Remove the ginger slices and the scallions.

"I will always treasure childhood memories of growing up in Hong Kong, especially the times when I was allowed to accompany Grandmother on afternoon shopping expeditions to the marketplace. I liked it best when she stopped at the shop with crates of colorful squawking chickens. I remember the skill and expertise she displayed in carefully selecting a healthy plump one to carry home for our evening meal. Just before cooking time, she killed it with her own hands to be certain that her prize fowl would yield the best flavor in her dishes. Watching her kill the chicken was always a frightening experience for me, but even so, I couldn't wait to taste the delicious dish she was going to turn that dead chicken into. I remember that her favorite parts of the chicken were the wings. She loved to cook them in a pot of wonderful smelling soup."
— Alice Cheng,
Washington, D.C.

Add the spinach and cook for 5 to 8 minutes until it is wilted. Add salt to taste.

Make the dipping sauce by combining the soy sauce and sesame oil and divide into individual small serving bowls.

Pour the soup into a large bowl or tureen and serve with the dipping sauce. Each person should get 2 or 3 chicken wings and some spinach. The dipping sauce may be spooned into individual bowls so that each person can dip the chicken wings.

HOT AND SOUR SOUP

Serves 4 to 6

¼ pound lean pork loin or pork butt
6 dried black Chinese or shiitake mushrooms or
   3 ounces fresh white mushrooms, coarsely chopped
1 tablespoon dried tree-ear mushrooms
8 dried tiger lily stems
¼ cup shredded bamboo shoots or broccoli stems
1 tablespoon plus 2 teaspoons light soy sauce
2 tablespoons plus 2 teaspoons cornstarch
2 tablespoons sesame oil
1 tablespoon dry sherry
1 tablespoon vegetable oil
5 cups chicken broth
2 to 3 tablespoons red wine vinegar
4 to 6 ounces fresh bean curd (tofu), cut into 1-inch pieces
1 teaspoon freshly ground pepper
2 eggs, lightly beaten
1 scallion, finely sliced, for garnish

Put the pork in the freezer for about 30 minutes until firm. Using a sharp knife, shred it so that the pieces are about 1/4 inch wide.

Put the dried mushrooms and the tiger lily stems in separate bowls. Pour enough very hot or boiling water over them to cover and let stand for 15 minutes until they are soft. Drain and then rinse the mushrooms to remove any sand. Squeeze dry and remove the tough stems and any hard spots. If you are using fresh mushrooms, do not soak them in hot water. Shred the mushrooms to about the same thickness as the pork, and cut the tiger lily stems in half.

Arrange the mushrooms, tiger lily stems and bamboo shoots in separate piles on a platter and set aside.

Put the shredded pork in a bowl with 1 tablespoon of the soy sauce, 2 teaspoons of the cornstarch, 1 tablespoon of the sesame oil and the sherry and stir well.

Heat a wok or a large skillet over high heat. Add vegetable oil. When it is hot, add the pork mixture, stirring to separate the strands.

Add the mushrooms, the tiger lily stems, and the bamboo shoots. Stir-fry for 1 minute and add the chicken broth. Adjust the heat so that the broth is simmering. Add the vinegar and the remaining 2 teaspoons of soy sauce and simmer for 5 minutes.

Dissolve the remaining 2 tablespoons of cornstarch in 3 tablespoons of water. Stir the cornstarch mixture into the broth. When it is thickened, add the bean curd and bring the mixture to the boil. Remove the pan from the heat and add the pepper and remaining tablespoon of sesame oil.

Pour the eggs into the wok in a thin stream, stirring gently in a circular motion so that they do not cook. Cover the pan and allow to sit for 1 minute. Sprinkle with the scallions and serve immediately.

nights when the old man would leave for his weekly dose of mah-jongg and I would be dispatched to a local restaurant for several dozen pot-stickers— wonderfully aromatic beef-filled pasta tubes— and a small vat of hot and sour soup to go. Hot and sour soup is one of those things I'll always enjoy but I don't think any subsequent experience can match the savor of those Friday nights. The two wives set out bowls and chopsticks, and their otherwise forbidden cigarettes, and there would ensue an hour of happy eating."— Barbara Tropp, San Francisco, California

SILVER EAR SWEET SOUP

"In China, it is common for three generations to live under one roof. When I was growing up, I lived with my grandmother, my parents, one brother, five sisters, an aunt and uncle, half a dozen cousins and a multitude of servants. My grandmother always enjoyed a snack in the middle of the night and so as not to disturb anyone else, she had a small 'self-service' unit at the edge of her three-sided, ornately carved and lacquered mahogany bed. This service consisted of a small pot, similar to a chafing dish, which burned hot with alcohol continuously. In it most often was her favorite dish, a thick soup of jujube red dates, longan and silver ears sweetened with rock sugar. As her favorite grandchild, I shared the cherished soup on many occasions. What I remember most was the subtle fragrance of the dates, the slight chewiness of the longan fruit and the smoothness of the silver ears. I make the soup still; the ingredients come dried and are easy to obtain."—
Florence S. Lin,
Bronx, New York

Serves 6

½ pound dried jujube red dates
2 ounces seedless dried longan (also called "dragon's eyes")
2 ounces dried silver ears
Rock sugar

Wash the jujubes and put them in a bowl. Cover with water and soak for 1 hour. Rinse them several times in cold water. Put the jujubes in a small saucepan, add 2 cups of water and cook over low heat for 1 hour. Set the jujubes aside.

Soak the longan in cold water for 1 hour. Drain, reserving and measuring the soaking water. Add enough water to make 3 cups.

Soak the silver ears in cold water for 30 minutes or until they have expanded fully. Put them in a saucepan, add 3 to 4 cups of cold water and cook over low heat for 2 hours or until very soft.

Combine the silver ears and their cooking water with the longan and water. Cook over low heat for 30 minutes. Add rock sugar to taste. Add the jujube dates and cook for 10 minutes more. Serve hot.

Note: Jujube dates have thick skins which are usually discarded during eating. They are left on during cooking because of their fragrance.

EGG DROP SOUP

Serves 4 to 6

2 eggs
2 tablespoons Japanese soy sauce
5 cups chicken broth
3 to 4 mushrooms, thinly sliced, or
watercress leaves, for garnish

Beat the eggs with the soy sauce in a small bowl.

Heat the broth in a saucepan over moderate heat. Add the mushrooms. Increase the heat to high and bring the soup to the boil. Stir the soup vigorously in one direction and pour in the eggs in a thin stream. Remove the pan from the heat, cover and allow to sit for 1 minute, until the egg threads rise to the surface. Serve the soup at once, garnished with the mushroom slices or watercress leaves.

"When I was a little girl, my grandparents took me with them on a long trip to meet our Chinese aunts, uncles and cousins. I loved the delicious food but I was astonished to discover that soup was served at almost every meal. Sometimes my aunt placed a large bowlful in the middle of the table and left it there throughout the meal. It was meant to replace the regular beverage. Our last meal was a more formal occasion and the soup was served at the end of the meal as the last course. Aunty May said it was an excellent aid to digestion. My favorite soup in Taipei was egg drop soup because it was so mild tasting and pretty to look at. My aunt gave me her recipe so that my mother could help me to make it when I was at home again. I will never forget the lesson she gave me on how to swirl the uncooked eggs into the hot stock, so they would explode into a sunburst of golden threads."—
Lilly Kuo, Cedarville, Ohio

27

OZOSUI
(THICK RICE SOUP)

Serves 4 to 6

6 cups chicken broth
3 to 4 cups cooked rice
1 large whole boneless, skinless chicken breast,
chopped into 1-inch pieces (about 2 cups)
2 tablespoons Japanese soy sauce
1 teaspoon grated fresh ginger
4 scallions, thinly sliced
Salt and freshly ground black pepper
1 egg, lightly beaten (optional)

Heat the chicken broth in a large pan over medium-high heat until it comes to the boil. Add the rice, chicken, soy sauce and ginger, reduce the heat to low and simmer for 10 minutes until the rice is very soft.

Add the scallions and season with salt and pepper to taste. Stir in the egg, if desired. Allow the soup to sit for 1 minute before serving.

MISO SHIRU
(BEAN SOUP)

Serves 4

4 cups water or chicken broth
2 to 3 tablespoons soy sauce
4 tablespoons white miso (fermented soybean paste)
½ pound fresh bean curd (tofu), cut into ½-inch cubes
2 to 3 tablespoons chopped scallions
¼ teaspoon crushed hot red pepper (optional)

Combine the water or broth with the soy sauce in a saucepan and bring to a simmer. Transfer 2 to 3 tablespoons of the simmering liquid to a small bowl, add the miso and stir to make a smooth liquid paste. Add the miso mixture back to the pan and keep at a simmer over moderate heat. Add the bean curd and heat through, stirring gently to keep the pieces intact.

Serve the soup sprinkled with the scallions and the hot red pepper if desired.

"In the morning when I was still in bed, I would hear my mother cooking. I would smell the miso shiru and hear the sound of chopping. These two things always told me it was time to get up. In Japan, breakfast is very simple. We always start with rice, then comes the miso shiru and some dried seaweed. My mother usually made the soup stock from bonito (dried shredded fish) and then added the miso, tofu and scallions. The scallions were what I heard her chopping from my bed." — Takami Yao, New York, New York

GRAVLAX

Serves 6

2 ½ to 3 pounds center-cut salmon, in one piece with skin on
3 tablespoons coarse salt
3 tablespoons sugar
1½ tablespoons white peppercorns, crushed
1 large bunch fresh dill

Cut the salmon in half lengthwise and remove all the bones. (An obliging fish store or butcher in the supermarket will do this for you.) Combine the salt, sugar and crushed peppercorns in a small bowl and mix well.

Put one piece of salmon in a glass or enamel dish, skin side down, and cover it evenly with the peppercorn mixture. Spread the dill on top of the seasonings. Set the other piece of salmon on top, skin side up. Wrap the fish in wax paper to enclose it completely and put it in a shallow dish. Weight the salmon evenly with cans or other heavy objects. (The weight and the salt will force the water out of the fish, leaving it firm and easy to slice.)

Put the salmon in the refrigerator and leave to marinate for 3 to 4 days, turning it every other day. Remove the salmon from its wrappings and gently scrape off the seasonings. Discard the dill and pat the fish dry.

Slice the salmon very thinly on the diagonal and lift the buttery-smooth slices from the skin.

It's a good and useful thing to pause from time to time and consider broad issues of life, and intimations of significant events— such as what to have for your 'last' supper. I myself have given this considerable thought, for I am of the opinion that it is wise to plan for the future. I have pretty much decided that on the menu will be a little Vivaldi and several slices of gravlax. Then I will moisten my lips with a strawberry … There may be a better send-off. But I haven't thought of one.

Caponata

Serves 6 to 8

2 pounds eggplant
Salt
½ cup olive oil
1½ cups finely chopped onion
1 large clove garlic, finely chopped
1¼ cups finely chopped celery
5 tablespoons wine vinegar
3 teaspoons sugar
4 anchovy fillets
3 cups drained canned plum tomatoes
2 tablespoons finely chopped parsley
2 tablespoons drained capers
¼ teaspoon freshly ground black pepper
3 tablespoons pine nuts

Cut the eggplant into 3/4-inch pieces, salt generously and put in a colander to drain for 30 minutes.

Heat 1/4 cup of the olive oil in a large heavy skillet over moderate heat. Add the onion and garlic and cook, stirring, for 3 to 4 minutes. Add the celery and continue to cook for about 10 minutes, until the celery and onion are softened and just beginning to brown. Remove them from the skillet with a slotted spoon.

Pat the drained eggplant dry with paper towels. Add the remaining olive oil to the skillet, increase the heat to high and cook the eggplant for 6 to 8 minutes, stirring constantly.

Stir the vinegar and sugar together. Rinse the anchovy fillets and chop very fine.

Return the onion mixture to the skillet. Add the vinegar, anchovies, tomatoes, parsley and capers. Season with 1 teaspoon of salt and the black pepper, and bring the mixture to a simmer. Reduce

"I've read that caponata is so named because it is a traditional Italian accompaniment to roast capon, but in our household it turned up on the table all the time— and capon almost never made an appearance. I find something mysteriously appealing about caponata. The combination of ingredients seems so unlikely, even arbitrary— eggplant, vinegar, sugar, anchovies, pine nuts, celery.... Yet the result is so savory that you realize there's nothing arbitrary about it. My mother learned her caponata recipe from her mother, and so on backward in time, and I guess it's been refined and perfected a little with each generation."— Jackie diPietra, San Pedro, California

the heat to low and let the caponata simmer, uncovered, for 10 to 15 minutes, stirring occasionally. Stir in the pine nuts and check the seasoning.

Transfer the caponata to a bowl, cool to room temperature and then chill for at least 5 hours. Remove from the refrigerator an hour before serving.

≋ COUNTRY TERRINE ≋

Serves 10 to 12

½ *pound ground pork*
½ *pound ground veal*
½ *pound pork fatback, finely chopped*
½ *pound chicken livers, finely chopped*
1 *tablespoon all-purpose flour*
1 *egg*
3 *to 4 tablespoons Cognac*
3 *cloves garlic, finely chopped*
½ *teaspoon dried thyme*
½ *teaspoon ground bay leaf*
6 *tablespoons finely chopped onions*
½ *tablespoon salt*
½ *teaspoon freshly ground black pepper*
½ *pound bacon*
3 *ounces thick sliced ham*

Heat the oven to 350 degrees.

Combine all the ingredients except the bacon and ham in a large bowl and mix well. To check for seasoning, fry a tablespoonful

"On Thursdays, a day off from school in France, my cousins and I would gather in the basement of my grandmother's house to help my uncles prepare charcuterie for the Marché des Capucins, the market in Bordeaux. My job was peeling kilos of shallots, onions and garlic for the pâtés and so I peeled and peeled until my eyes watered so much I could hardly see the pile in front of me.
"Once all the ingredients were chopped and mixed,

Opposite: Chirashi Sushi (page 48)
Page following: Melitzanosalata (page 41)

of the mixture in a little hot oil and then taste it. It should be highly seasoned.

Line a 6-cup terrine mold with the bacon strips, overlapping them to form a seal. Reserve a few strips for the top. Cut the ham into strips about 1/3 inch wide.

Pack a third of the terrine mixture into the mold and layer with half the ham strips. Repeat and then pack the remaining terrine mixture on top of the ham strips. Cover the top of the terrine with the remaining bacon, again making sure that the strips overlap. Cover the mold tightly with aluminum foil.

Half fill a baking pan with boiling water and set the mold in the pan. Put the pan in the heated oven and bake for 1 1/4 to 1 1/2 hours, or until the juices run clear when the terrine is pierced with a knife. Remove the mold from the baking pan and allow it to cool to room temperature.

Leaving the foil in place, weight the top of the terrine (you can use a couple of 1-pound cans or a brick, if you have no weights) and chill for at least 24 hours.

the pâtés were baked and then cooled on racks. While they cooled, my uncles napped— and we nibbled. I would snack on the crusty tops of the loaves, carefully breaking off a tiny piece here and there, hoping that my uncles wouldn't notice. I'm sure they did, but they never said a word about it — after all, who else would they find to peel all those shallots?"—
Jean-Pierre Pradie,
New York, New York

Opposite: Saltimbocca di Pollo (page 54)
Page preceding: Spanikopita (page 77)

STUFFED GRAPE LEAVES

Serves 6

8-ounce jar vine leaves in brine
4 ounces uncooked rice
½ cup boiling water
1 tomato, peeled, seeded and chopped
8 ounces ground beef or lamb
1 small onion, finely chopped
3 tablespoons finely chopped parsley
Salt and freshly ground black pepper
2 cloves garlic, cut into slivers
Juice of 1 lemon
Water

Soak the vine leaves in boiling water for 20 minutes. Drain them and soak in fresh cold water. Repeat the process to make sure all the excess salt is removed, and set the leaves aside.

Put the rice in a bowl and add the boiling water. Let the rice stand until the liquid is absorbed. Turn the rice into a sieve and rinse under cold water.

Combine the rice, tomato, ground meat, onion and parsley in a bowl and mix well. Season with salt and pepper to taste. Set the vine leaves veined side up on a work surface. Put 1 heaping teaspoon of filling in the center of each leaf near the stem (bottom) end and fold the stem end up over the filling. Fold both sides of the leaf toward the middle and roll the vine leaf up tightly, like a cigar. Squeeze each stuffed vine leaf gently in the palm of your hand after rolling.

Line the bottom of a large saucepan with the remaining vine leaves to prevent the stuffed ones from sticking to the bottom. Arrange the stuffed leaves close together in the pan, in layers if necessary. Wedge slivers of garlic between the stuffed leaves. Sprinkle with lemon juice and about 1/2 cup of water. Put a plate on top of the leaves to prevent them from unrolling. Cover the pan and cook over very low heat for about 2 hours, adding more water as necessary to keep moist.

TARAMASALATA

Serves 6 to 8

3 slices Italian bread, crusts removed
½ cup tarama (salted roe) or smoked cod roe
4 tablespoons lemon juice
2 tablespoons finely chopped onion
1 cup olive oil
1 tablespoon finely chopped parsley

Soak the bread in water to barely cover it and squeeze dry.

Put the bread, tarama or cod roe, lemon juice and onion in a food processor or blender. Add 1/3 cup of the oil and blend until smooth. With the motor running, slowly add the remaining oil and continue processing until the mixture is smooth and creamy. Heap the taramasalata in a serving dish and garnish it with parsley.

"I clearly remember the first time I tasted taramasalata. I was nine, and with my parents was visiting my father's bother Nikos in Athens. Nikos took us to one of his favorite tavernas and the owner, with a booming Kalin Orexi! (Hearty appetite) to the visitors, placed an assortment of appetizers on the table— chunks of feta, astringent black olives, plump little dolmas, and savory phyllo pastries. I first tasted the taramasalata with a mixture of delight and shock; with its creamy-salty-fishy pungency it was totally unlike anything I'd ever eaten. Over the ensuing years I have become practically addicted to taramasalata. For Greek dinners I serve it with a big assortment of other starters, with bread and pitas for dipping; if I'm hosting an American-style cocktail party I serve it with crackers and crudites. With its rich flavors of roe, lemon juice and olive oil, I can't imagine a more quintessentially Greek dish."— Georgia Joannou, St. Louis, Missouri

HUMMUS

"My first trip to Israel was a thrill in so many ways—the sights, the history, the tradition, the people, and the food all delighted me!

"I remember eating falafel on the street in Tel Aviv, St. Peter's fish in Galilee, and roast baby lamb in Jericho. And with every meal, hummus was an obligatory appetizer. Eggplant salad, Tahina dip, Tarama (Greek caviar dip), and hummus were always put on the table at the start of each meal and we would all dive in with pieces of fresh pita bread and crisp, cut-up, raw vegetables. A wonderful start for any meal—made even more wonderful because we were in Israel!"— Herb Giat, Flushing, New York

Serves 8

½ cup sesame paste (tahini)
2 large cloves garlic, finely chopped
½ to ¾ cup lemon juice, to taste
1 teaspoon salt
1 cup cooked chick peas or canned cooked chick peas, drained
1½ tablespoons olive oil
2 tablespoons finely chopped parsley

Put the tahini in a bowl and stir until the paste and its oil are well mixed.

Put the garlic, lemon juice and salt in a blender. With the motor running on medium speed, add the chick peas a spoonful at a time. Gradually add the oil and the tahini. The mixture should be creamy and smooth – if it becomes too thick, add a little water. Check the seasoning and add more lemon juice, salt or garlic, to taste. Sprinkle chopped parsley over the hummus before serving.

EL PASO GUACAMOLE

Makes 4 cups

4 ripe, soft avocados
½ to 1 cup hot, chunky red or green salsa
Juice of 2 limes
Salt

Cut the avocados in half and scoop out the flesh. Mash with a fork or process in a blender until smooth. Transfer to a serving bowl. Add salsa and lime juice to taste. Add salt to taste. Serve with corn chips.

TSATSIKI
(CUCUMBER DIP)

Serves 6

3 cups plain yogurt
2 large cloves garlic, finely chopped
1 tablespoon chopped fresh mint
4 tablespoons olive oil
2 tablespoons lemon juice
½ teaspoon salt
White pepper
2 medium-size cucumbers, peeled, seeded and chopped

Put the yogurt in a bowl. Add the garlic, mint, olive oil, lemon juice, salt and pepper to taste and stir well. Add the cucumber and toss to combine.

For a smoother dip, combine all the ingredients in a food processor or blender and process briefly until blended.

Put the dip in a serving bowl, cover with transparent wrap and chill thoroughly. Serve with warm pita bread.

"Cucumbers in yogurt always bring back memories of annual summer visits to grandmother's villa in Greece. She served a dish of it in one way or another almost every day. On warm afternoons, I loved to sit on the upstairs balcony overlooking the Aegean Sea, enjoying a snack of Grandmother's creamy cucumber and yogurt dip with wedges of fresh pita bread. Sometimes she served it during our meals in the form of a salad. I remember Grandmother telling me that yogurt was nutritious and I should eat it regularly to stay healthy. Grandmother would be proud because I have faithfully followed her advice and continued to eat cucumbers and yogurt throughout the years."—
Caroline Tassos,
Altamonte Springs, Florida

Gurken in Tomatensossen
(Cucumbers in Tomato Sauce)

Serves 4

3 cucumbers, peeled, cut in half lengthwise and cut into ¼-inch slices
4 strips bacon, cut into ½-inch pieces
½ medium-size onion, finely chopped
½ cup tomato puree
1 tomato, coarsely chopped
1 tablespoon grated Swiss cheese
1 tablespoon grated Parmesan cheese
Freshly ground black pepper
2 to 3 tablespoons chopped parsley

Put the sliced cucumbers in a bowl and sprinkle generously with salt. Put a plate on top, weighted with cans or kitchen weights, and let sit for at least 30 minutes or, preferably, 2 to 3 hours.

Rinse and drain the cucumbers thoroughly. Pat them dry with paper towels.

Put the bacon in a heavy skillet over moderate heat and cook until lightly browned. Remove the bacon from the pan and set it aside. Add the cucumbers to the skillet and cook until lightly browned. Remove them with a slotted spoon and set aside.

Add the onion to the pan and cook for 2 to 3 minutes, until softened. Add the tomato puree and the chopped tomato. Lower the heat and cook for 10 minutes.

Return the bacon and cucumber to the pan. Stir in the cheese, add pepper to taste and sprinkle with the parsley.

TIROPITAKIA
(CHEESE TRIANGLES)

Makes 30 pieces

½ pound feta cheese
4 ounces cream cheese
½ pound Swiss cheese
2 scallions, finely chopped (optional)
2 eggs
⅛ teaspoon freshly ground black pepper
½ pound phyllo dough
6 ounces (¾ cup) butter, melted

Heat the oven to 375 degrees.

Combine the cheeses, scallions, eggs and pepper in a bowl and stir until well blended.

Put a sheet of phyllo dough on a work surface and brush generously with melted butter. Put another sheet of dough on top and brush with more melted butter. Top with a third sheet of dough. Starting from one of the shorter edges, cut the layered dough into 6 equal strips.

Put 1 tablespoon of the filling at the bottom of each strip. Fold a corner of each strip over to form a triangle and cut with a sharp knife to separate. Put another tablespoon of filling at the bottom of each strip and fold the dough over into a triangle as before. Continue this process until all the dough is used.

Put the filled triangles on a baking sheet and brush them with melted butter. Bake for 20 minutes or until golden brown.

"The women in my family have always been skillful at making the exquisite pastries which are such an important part of our Middle Eastern heritage. I began learning to make pastries and desserts with ultra-thin sheets of homemade phyllo dough from my Greek grandmother when I was only five years old. Tiropitakia, a small traditional Greek cheese pastry has always been one of our family's favorite recipes, and especially of my two brothers. Grandmother taught me how to fill and fold the delicate pastry triangles with her savory mixture of three cheeses and green onions. When they were in the oven, sometimes grandmother would allow me to peek. To me it was like watching a magic act to see those flat little pastries expand into puffy golden triangles with tissue-paper-thin layers."—
Susanne Augustauskas, Washington, D.C.

SAGANAKI
(FRIED CHEESE)

Serves 4 to 6

½ pound kasseri, kefalotiri or feta cheese, chilled
3 to 4 tablespoons butter
3 tablespoons lemon juice

Cut the cheese horizontally into 1/4-inch-thick slices.

Heat 3 tablespoons of butter in a heavy skillet over moderately high heat. Add the cheese and cook until lightly browned on each side, about 2 minutes in all. Remove the pan from the heat. Sprinkle the cheese with lemon juice, cut into bite-sized pieces and serve at once.

Cook the remaining cheese in the same way, adding more butter to the skillet if necessary.

Melitzanosalata
(Greek Eggplant Salad)

Terrible

Serves 4 to 6

2 medium-size eggplants
1 medium-size onion, grated
1 clove garlic
2 tomatoes, peeled, seeded and finely chopped
2 tablespoons chopped parsley
½ cup olive oil
3 tablespoons wine vinegar or lemon juice
½ teaspoon salt
Freshly ground black pepper
Black olives, for garnish
1 green pepper, cut into rings, for garnish

Heat the oven to 350 degrees.

Put the eggplants in a roasting pan and bake, in their skins, for about 1 hour or until softened.

While the eggplants are still warm, remove the skins and chop the pulp finely. Put the chopped pulp in a serving bowl. Add the onion, garlic, tomatoes and parsley. Toss gently to combine all the ingredients.

Put the olive oil in a small bowl. Add the vinegar, salt and pepper to taste and whisk briefly to blend. Pour the dressing over the eggplant mixture and toss to combine. Cover the bowl with transparent wrap and chill thoroughly.

Garnish the salad with olives and green pepper rings before serving.

"I have often wondered what direction Greek cooking would have taken if there were no such thing as eggplant. My family must have eaten eggplant in some form or other at least four times a week— stuffed, in moussaka, braised with liver, even broiled and mashed like potatoes— and we never got tired of it. In our backyard in Queens, there was just enough room for my father to plant a few rows each of eggplant and tomatoes, and they would take us through most of the summer and fall."— Marina Costas Nathan, Jamaica Plains, Massachusetts

GREEK SALAD

Serves 6

1 medium-size red onion, thinly sliced
6 ripe medium-size tomatoes, quartered
1 cup thinly sliced cucumber
1 large green pepper, seeds and ribs removed, sliced
1 large red pepper, seeds and ribs removed, sliced
½ pound feta cheese, broken into ½-inch pieces
6 ounces black oil-cured olives
½ cup olive oil
3 tablespoons red wine vinegar
1 tablespoon finely chopped parsley
1 tablespoon finely chopped fresh oregano
1 tablespoon finely chopped fresh mint
Salt and freshly ground black pepper

Soak the onion slices in cold water for 15 minutes. Remove them from the water and drain on paper towels. This takes away their sharpness.

Combine the onion, tomatoes, cucumber, red and green peppers, cheese and olives in a large shallow bowl and toss gently together.

Combine the olive oil and vinegar in a small bowl and blend with a wire whisk. Add the herbs, salt and pepper and stir well. Pour the dressing over the salad, toss well and serve immediately.

Milanese Stuffed Artichokes

Serves 6

6 large artichokes
2 teaspoons butter
¼ cup finely chopped onion
1 clove garlic, finely chopped
½ cup chopped pancetta or bacon
2 cups fresh bread crumbs
4 tablespoons grated Parmesan cheese
2 tablespoons finely chopped basil leaves
2 tablespoons finely chopped parsley
1 teaspoon dried thyme
Salt and freshly ground black pepper
2 tablespoons olive oil

Cut the stems from the artichokes and cut about 2 inches off the top of each one. Remove the choke, which is the fuzzy part in the center, and enough of the leaves around it to make a cavity for the stuffing. Trim the outer leaves and set the artichokes aside.

Heat the butter in a skillet over moderate heat, add the onion and garlic and cook for about 5 minutes, stirring occasionally, until softened and translucent. Remove the onion and garlic to a medium-sized bowl, using a slotted spoon. Add the pancetta to the pan and cook until lightly browned. Remove with a slotted spoon and add it to the onion mixture. Add the bread crumbs, cheese and herbs, mix well and season with salt and pepper to taste.

Heat the oven to 350 degrees.

Fill each artichoke with the stuffing. If there is any left over, push it gently down between the outer leaves. Put the artichokes in a shallow baking dish and drizzle the olive oil over the top. Pour in enough water to come barely halfway up the sides of the artichokes. Cover with foil and bake for 1 1/2 hours. Serve warm or at room temperature.

A pompous friend once pronounced in my hearing, though I was trying not to pay any attention at all to him, that the world is divided into those who do and those who do not adore artichokes. To my mind, it was the only thing he ever said worth listening to, for I believe him to have been right in his assessment of the human race.

I do adore artichokes, and from this old bore I learned how to eat them, laying down each nibbled leaf with infinite care so that one overlaps the other to form a perfect circle around the plate. I pretend, always, when I do this in fine restaurants, not to notice the look of astonishment on the waiter's face when he comes to remove the plates. I act quite nonchalantly and never tire of playing this little game, nor of the delight of discovering the next artichoke— and the next.

≋ CLAMS OREGANATA ≋

Serves 4 to 5

*"My father's sister, Aunt Tessie, was famous for her clams oreganata, and was called upon to make them for every conceivable occasion— block parties, baptisms, Christmas Eve dinner, you name it. I don't think she ever bothered preparing fewer than 100 clams at a time, and she had the procedure down to assembly-line precision. The one task she would sometimes enlist help for was grating cheese. It wouldn't have occurred to her to use other than freshly grated Parmesan, and she always made a point of remarking on the otherwise unmentioned 'touch of arthritis' in her elbow when it was time to call the grater into action."—
Richard LaRosa,
Pittsburgh, Pennsylvania*

30 littleneck clams, in the shells
3 slices firm white bread
½ cup grated Parmesan cheese
1 small clove garlic, finely chopped
1½ teaspoons dried oregano
1 teaspoon dried thyme
1 tablespoon chopped parsley
Freshly ground black pepper
Pinch of cayenne
1 teaspoon lemon juice
½ cup clam juice, reserved from the clams or bottled
¾ cup white wine
½ cup olive oil

Heat the oven to 425 degrees.

Open the clams and loosen them from the shells without removing them completely. (You might want to ask the fishmonger to do this for you.) Discard the top shells. Save any clam juice. If you do not have 1/2 cup, add bottled juice or water.

Trim the crusts from the bread, put the slices in a blender or food processor and process into fine crumbs. If you are using a blender, you may have to make the crumbs in several batches.

Put the bread crumbs in a bowl and add all of the remaining ingredients except 2 tablespoons of the olive oil.

Lay the clams in their shells in a shallow baking pan large enough so that they fit snugly but are not crowded. Using your fingers or a spoon, spread the bread crumb topping on top of the clams. Sprinkle the remaining 2 tablespoons of olive oil over the clams and bake for 8 to 12 minutes until the topping begins to brown. If you want a crispy finish, put the clams under the broiler for a minute or two just before serving.

≋ CHOPPED CHICKEN ≋ LIVERS

Makes 2 cups

2 hard-cooked eggs
¼ cup vegetable oil
¾ cup finely chopped onion
1 pound chicken livers
1 teaspoon salt
1 teaspoon freshly ground black pepper

Peel the eggs under cold running water and set them aside. Heat the oil in a medium-sized skillet, add the onion and cook until softened and translucent. Remove the onion with a slotted spoon and set aside.

Add the livers to the skillet and cook over moderate heat for about 10 minutes, stirring occasionally. The livers should still be slightly pink in the center.

Put the livers in a food processor. Add the eggs, onion, salt and pepper. Process for 10 seconds for coarsely chopped livers, or longer for a smoother paste. Chill for at least 4 hours before serving.

"I make chopped chicken livers the same way my mother did— only difference is she always used chicken fat and I use vegetable oil. I cook quartered onions in the oil, just as she did in the chicken fat, until they are yellow, not browned. This takes out the sting. Then I lift them out of the pan and put in the livers. I don't like the onions to get black from the blood from the liver. I chop up a lot of eggs and mix them with the chicken livers, and so did she. I love them this way."—
Florence Jurgrau,
Boca Raton, Florida

BLINI

Makes about 34 3-inch blini

1 envelope active dry yeast
1 teaspoon sugar
⅓ cup warm water (100 degrees Fahrenheit)
3 tablespoons butter
1⅔ cups milk
3 eggs, at room temperature, separated
2 cups all-purpose flour
1 teaspoon salt
Melted butter, for frying

Combine the yeast, sugar and water in a small bowl and let stand for about 15 minutes or until the mixture starts to bubble.

Put 3 tablespoons of butter in a small saucepan. Add the milk and heat to lukewarm. Stir until the butter has completely dissolved. Add the egg yolks to the milk mixture, beating with a wire whisk until well blended.

Put the flour and salt in a food processor. Pour in the yeast mixture and the warm milk and process until smooth. Transfer the batter to a large bowl, cover with transparent wrap and set in a warm place to rise for 1 hour, or until the mixture has doubled in volume.

Heat the oven to 200 degrees.

Beat the egg whites until stiff peaks form. Fold them gently into the risen batter, cover and allow to rest for a further 15 minutes.

Brush a heavy skillet or griddle with melted butter. When the butter is sizzling, spoon tablespoonfuls of the batter onto the griddle, about 2 tablespoons for each pancake. When the first side is golden brown, turn the pancake over and cook briefly on the other side. Arrange the cooked blini in a warm, ovenproof dish and keep warm in the oven while you cook the remaining batter in the same way, adding more butter to the griddle as necessary.

GEFILTE FISH

Serves 6 to 8

3 pounds white fish (preferably a mixture of fat and
   lean fish such as carp and pike), filleted, trimmings reserved
3 medium-size onions, sliced
2 carrots, sliced
1 stalk celery, sliced
1 bay leaf
¼ teaspoon dried thyme
2 sprigs parsley
2 eggs, lightly beaten
¼ cup matzoh meal
Salt and pepper

Put the fish trimmings in a medium-sized pan and add enough water to cover, about 4 cups. Add 2 of the onions, the carrots, celery, bay leaf, thyme and parsley and bring to the boil. Lower the heat and simmer, uncovered, for 30 minutes.

Meanwhile, put the fish fillets in a food processor together with the remaining onion slices. Process for 10 seconds. Transfer the mixture to a medium-sized bowl, add the eggs, matzoh meal and 1/4 cup water and mix well. Season with salt and pepper. The mixture should be slightly sticky.

With wet hands, shape the fish mixture into balls. When the fish broth has simmered for 30 minutes, add the fish balls, cover the pan and cook gently over very low heat for 1 hour. At the end of the cooking time, leave the fish balls in the broth until they are slightly cooled, then transfer them to a shallow serving dish. Strain the broth and pour it over the fish. Garnish with some of the onions and carrots from the broth.

"I grew up in the Bronx and I still remember my mother coming home from the market with a big, live carp to make gefilte fish. We kept the fish in the bathtub until time to kill it, after which my mother put it through a meat grinder. She put the ground fish in a bowl and chopped it some more until it was a consistency she liked."—Lily Liss, Queens, New York

CHIRASHI SUSHI
(MIXED SUSHI)

Serves 3 to 4

Seasoned vinegar:
1 cup rice vinegar
1 cup sugar
Sushi rice:
1 recipe Japanese Cooked Rice (see recipe page 198)
⅓ cup seasoned vinegar, above
8 dried black mushrooms, or 8 fresh white mushrooms
1 medium-size carrot, peeled and cut into ⅛-inch-thick strips
2 tablespoons soy sauce
4 tablespoons water
2 tablespoons sugar
¼ pound green beans or snow peas, trimmed, blanched and shredded
¼ cup thinly sliced pickled red ginger
3 Thin Egg Omelettes cut into ⅛-inch-wide ribbons
   (see recipe page 49) or 3 hard-cooked eggs, crumbled
8 to 10 medium-size shrimp, cooked and peeled

     To make the seasoned vinegar, combine the vinegar and the sugar in a small saucepan. Bring to the boil over high heat and stir until the sugar dissolves. Remove from the heat and use hot or cold.

     To make the sushi rice, transfer the freshly cooked hot Japanese rice to a large bowl. Sprinkle the 1/3 cup seasoned vinegar over the rice and toss gently. (Reserve the remaining seasoned vinegar for another use.) Continue to toss the rice occasionally until it cools to room temperature. Set the sushi rice aside.

     Put the dried mushrooms in a bowl and pour enough hot water over them to cover. Let the mushrooms soak until softened, about 15 minutes. Rinse them, remove the tough stems and slice them. (If you are using fresh mushrooms, it isn't necessary to soak them.) Combine the sliced mushrooms, carrot strips, soy sauce and

water in a small skillet. Bring to the boil over high heat. Reduce the heat to low, cover the pan and simmer for 5 minutes. Add the sugar and simmer for 5 minutes longer. Remove the cover, increase the heat to high and cook, shaking the pan, until most of the liquid has evaporated. Allow the vegetables to cool.

Scatter the mushroom mixture, the green beans or snow peas and the ginger over the seasoned rice and toss well. Garnish with the sliced omelette or hard-cooked egg, and the cooked shrimp.

TAMAGO
(THIN EGG OMELETTE)

Serves 1

1 egg
1 teaspoon sugar
Vegetable oil

Beat the egg and the sugar together.

Heat the skillet over medium-high heat. Using a paper towel, coat the bottom of the pan with a thin film of oil. The oil should be hot enough to make a drop of egg sizzle, but it should not be smoking.

Remove the pan from the heat and pour in the egg mixture, tilting the pan so that it is coated with a thin, even layer of egg. Return the pan to the heat and cook until the edges of the omelette are dry and the middle is set. Carefully flip the sheet over and cook the other side for 10 seconds. Turn the omelette out on a flat dry surface to cool. Serve with sushi.

"I remember my mother making these omelettes for us when we lived on Oahu in Hawaii. She had her own way of making it— she liked to crumble some sweet nori (seaweed) into the egg, just to give it a little color."— Bea Wakida, New York, New York

YAKITORI
(GRILLED SKEWERED CHICKEN)

"When I was a small boy growing up in Japan, my parents owned a chicken pub or yakitori-ya. Everyone recognized it by the big red lantern hanging outside the front door. In our restaurant we specialized in serving small pieces of foods skewered on bamboo sticks, then cooked over a charcoal grill. Although we offered many skewered foods such as vegetables, pork heart, quail, and meatballs, my favorite was the chicken. Sometimes Mother alternated pieces of chicken with chicken liver or scallion. The good taste of the yakitori came from the tare, or special sauce made up primarily of soy sauce, rice wine, and sugar. My mother always prepared the sauce with her own hands; the recipe a closely guarded secret never entrusted to anyone. Only after I was grown and married did my mother write down the recipe for me."—
Yatsuhiro Kaiede,
Gifu Prefecture, Japan

Serves 4 to 6

½ cup soy sauce
5 tablespoons sugar
1 tablespoon rice wine or dry sherry
1 clove garlic, finely chopped
½ pound boneless, skinless chicken, white or dark meat,
    cut into 1½-inch pieces
½ pound chicken livers, trimmed of all fat and membranes
6 large scallions, cut into 1-inch lengths (optional)

Combine the soy sauce, sugar, rice wine and garlic in a shallow glass dish. Add the chicken and the chicken livers and marinate for 30 minutes.

Soak 8 to 10 bamboo skewers in water for 10 minutes. Remove the chicken and livers from the marinade and reserve the liquid. Thread alternating pieces of meat, livers and scallions onto the skewers.

Prepare a charcoal fire in an outdoor grill or heat the broiler to high.

Heat the reserved marinade in a saucepan over moderate heat for about 5 minutes until it is slightly thickened.

Grill or broil the skewered chicken 4 to 5 inches from the heat for 3 to 4 minutes, brushing occasionally with the thickened marinade. Turn the skewers and grill for 5 minutes longer. Continue grilling, turning occasionally, brushing with more sauce every minute or so for another 5 minutes until the chicken is cooked through.

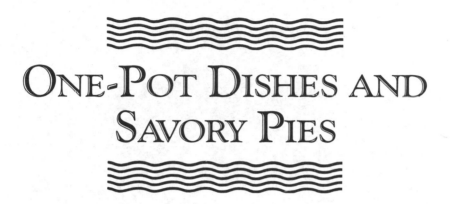

One-Pot Dishes and Savory Pies

≋ QUICHE LORRAINE ≋

Serves 4 to 6

Pastry
6 slices bacon, cut into small pieces
4 eggs
1 tablespoon all-purpose flour
1 cup half-and-half
1 cup grated Gruyère or Swiss cheese
½ teaspoon salt
¼ teaspoon freshly ground black pepper
Dash cayenne pepper

Remove the pastry from the refrigerator. Set it on a well-floured work surface and roll it out into a 12-inch circle, about 1/8 inch thick. Line an 8-inch quiche pan with the dough, trim the edges and prick the bottom several times with a fork. Allow to rest in the refrigerator for at least 15 minutes.

Heat the oven to 450 degrees.

Line the pastry shell with aluminum foil, weight with dried beans or pie weights, and bake in the oven for 8 to 10 minutes. Carefully lift out the foil and beans, brush the shell with the egg yolk wash and continue to bake for 5 minutes more. Remove the shell from the oven and allow it to cool slightly while you prepare the filling. Reduce the oven temperature to 350 degrees.

Fry the bacon in a skillet over moderate heat, stirring, until browned and crisp. Remove with a slotted spoon and drain on paper towels. Mix together the eggs, flour and half-and-half. Stir in the cheese, seasonings and bacon pieces. Pour the filling into the pastry shell; it should come to within 1/4 inch of the top.

Place the quiche in the top half of the oven and bake for about 45 minutes, until the filling has set and is lightly browned. The quiche will become a little firmer as it cools. Serve warm or at room temperature.

Frittata

Serves 4 to 6

3 tablespoons butter
1 cup sliced zucchini
½ cup finely chopped onion
1 clove garlic, finely chopped
8 eggs
1 cup prosciutto, cut into small pieces
2 medium-size tomatoes, peeled, seeded and coarsely chopped
1 teaspoon salt
½ teaspoon freshly ground black pepper
¼ teaspoon dried basil
½ teaspoon dried oregano
½ teaspoon dried marjoram
½ cup grated Parmesan cheese

Heat 2 tablespoons of the butter in a large heavy skillet. (Make sure the skillet will fit under the broiler, because the last step of the recipe is to melt the cheese over the top of the frittata.) Add the zucchini and cook until soft and lightly browned. Remove the zucchini with a slotted spoon and set aside to cool. Add the onion and garlic to the pan and cook, stirring occasionally, until softened and translucent. Remove with a slotted spoon and set aside.

Beat the eggs in a large mixing bowl until well blended. Add the cooled zucchini, the onion mixture, the prosciutto, tomatoes, salt, pepper and herbs and mix well.

Wipe the skillet with a paper towel. Add the remaining tablespoon of butter and melt, tilting the skillet so that the bottom is evenly coated. When the butter foams, pour the egg mixture into the pan and cook over low heat until the eggs are almost set on top. Meanwhile, heat the broiler.

Sprinkle the cheese on top of the frittata and place the skillet under the broiler. Cook until the cheese has melted, about 2 minutes. Serve at once.

"A couple of times each summer, when the cantaloupes were at their peak, my dad liked to splurge on a good-sized hunk of prosciutto. We'd gorge on paper-thin slices of the prosciutto with melon, and my mother would use the meat trimmings in other dishes— pizza, soups and frittata. It's impossible to give a strict recipe for frittata because it's a little different every time, but in our house it usually included tomatoes, cheese and a green vegetable or two. If there's no prosciutto on hand, a little bacon, sausage or another kind of ham is also delicious."—
Kitty LaCapra Heidler,
Indianapolis, Indiana

≋ SALTIMBOCCA DI ≋ POLLO

Serves 4 to 6

4 whole skinless, boneless chicken breasts
8 thin prosciutto slices, cut in half
½ cup grated Parmesan cheese
½ cup coarsely grated mozzarella cheese
8 fresh sage leaves
2 tablespoons butter
2 tablespoons olive oil
¾ cup white wine
Salt and freshly ground black pepper

Cut each chicken breast lengthwise into 3 or 4 pieces. Place the pieces between 2 sheets of wax paper and pound them until they are 1/8 inch thick.

Cover each chicken piece with a slice of prosciutto, 2 teaspoons of Parmesan, 2 teaspoons of mozzarella and half a sage leaf. Roll each piece lengthwise and secure with a toothpick.

Put the butter and olive oil in a large skillet and heat until bubbling. Cook the chicken rolls, 8 at a time, for 4 to 5 minutes or until lightly browned. Remove the cooked chicken from the pan and cook the remaining pieces. Remove the second batch from the pan.

Add the wine to the skillet and simmer for 2 to 3 minutes. Return the chicken to the pan and simmer for 3 to 4 minutes more, until tender. Spoon the pan juices over the chicken to serve.

CHICKEN PAPRIKAS

Serves 4 to 6

2 tablespoons butter
1 large onion
3-pound chicken, cut into serving pieces
1 large tomato, peeled, seeded and chopped
1 green pepper, cut into strips
1 tablespoon paprika
1 teaspoon salt
½ cup water
1 tablespoon all-purpose flour
½ cup sour cream

Heat the butter in a heavy casserole over moderate heat. Add the onion, reduce the heat to low and cook, covered, for 10 to 15 minutes until the onion is very soft but not brown.

Increase the heat to moderate. Add the chicken to the pan and cook, turning occasionally, for 10 minutes. Reduce the heat to low. Add the tomato and green pepper and stir in the paprika and salt. Add the water and cook, covered, for 20 minutes. Remove the lid and cook for 10 to 15 minutes more, stirring occasionally, until the chicken is tender. Remove the chicken from the pan to a serving dish and keep warm.

Stir the flour into the sour cream until well blended. Add the mixture to the pan and cook for 4 to 5 minutes, stirring occasionally, until it starts to thicken. Pour the sauce over the chicken and serve at once.

"Each time I cook something new in my kitchen, I am aware of a certain sense of magic and romance at work. I always know that I have inherited the same love for cooking that so enchanted my Hungarian grandmother's gypsy soul. When I prepare her favorite dish, Chicken Paprikas, I cook the onions slowly until they are light golden but never browned, just the way she carefully taught me. My grandmother told me that fine sweet Hungarian paprika gave this dish its special appearance and flavor. When we shopped for paprika at the market, she explained that the best paprika should have a sweet and lively taste, yet never be sharp tasting or bitter. I greatly loved and admired my little grandmother. I have special memories of the wonderful times she spent sharing gems of kitchen wisdom and cooking lore with me."—
Maria Puck,
Newport, Rhode Island

CHICKEN POT PIE

Serves 4
Pastry:
1½ cups all-purpose flour
2 teaspoons salt
8 tablespoons butter, cold
¼ cup ice water
Filling:
1½ cups chicken broth
1 pound boned, skinless chicken breast, cut into 1-inch pieces
4 tablespoons butter
1 small onion, finely chopped
3 tablespoons all-purpose flour
1 cup coarsely chopped carrot
¾ cup fresh or frozen, defrosted peas
1 tablespoon finely chopped parsley
2 teaspoons finely chopped chives
1 teaspoon dried tarragon or sage
Salt and freshly ground black pepper
1 egg yolk, lightly beaten with 1 tablespoon milk

To make the pastry, sift together the flour and salt and place in a food processor. Add the butter and process for 7 or 8 seconds (it is not necessary for the butter to be fully incorporated). Add the water and process for 2 to 3 seconds more, until the dough starts to hold together on the blade. Do not overprocess or the dough will be tough.

Turn the dough out onto a floured work surface. Using the heel of your hand, spread the dough out 6 to 8 inches in front of you, a little at a time, to finish incorporating the butter. Make the dough into a disk, wrap it in transparent wrap and chill for at least 2 hours.

To make the filling, pour the chicken broth into a saucepan and bring to the boil. Add the chicken pieces, lower the heat and simmer for 10 to 15 minutes until just tender. Remove the

chicken with a slotted spoon and set aside. Keep the chicken broth warm.

Heat the butter in a medium-sized saucepan over low heat. Add the onion and cook for 4 to 5 minutes, until softened. Sprinkle the flour over the onion and stir to combine. Continue to cook for 2 more minutes, stirring continuously.

Slowly add the warm chicken broth to the onion mixture, stirring until the sauce thickens. Add the carrots and simmer for 5 minutes. Add the peas, the reserved chicken and the herbs; season with salt and pepper to taste. Pour the filling into a deep 2-quart pie dish.

Heat the oven to 350 degrees.

Remove the pastry from the refrigerator and roll it out on a floured work surface to make an 1/8-inch-thick circle, 2 inches larger that the pie dish. Spread the pastry over the filled pie dish, trim and crimp the edges and make several slits in the top to allow steam to escape. Brush the surface with the egg yolk wash. Put the pie on a baking sheet and bake for 30 to 35 minutes, or until the pastry is golden.

"During the Depression, when times were hard for our family (as they were for many others, of course), Mom tried to make the most economical meals possible to feed our large family.
"One of Mom's favorite ways to use leftover chicken was in chicken pot pie. The flaky pastry and bubbling vegetables and chicken were a special treat— we never thought of it as 'eating leftovers' and Mom would put all kinds of things in the pie to make it more filling— carrots, string beans, pieces of cooked potatoes, and of course, the chicken."—
Herb Weinberg,
Dix Hills, New York

IRI DORI
(CHICKEN SAUTÉED WITH VEGETABLES)

"My grandparents lived on the Northern coast of Kyushu. Winters could be bitterly cold from the cold Siberian winds. For Grandmother and Grandfather, like other country folks, the pleasures of eating became an enjoyable winter pastime. I remember Grandmother loved to prepare a regional specialty, called iri dori. It was made with chicken and vegetables. She always varied the vegetables depending on what was available or in season. I can still see her deftly stir-frying the ingredients to seal in the flavors. Then she sprinkled in some soy sauce and other seasonings. A big iron kettle of freshly cooked rice always hung on a chain in the hearth. I remember how delicious it all tasted as we tucked our cold legs under the colorful quilt on the kotatsu, a low table with a charcoal box burning in the center. Grandmother's iri dori was very nourishing and warming on a cold winter's eve."— Terumi Ohya, Irvine, California

Serves 4

8 dried black mushrooms, or 8 fresh white mushrooms
2 tablespoons vegetable oil
1 pound boneless, skinless chicken breasts, cut into ½-inch pieces
1 cup ½-inch pieces of bamboo shoots
2 carrots, peeled and cut diagonally into ⅛-inch slices
3 tablespoons Japanese soy sauce
2 tablespoons sugar
½ cup snow peas (or other green vegetable such as broccoli, brussels sprouts or zucchini)
2 to 3 cups hot cooked rice

Put the dried mushrooms in a bowl and pour enough hot water over them to cover. Let them soak until soft, about 15 minutes. Rinse the mushrooms, remove their tough stems and slice. If using fresh mushrooms, it isn't necessary to soak them.

Heat the oil in a skillet over high heat. Add the chicken and stir-fry for 3 minutes until it is no longer pink. Add the bamboo shoots, carrots and mushrooms and stir for 2 minutes.

Add the soy sauce and sugar to the skillet. Lower the heat to moderately high and continue to cook, stirring, for about 5 minutes until the chicken and vegetables are cooked. Add the snow peas and stir for 3 minutes more.

Increase the heat to high and cook until the liquid is thickened and forms a glaze. Remove from the heat and serve immediately with the rice.

Stir-Fried Noodles with Chicken and Shredded Vegetables

Serves 4 to 6

Marinade:
1 tablespoon light soy sauce
1 tablespoon rice wine or dry sherry
1 teaspoon sesame oil
1 teaspoon cornstarch
1 pound boneless, skinless chicken or turkey breast,
    cut into ¼-inch pieces

Vegetables:
8 to 10 dried Chinese black mushrooms or
¼ pound fresh white mushrooms, coarsely chopped
1 tablespoon finely chopped garlic
1 tablespoon finely chopped fresh ginger
2 cups fresh bean sprouts, rinsed and drained
3 to 4 scallions, shredded

Sauce:
2 cups chicken broth
3 tablespoons light soy sauce
2 tablespoons rice wine or sherry
1 teaspoon sesame oil
Freshly ground black or white pepper
1 teaspoon cornstarch
2 tablespoons vegetable oil
½ pound fresh or dried noodles,
    such as lo mein or spaghettini, cooked al dente

Combine the marinade ingredients. Stir the chicken pieces into the marinade and toss to coat.

Pour enough very hot or boiling water over the mushrooms to cover and let them soak for 15 minutes, until the mushrooms are soft. Rinse to remove any sand, remove the tough stems and shred

"Many years ago, I had the good fortune of having a wonderful Chinese friend, Lin Chung, with whom I went to school. Her entire family was involved in their family restaurant business. Since she came from a large family, nine children in all, there was a lot of work for each member, considering that there were also household chores to be taken care of, as well as the restaurant. Suprisingly enough, though, no one seemed to mind— but I did feel very sorry for my friend because she did not have as much free time as the rest of our group of friends. However, on one occasion my friend invited several of us to her restaurant for Friday night supper— and then, from then on, in my childish ways, I believe I envied her.

the mushrooms. If you are using fresh mushrooms, there is no need to soak them.

Put the mushrooms, garlic, ginger, bean sprouts and scallions in separate piles on a platter. Combine the sauce ingredients in a small bowl. Have the vegetables and sauce ready at the stove.

Heat the vegetable oil in a wok, large heavy pot or deep skillet over high heat until it is very hot but not smoking. Add the marinated chicken and stir-fry for about 3 minutes until the chicken whitens and separates into shreds. Remove the chicken from the pan using a slotted spoon, allowing the oil to remain in the pan.

Add the garlic and the ginger, stir for 10 seconds, and add the mushrooms. Stir-fry for about 1 minute until the mushrooms are slightly softened.

Add the noodles, bean sprouts, scallions and chicken. Pour in the sauce and bring the mixture to a simmer, stirring gently for about 2 minutes until slightly thickened. Serve immediately.

KREPLACH

Makes 24

Dough:
2 cups all-purpose flour
½ teaspoon salt
2 large eggs
2 to 3 tablespoons iced water
Filling:
1 cup cream cheese
1 egg
½ teaspoon salt
¼ teaspoon freshly ground black pepper
⅛ teaspoon paprika
10 cups chicken broth

To make the dough, put the flour and salt in the bowl of a food processor fitted with a steel blade. Pulse for 2 seconds to combine. Lightly beat the egg in a small bowl and add to the flour along with 2 tablespoons of iced water. Process for about 10 seconds, until a stiff dough is formed, adding more iced water if necessary. Remove the dough from the food processor and allow to rest in the refrigerator while you make the filling.

Put all the filling ingredients except the chicken broth in a bowl and mix well.

Roll the dough out very thin and cut into 2-inch squares. There should be enough dough to make 24 squares.

Put a teaspoon of filling in the middle of each square of dough. Fold each square in half to form a triangle and seal the kreplachs by pressing the edges together with the tines of a fork.

Put the broth in a large pan and bring to the boil. Add the kreplachs in 2 batches and cook them until they rise to the surface. Keep the first batch warm while you make the second. When the second batch is done, transfer the broth and kreplachs to a warmed soup tureen and serve.

"I have inherited a wonderful old wooden chopping bowl and chopper, a 'mezzaluna,' and also the memories that go along with it. My Aunt Shirley was the official family kreplach maker and whenever her friend Arthur (also known as 'Arthur-itis') came to visit, she asked her nieces to stop by and help her make kreplach. We would chop the meat and onions, roll the dough, and, most importantly, taste for seasoning. Aunt Shirley also used the same bowl and chopper to make her gefilte fish.
I am not sure why she chose me to inherit the bowl and chopper. I like to believe it is because kreplach became my son's favorite food and Aunt Shirley wanted me to carry on the tradition of family kreplach maker. I don't know who will inherit it from me— my son or my daughter."—
Bailee Kronowitz, Savannah, Georgia

 # PIEROGI

Makes 18 pierogi

Dough:
2 eggs
⅓ cup cold water
2 cups all-purpose flour
½ teaspoon salt
Filling:
¼ pound kielbasa
1 tablespoon vegetable oil
1 tablespoon finely chopped onions
1 cup mashed potatoes
1 tablespoon finely chopped parsley
Salt and freshly ground black pepper
4 tablespoons butter, melted

To make the dough, mix the eggs with the water in a small bowl. Put the flour and salt in a food processor fitted with the plastic blade. With the motor running, pour in the egg mixture and process until the dough is smooth and not sticky. If necessary, add a little more flour. Remove the dough from the processor, wrap in plastic and set aside.

To make the filling, put the kielbasa in the food processor and process until finely chopped. Heat the oil in a small skillet over low heat. Add the kielbasa and onions and cook, stirring occasionally, until the onions are softened. Using a slotted spoon, transfer the kielbasa and onions to a bowl. Add the mashed potatoes and parsley to the bowl, mix well and season with salt and pepper to taste.

Divide the dough in half and roll one half out to a thickness of 1/8 inch on a lightly floured work surface. Using a 3-inch cookie cutter or upturned glass, cut out rounds of dough, reserving the trimmings. Repeat with the remaining dough. Combine the trimmings from both to make more rounds.

Moisten the rim of each round with a little water and put 1 teaspoon of the filling on each, slightly off center. Fold in half to cover the filling and seal the edges, using the tines of a fork to press them together. Turn the pierogi over and seal again on the other side.

Fill a large saucepan with water, add 1 teaspoon of salt and bring to the boil. Using a slotted spoon, add the pierogi to the pan, a few at a time. Do not overcrowd the pan or the pierogi may stick together. Remove the pierogi from the pan as soon as they rise to the surface and keep them warm while you boil the remainder.

Before serving, drizzle the melted butter over the pierogi. Alternatively, you can fry them in the butter until they are lightly browned.

"I often make pierogi today instead of potatoes, as a side dish, or even as a main course for a casual supper. I learned how to make them as a child from my grandmother. Unfortunately, she never told me her recipe, and I never wrote down anything she did, so I experimented and attempted to reconstruct the recipe for years before I was able to match what I thought was her recipe. My sister agrees with me that it is very close and we often reminisce about our childhood and the good times we had in our grandmother's kitchen, learning to cook and bake, and enjoying her warmth and love."— Lorraine Partridge, Salem, North Carolina

 # MEATLOAF

"To this day, my favorite way to eat meatloaf is cold in a sandwich with mayonnaise. My mother must have made meatloaf and mashed potatoes for supper at least once a week, maybe more. I remember finding meatloaf sandwiches in my lunch box all the time. My mother always added a little nutmeg, which helped bring out the flavor, and usually made it with a mixture of beef and pork."— Alice Ayers, Harrisburg, Pennsylvania

Serves 8

1 pound ground pork
1 pound ground beef
1 cup fresh bread crumbs
1 cup finely chopped onion
¼ cup chopped parsley
2 eggs, lightly beaten
¼ cup chicken broth
1½ teaspoons salt
1 teaspoon white pepper
¼ teaspoon dried thyme
½ teaspoon grated nutmeg
1 teaspoon Worcestershire sauce

Heat the oven to 350 degrees.

Combine all the ingredients in a large bowl and mix thoroughly with your hands. Lightly oil a 9-by-5-by-3-inch loaf pan. Pack the meatloaf mixture into the pan and press it down lightly, but don't lean on it or the meat will become too compact and dry.

Bake the meatloaf for 1 to 1 1/2 hours or until it starts to shrink away from the sides of the pan and the top is well browned.

Opposite: Fritatta (page 53)
Page following: Lasagne (page 123)

≋ Steak and Kidney Pie ≋

Serves 4 to 6

2 tablespoons vegetable oil
1½ pounds chuck steak, trimmed of fat and cut into ½-inch pieces
½ pound beef kidney, trimmed and cut into ½-inch pieces
1 tablespoon butter
½ pound mushrooms, cut into quarters
¼ cup all-purpose flour
½ teaspoon freshly ground black pepper
2 cups beef broth
½ pound (about 10) fresh white pearl onions
1 pound frozen or refrigerated puff pastry or pie pastry
2 to 3 tablespoons water
1 egg, lightly beaten with 1 tablespoon milk

Heat the oven to 400 degrees.

Heat the oil in a deep skillet and sear the steak over high heat, stirring until browned. Remove the meat to a large plate. Add the kidney pieces to the pan and brown them over medium-high heat for 3 minutes, stirring. Remove to the plate with the steak.

Heat the butter in the skillet over high heat, add the mushrooms and toss for 3 to 4 minutes until browned. Return the steak and the kidneys to the pan. Sprinkle with the flour and pepper and stir to coat the meat. Add the beef broth to the pan and stir in the onions. Bring the mixture to the boil, reduce the heat to medium-low and simmer, uncovered, for 20 minutes.

Roll the pastry out so that it is at least 2 inches larger all around than a deep 9- or 10-inch pie dish. Cut a 1-inch-wide circle from the outer rim of the pastry. Wet the edges of the pie plate with a little water and lay the pastry strip around the rim.

Pour the meat filling into the pie dish. Add the water to the skillet and heat gently, stirring and scraping the bottom and sides of

When I lived in North Carolina, I was astonished to watch grown people melt in an abstraction of longing when mention was made of ham and red-eye gravy. Brisk discussion would inevitably follow with the flow of bourbon as memories of ham biscuits would interrupt each other in their anxiety to be heard.

Where I grew up, in England, decent folk didn't call each other by their first names, though they could have been neighbors for years. Nor did they talk about their food, It's a pity, because if talk were to start about, say, steak and kidney pie, an entire body of culinary literature would enrich those who have never, even once, experienced this noble British birthright.

the pan to loosen any browned particles. Add the pan juices to the filling in the pie dish.

Brush the pastry strip around the rim of the dish with water and lay the pastry round over the whole dish. Crimp the edges of the pastry to seal and brush the surface with the beaten egg-milk mixture. Make a small hole in the center of the pie to release the steam.

Bake at 400 degrees for 10 minutes, then reduce the heat to 350 degrees and bake for 1 hour longer, until the pastry is golden brown.

SHEPHERD'S PIE

Serves 4

1½ pounds potatoes
2 tablespoons butter
¼ cup milk or heavy cream
1 tablespoon vegetable oil
1 large onion, finely chopped
1 pound ground cooked lamb roast or lean ground lamb
3 medium-size carrots, thinly sliced
1 teaspoon salt
½ teaspoon freshly ground black pepper
1 tablespoon chopped parsley
2 cups beef

Heat the oven to 350 degrees.

Peel the potatoes, cut them in half and put them in a medium-sized saucepan with enough salted water to cover. Bring to the boil and cook for 15 to 20 minutes until tender. Drain the potatoes and mash them thoroughly with the butter and milk or cream. Set them aside.

Heat the oil in a large heavy skillet over moderate heat. Add the onion and cook until softened and translucent, but not browned. If you are using ground meat that has already been cooked, move directly to the step of adding the vegetables. If you are using uncooked lean ground lamb, add it to the pan and cook for 6 to 8 minutes, stirring constantly, until the meat is no longer pink. Pour off any excess fat. Add the carrots, salt, pepper, parsley and broth. Bring to the boil, stirring constantly. Lower the heat and simmer for 10 minutes or until the carrots are tender.

Remove the pan from the heat and transfer the meat mixture with a slotted spoon to a large, deep ovenproof dish. If you are using ground cooked meat, lift the vegetables from the broth with the slotted spoon and combine them thoroughly with the meat mixture in the dish. Add enough of the remaining broth to moisten the meat thoroughly – but avoid using too much liquid or the potato topping will sink in. Spread the mashed potato over the meat and make a ridged design on the top with the back of a fork. Bake for 40 minutes or until the top is golden brown.

"What I remember most about shepherd's pie is that we always had it on Mondays or Tuesdays, since it was a good way to use up the leftover mutton or lamb from Sunday dinner. Monday was wash day, too, and since shepherd's pie is quick and easy to put together, my mother liked to make it because she had so little time for cooking when she was doing the laundry. Or, she might give us cold meat for Monday supper and make shepherd's pie on Tuesday."
— Mary Thomson, Westport, Connecticut

Ropa Vieja
(Shredded Beef)

Serves 6 to 8

2 pounds chuck, flank steak or London broil
2 teaspoons cider vinegar
1 teaspoon lemon or lime juice
1 clove garlic, crushed
Salt and freshly ground black pepper
2 tablespoons peanut oil
¼ cup chopped onion
¼ cup chopped green pepper
3 cloves garlic, finely chopped
1¼ cups tomato sauce
1 cup chopped tomatoes

Put the beef in a large pot and add enough cold water to cover. Simmer for about 1 1/2 hours, until the meat is very tender. Lift the meat from the pot, reserving the liquid. When the beef is cool enough to handle, shred it with a fork or a knife and fork.

Combine the vinegar, lemon juice and crushed garlic in a ceramic or glass bowl. Add the shredded beef and stir to coat well. Add salt and pepper to taste and let the meat marinate for at least 45 minutes.

Heat the oil in a deep skillet. Add the onion and green pepper and cook over moderate heat, stirring, for about 5 minutes until the vegetables are softened. Add the chopped garlic and cook for 2 to 3 minutes more. Add the tomato sauce, chopped tomatoes and 1 cup of the reserved cooking liquid from the beef. Season to taste with salt and pepper. Cook over moderate heat for about 20 minutes, stirring occasionally. Lift the beef from the bowl with a slotted spoon and add it to the sauce. Stir gently and simmer for about 10 minutes to heat the beef through. Serve over rice.

≋ Swedish Meatballs ≋

Serves 6 to 8

3 tablespoons butter
¼ cup finely chopped onion
¼ cup mashed potato
½ pound ground beef
¼ pound ground veal
¼ pound ground lamb
bread crumbs
1¾ cups light cream
1 egg, lightly beaten
1 teaspoon salt
¼ teaspoon ground nutmeg
2 tablespoons vegetable oil
2 tablespoons all-purpose flour
Freshly ground black pepper

Heat 1 tablespoon of the butter in a heavy skillet and cook the onion until softened and translucent. Remove them to a large bowl with a slotted spoon. Add the mashed potato, ground meats, bread crumbs, 1/4 cup of the cream and the egg. Stir in the salt and nutmeg and mix thoroughly. Take one rounded teaspoonful of the mixture at a time and roll between the palms of your hands to form small balls. Put the meatballs on a baking sheet, cover with wax paper and refrigerate for 1 hour.

Heat the oven to 200 degrees.

Heat the remaining 2 tablespoons of butter with the oil in a large heavy skillet over moderate heat. Cook the meatballs in batches until browned, shaking the skillet frequently to prevent them from sticking. Remove the meatballs to a warmed dish as they are cooked and keep them warm in the oven.

"Both my grandmothers gave me a taste of Old World cooking. My mother's mother hailed from County Mayo in Ireland and my dad's mom was born in Uppsala, Sweden. At her house we always enjoyed, among other good things, delicate, flavorful Swedish meatballs as a dinner appetizer or over noodles. She also baked Swedish coffee cakes for breakfast (she arose at 5 a.m. each day). I still treasure my luck in having immigrant grandmothers whose cooking brightened my earliest eating experiences."—
Michael Bartlett,
Des Plaines, Illinois

Pour all but 1 tablespoon of fat from the skillet. Stir in the flour and cook for 1 minute, stirring constantly. Whisk in the remaining 1 1/2 cups of cream, bring to the boil and cook for about 2 minutes. Season with salt and pepper to taste.

Pour the sauce over the meatballs and serve at once.

≋ RED FLANNEL HASH ≋

Serves 4

4 medium-size potatoes
4 to 5 small beets, unpeeled, with at least 1 inch of stem attached
2 cups cooked corned beef, cut into ½-inch pieces
1 medium-size onion, finely chopped
½ cup heavy cream
1 tablespoon chopped parsley
1 teaspoon Worcestershire sauce
1 teaspoon salt
1 teaspoon freshly ground black pepper
¼ teaspoon cayenne pepper
4 tablespoons butter

Cook the potatoes in enough boiling salted water to cover generously for 15 to 20 minutes, or until tender but not mushy. Drain and cool them slightly, then cut into 1/2-inch pieces.

Cook the beets, covered, in boiling salted water for 35 to 45 minutes, until tender. Drain and cool just until you can handle them and then rub off the skins. Cut the beets into 1/2-inch pieces.

Combine the corned beef, potatoes, beets and onion in a bowl. Stir to mix well and set aside.

Combine the cream, parsley, Worcestershire sauce, salt, pepper and cayenne in a small bowl. Add the cream mixture to the corned beef mixture and toss until well coated.

Heat the butter in a large heavy skillet over moderate heat until foamy. Add the corned beef mixture, spreading it out with the back of a wooden spoon to cover the bottom of the pan. Reduce the heat to low and cook for 10 minutes or until a crust has formed on the bottom of the pan. Remove from the heat.

Invert the hash onto a large platter and then slide it carefully back into the skillet to cook on the other side. Cook the hash for a further 10 minutes or until a crust has formed. Transfer to a warmed serving dish and serve immediately.

"Red Flannel Hash is an earthy, hearty dish that was always a great favorite with my father. He worked hard all week and especially liked to sit down to a meal with his large family around him, eating his favorite food and drinking a glass (or two) of foamy beer. When he knew Mom was making hash, he always tried to be home a little earlier and he would hustle us all to the table, even before Mom was ready to serve. Then he would wait impatiently, glaring at the closed kitchen door until Mom pushed it open with her shoulder and triumphantly carried the platter to the table for His Nibs to dive into." — *Charles O'Brien, Omaha, Nebraska*

MIZUTAKI
(MEAT AND VEGETABLES WITH DIPPING SAUCES)

*"Many years have passed since I became a foreign bride in Japan, once a strange and unfamiliar land to me. My initiation into the world of Japanese food preparation was a shock—but fortunately for me, my sympathetic mother-in-law took me under her wing and taught me every-thing she knew. One of her favorite styles of cooking was nabemono or casserole cooking. It was always easy for her to prepare this type of dish at home when family or friends would drop by. In the kitchen she arranged the uncooked foods attractively on beautiful blue and white platters and the sauces in colorful bowls. At the table, everyone gathered around the food in friendly communion so that Mother Kyoko could cook for everyone in a large central pot. somehow the foods always tasted better when she cooked them this way, then served them steaming hot right out of the pot."—
Elizabeth Tanaka,
Toki City, Japan*

Serves 4 to 6

Soy dipping sauce:
½ cup Japanese soy sauce
¼ cup Japanese rice wine vinegar
¼ cup grated daikon
2 tablespoons water
Sesame dipping sauce:
6 tablespoons white sesame seeds
2 teaspoons salt
6 tablespoons Japanese rice wine vinegar
4 tablespoons water
2 tablespoons sesame oil
Meat and vegetables:
1½ quarts chicken or beef broth, or water
2 carrots, peeled and cut diagonally into ⅛-inch-thick slices
1 pound fresh tofu, cut into ½-inch squares
1 cup sliced bamboo shoots
1 cup thinly sliced mushrooms
1 bunch spinach, stemmed and torn into pieces, or
1 small head Chinese cabbage, cut into 1-inch pieces
6 scallions, trimmed and cut into 1-inch lengths,
  or 1 onion, thinly sliced
1 pound lean steak, such as London broil, cut into thin slices

To make the soy dipping sauce, combine the ingredients in a bowl and divide among individual dishes for dipping.

To make the sesame dipping sauce, grind the sesame seeds with the salt in a blender at high speed, adding the liquid ingredients gradually to make a creamy sauce. Pour the sauce into individual bowls or saucers. Have both sauces ready for dipping as soon as the meat and vegetables are served.

Heat the broth or water in a chafing dish or electric frying pan, or on the stovetop. Working in batches, add the carrots, tofu and bamboo shoots and heat for 1 minute. Add the mushrooms, spinach and the scallions and simmer for 2 to 3 minutes, until the spinach is wilted. Add the beef and cook for 1 to 2 minutes. Remove the meat and vegetables to individual serving bowls, to be dipped in the sauces.

Spoon the remaining broth into separate serving bowls and season with dipping sauce to taste as a light soup to accompany the meat and vegetables.

KATSO DONBURI
(PORK CUTLETS WITH RICE AND BEAN SPROUTS)

Serves 4

Sauce:
½ cup water
¼ cup soy sauce
3 tablespoons sugar
3 tablespoons rice wine or dry sherry
Pork:
4 3-ounce pork cutlets, about ⅛-inch thick
2 eggs, beaten
1½ cups white bread crumbs
Vegetable oil for frying
4 eggs
1 medium-size onion, thinly sliced, or 6 scallions, sliced
1 pound fresh bean sprouts, rinsed and drained
2 to 3 cups hot cooked rice

*"My Japanese grandmother often told me stories her grandmother had told her about life during the Meiji Restoration. I loved to hear of the time the ban on meat-eating was lifted in Japan and great-great Grandmother ate meat for the first time. Tonkatsu, or breaded fried pork cutlets quickly became popular. (Ton means pork—katsu refers to cutlet.) Katsu donburi is a closely related cousin and came later. No one could make it better than Grandmother. She would generously fill each individual serving bowl (donburi) with hot steaming rice. Then she placed a small portion of cooked egg and vegetable on top. Finally she topped it all off with a sliced fried pork cutlet and a spoonful of delicious sauce. This type of meat-in-a-bowl was always a real favorite among our family as well as everyone else in Japan. Even foreigners like this type of Namban-ryori or foreign devil's food."—
Yukari Robb,
Richmond, Virginia*

Combine all the sauce ingredients in a small saucepan over moderate heat and stir until the sugar dissolves. Set the sauce aside.

Heat the oven to 200 degrees.

Dip the pork in the beaten eggs and then in the bread crumbs, patting the cutlets so that the coating adheres. Set the cutlets aside for 20 minutes to allow the coating to set.

Heat 1/2 inch of vegetable oil in a large skillet over moderately high heat. Cook the cutlets one at a time until brown on both sides, turning once. Drain on paper towels and keep warm in the oven.

Beat the eggs, adding any of the beaten egg left from coating the pork.

Heat 2 tablespoons of oil in a skillet over moderately high heat and add the onion or scallions. Cook, stirring, for 5 minutes until softened. Add the bean sprouts and stir for 2 to 3 minutes until softened. Pour in the eggs and cook, stirring, until just set.

Cut the pork into 1/8-inch strips.

To serve, put a spoonful of hot rice in each serving bowl. Spoon the bean sprout mixture on top and pour some of the sauce over the bean sprouts. Top each serving with strips of pork. Serve immediately.

SPANIKOPITA
(SPINACH SQUARES)

Makes 16 to 20 squares

Béchamel sauce:
2 tablespoons butter
2 tablespoons all-purpose flour
1 cup milk
Spinach filling:
3 10-ounce packages frozen chopped spinach, thawed
½ onion, finely chopped
½ pound feta cheese, crumbled
½ cup grated Parmesan cheese
4 eggs
Freshly ground black pepper
1 cup butter, melted
½ pound (14 to 16 sheets) phyllo dough

Heat the oven to 350 degrees.

To make the béchamel sauce, heat the butter in a saucepan over low heat. Add the flour and stir until the mixture is smooth. Remove the pan from the heat and gradually stir in the milk. Return the pan to the heat and stir until the mixture thickens and just comes to the boil. Remove from the heat and pour into a mixing bowl.

Add the spinach, onion and cheeses to the béchamel and stir to combine. Stir in the eggs and season with pepper to taste.

Brush a 9-by-12-inch pan with a little of the melted butter. Put one phyllo sheet in the pan and brush with more melted butter. Repeat with 6 more sheets of dough, brushing each one with butter. Spread the filling evenly over the dough. Cover the filling with 6 to 7 more sheets of dough, brushing each one with melted butter. Tuck the edges under to form a neat edge. and brush with the remaining butter. Cut into squares and bake for 30 to 35 minutes or until browned.

"I have to confess that spinach, in most of its forms, is not something I find very exciting. In the extended household in which I grew up, all the cooks (and there were a handful— my mother, both grandmothers and/or three aunts, depending on the occasion) seasoned everything lavishly, and they would have presented salad without dressing. But the humble vegetable was deemed worth eating when it was made into spanakopita, enriched as it is with cream sauce, eggs, cheese, butter and phyllo pastry. Non-Greek cooks who only discover phyllo as adults are often overawed by it, but the women in my family went through packages of the paper-thin pastry at an astonishing rate; it was practically as essential to our diet as bread would be to that of most Americans."—
Florence Callas,
Astoria, New York

 # MOUSSAKA

Serves 6

1½ pounds eggplant
¼ cup salt
3 tablespoons butter
2 small onions, finely chopped
1 clove garlic, finely chopped
1½ pounds ground lamb
28-ounce can whole tomatoes, drained, juice reserved
3 tablespoons tomato paste
1 teaspoon dried thyme
½ teaspoon ground nutmeg
1 teaspoon freshly ground black pepper
¾ cup vegetable oil
3 eggs
1 cup light cream
1 cup grated Parmesan cheese

Heat the oven to 350 degrees.

Slice the eggplant lengthwise and spread the slices on paper towels. Sprinkle with half the salt and let them drain for 10 to 15 minutes. Turn the pieces over and repeat with the remaining salt.

Heat the butter in a large pan over moderate heat. Add the onions and garlic and cook until they are softened and translucent, about 5 minutes. Add the lamb and continue to cook for about 10 minutes or until the meat is no longer pink.

Chop the tomatoes coarsely and add them to the meat. Stir in the tomato paste, half the reserved tomato juice, the thyme, nutmeg and pepper. Cook over moderate heat for 5 minutes. Check the seasoning and add more salt and pepper if desired.

Pat the eggplant slices dry with paper towels. Heat 1/4 cup of the oil in a large skillet, add a third of the eggplant slices and fry

until golden brown on both sides. Remove them from the skillet with a slotted spoon and drain on paper towels. Fry the remaining batches of eggplant slices in the same way.

Place alternate layers of meat and eggplant in an ovenproof casserole, ending with a layer of eggplant. Cover and bake in the 350-degree oven for 40 minutes.

Whisk together the eggs and the cream in a small bowl. Stir in the cheese. Remove the lid from the casserole and pour the egg mixture over the top of the moussaka. Return it to the oven and cook for a further 15 minutes, uncovered, until the topping is puffed and golden.

KASHA VARNISKES

Serves 4 to 6

1 cup kasha
1 egg, lightly beaten
2 cups boiling water
2 tablespoons butter or chicken fat
½ onion, chopped
¼ pound small bow-tie noodles, cooked
Salt and freshly ground black pepper

Combine the kasha and egg in a saucepan or skillet and stir over moderate heat until the ingredients are blended and the kasha is evenly coated. Add the boiling water, cover tightly and simmer for 15 to 20 minutes, until the kasha is tender. If any cooking liquid remains, remove the cover and continue to cook until all the liquid is absorbed.

"My mother made kasha varniskes when I was a child, mostly because my father liked it so much. My brother and I especially loved the bow-tie noodles, and when we got older, we asked our grandmother to teach us how to make it (we figured since she had taught my mother, she would be the best resource). We both made this a lot during our college years, because it was so easy on the budget and on our appetites."—
Melanie Falick,
New York, New York

Heat the butter in a small pan over moderate heat. Add the onion and cook, stirring, for 3 to 4 minutes until softened and translucent.

Add the noodles and the onions to the kasha. Season with salt and pepper to taste.

KEDGEREE

There are some things you simply have to grow up with to appreciate fully. One of these is kedgeree, which could fairly accurately be described as a mess of rice, fish and peas. It's one of those dishes that is a hangover from Britain's role as defender of the Empire in general, and India in particular. It has come to be associated with hunt breakfasts and romantic memories of hounds and horses and red-coated, black-hatted riders who tally-ho lustily into the morning mists. On the sideboard awaiting their return are arrayed covered silver tureens of the finer things of life: kidneys and fried tomatoes, bacon and roast potatoes and, of course, kedgeree.

Serves 4

5 cups water
1 bay leaf
4 peppercorns
1 pound smoked haddock fillets
Salt
1½ pounds uncooked long-grain rice
4 tablespoons butter
½ cup heavy cream
1 cup (4 ounces) frozen peas
4 hard-cooked eggs, shelled and roughly chopped
½ cup chopped parsley
Freshly ground black pepper

Bring 4 cups of water to the boil in a deep skillet with the bay leaf and peppercorns. Reduce the heat and poach the haddock in the barely simmering water for 4 to 5 minutes, until the flesh is opaque and flakes easily. Transfer the fish to a plate with a slotted spatula.

Strain the poaching liquid and add the remaining 1 cup of water, or enough to make 5 cups in all. Pour the water into a medium-sized saucepan, add 1 teaspoon of salt and bring to the boil.

Add the rice, stir once and cook, covered, over medium-low heat for 15 to 20 minutes.

Heat the butter with the cream in a small pan and boil gently for 3 to 5 minutes, until slightly thickened. (Take care that the cream does not boil over, though.)

Combine the rice and the peas in a large pan. Stir in the thickened cream mixture. With the pan over low heat, flake the fish into the rice. Add the chopped eggs, parsley and salt and pepper to taste. Toss gently together and serve immediately.

PASTA DOUGH

Makes enough for 6 main-course servings

2½ to 3 cups all-purpose flour
⅛ teaspoon salt
3 large eggs
2 teaspoons olive oil
Water
Cornmeal and cornstarch for rolling

Put the flour and salt in a mixing bowl and make a well in the center. Add the eggs and beat lightly with a fork. Gradually incorporate the flour to form the sides of the well until the eggs have absorbed enough to make a soft dough. Add the oil and a few drops of water. Continue to work in more flour to make a manageable dough. If the dough is too dry, add more water, a few drops at a time. Turn the mass out onto a floured board and knead vigorously for about 10 minutes, adding more flour as needed until the dough is

"I have to chuckle when I see all the gizmos available today for making pasta dough—rolling machines, extrusion machines, mixer attachments… . A neighbor of mine recently paid more than $300 for an electric gadget that takes the flour and water and churns out the finished dough. My mother and grandmother might not have laughed outright, but they certainly would have been astonished by all the fancy paraphernalia. They used a long, thin rolling pin, a big board for mixing and rolling the dough, and a couple of broomsticks for hanging it dry. After my grandmother was widowed and she moved in with us, they made a joint venture of pastamaking every week. Usually Mom would do the mixing, though sometimes Grandma would do it just to keep her hand in. Then they would take turns rolling out the dough on the big board, after having conferred on what they'd need that week— would we have a lasagna on Sunday? Were we running low on linguine? On the rare occasions that I made homemade pasta myself,

firm, smooth and resilient. Allow the dough to rest for at least 30 minutes before rolling it.

To roll the pasta by hand: Cut the dough in half and pat each piece into a flat disk. Dust the work surface and the rolling pin with flour. Roll the rolling pin over the disk in a firm back-and-forth motion to flatten the dough further. Give the dough a quarter turn and roll until it is roughly as long as it is wide. Dust the dough lightly with flour and turn over. Roll and give the dough another quarter turn. Continue the rolling and turning process about 5 times, flouring lightly each time the dough is flipped, until the dough is about 1/16 inch thick. As the sheet of dough becomes thinner, take special care to keep the edges the same thickness as the rest of the sheet. As the piece of dough gets larger, fold it over the rolling pin to help turn it over. When the dough is finished, brush off any excess flour.

Place the dough on a clean cloth and allow it to dry for about 20 minutes, depending on the weather, before cutting it.

To cut the dough: Dust the sheet of dough lightly with cornstarch and cornmeal to keep the noodles from sticking together. Roll the dough loosely into a long cylinder. Cut the cylinder crosswise into the desired widths for flat noodles. Unroll the noodles as they are cut and lay on a towel or a rack to dry.

If you have a pasta machine, cut the dough into quarters after it has rested and flatten one of the pieces with your hand. Keep the other pieces covered with a cloth. Feed the flattened dough into the machine, rolling it into a flat sheet. Repeat with the other three pieces. Fit the machine with the size blade you wish to use and feed the flattened pieces of dough through the machine, which will cut the pasta to the desired width.

SPAGHETTI AND MEATBALLS

Serves 6

1 pound ground chuck beef
½ pound ground pork
½ pound sweet Italian sausage
½ cup grated Parmesan cheese
1 cup fresh bread crumbs
1 tablespoon dried oregano
1 medium-size onion, finely chopped
1 clove garlic, finely chopped
1 egg
3 tablespoons finely chopped parsley
3 cups tomato sauce
1¼ pounds thin spaghetti
Freshly grated Parmesan cheese

Combine all the ingredients except the tomato sauce, spaghetti and Parmesan in a bowl and mix thoroughly. Chill the mixture for about 30 minutes to make it easy to handle. Take tablespoonsful of the chilled mixture and form into 1/2-inch balls.

Heat the tomato sauce in a saucepan over moderate heat. Add the meatballs, bring to a simmer and cook for about 30 minutes.

Cook the spaghetti in 6 to 8 cups of boiling salted water for about 8 minutes or until tender. Drain well and serve with the meatballs and sauce. Accompany with freshly grated Parmesan cheese.

"I'm not Italian, but when I was growing up around Boston everybody ate spaghetti and meatballs or spaghetti and meat sauce at least once a week. I know we did— my brother and I always told our mother it was our favorite supper. It might still be my favorite"—
Charles Marshall,
Dedham, Massachusetts

Manicotti

Serves 4 to 6

8 to 10 manicotti
Sauce:
2 tablespoons olive oil
1 small onion, chopped
2 cloves garlic, finely chopped
2 cups canned crushed tomatoes, with juice
½ cup tomato sauce
4 tablespoons tomato paste
1 teaspoon dried basil
2 teaspoons dried oregano
½ teaspoon salt
¼ teaspoon freshly ground black pepper
Filling:
2 cups ricotta cheese
1 cup mozzarella cheese, coarsely grated
⅓ cup grated Romano or Parmesan cheese
3 egg yolks, lightly beaten
3 tablespoons chopped parsley
Salt and freshly ground black pepper
¼ cup grated Parmesan cheese, for sprinkling

*"I've never met anyone, Italian or not, who didn't love manicotti. It's a shame that people think it is too hard or time-consuming to make often just because there are a few steps involved. It always fell to my grandmother to make the manicotti for Sunday dinners and special occasions, and it seemed very simple because she made the sauce and filling at a leisurely pace the evening before. Then an hour or so before the meal, she'd cook the manicotti shells and assemble the dish— I liked to spoon in the filling, so I usually got that job. There's something about stuffed pasta that seems elaborate and extra-special, but it's really simple to do if you just plan ahead a little."—
George Spano,
Kansas City, Missouri*

Cook the manicotti in boiling water until al dente, following the package directions. Drain and set aside.

Heat the olive oil in a large frying pan over moderately high heat. Add the onion and cook, stirring, for about 5 minutes until softened. Add the garlic and cook for 1 to 2 minutes longer, being careful not to burn the garlic. Add the crushed tomatoes, tomato sauce, tomato paste, basil, oregano and salt and pepper. Stir well, lower the heat, and cook uncovered for 15 to 20 minutes until the sauce thickens.

Meanwhile, make the filling by mixing the cheeses, egg yolks and parsley and salt and pepper to taste. Stir until the mixture

is soft and is the right consistency for spooning into the manicotti easily.

Heat the oven to 350 degrees.

Spread a layer of sauce (about 1 cup) over the bottom of a shallow baking dish large enough to hold the manicotti in a single layer. You may want to use two baking dishes. Holding a manicotti in one hand, carefully spoon the cheese filling into it, stuffing it as full as possible. Lay the filled pasta on the sauce. Continue stuffing all the manicotti. Spoon about 1/2 cup of the sauce over pasta. Cover the baking dish and bake for 25 to 30 minutes. Uncover the dish, sprinkle with Parmesan cheese and bake for 5 to 10 minutes more until the cheese melts. Serve with the remaining sauce on the side. Be sure to reheat the sauce before passing it.

"Of all the delightful pasta dishes I enjoyed as a child at my Uncle Joe's restaurant in Little Italy, the one I enjoyed the most was manicotti. Uncle Joe was the owner-chef of the restaurant and I know he always took a little more care when he prepared the manicotti for my brother and me. There was always so much cheese in the filling that it poured out of the pasta when we cut into it and I loved to scoop it up with chunks of fresh Italian bread. I would wolf it down, dribbling some on my shirt on the way. Pasta has never been so good since!"—
Albert Musumeci,
Troy, New York

83

CANNELLONI

Serves 4 to 6

Pasta:
2 ½ cups all-purpose flour
1 teaspoon salt
3 eggs, lightly beaten
1 tablespoon vegetable oil
Filling:
3 tablespoons olive oil
2 tablespoons chopped onion
1 clove garlic, finely chopped
½ pound lean ground beef
1 teaspoon salt
1 teaspoon freshly ground black pepper
1 tablespoon chopped fresh basil or 1 teaspoon dried
2 tablespoons chopped parsley
Béchamel sauce:
2 ¼ cups milk
3 tablespoons butter
2 tablespoons all-purpose flour
¼ teaspoon salt
1 cup grated Parmesan cheese, for sprinkling

"Both sides of my family are from Peidmont, in the north of Italy, so we tend to stick with pasta dishes that don't have a lot of tomatoe sauce and olive oil. In fact, cannelloni makes me think of french food, and some people even make them with crepes instead of pasta dough— but my mother prefered pasta because it holds up better to the filling and sauce without becoming soggy. Cannelloni are impressive but really easy to prepare if you just take the steps one at a time and do as

To make the pasta, mound the flour on a clean, dry work surface. Stir in the salt. Make a well in the center of the flour and add the eggs and oil. Using a spoon or your fingertips, gradually mix the liquid ingredients with the flour. When the dough starts to hold together, brush away any unused flour and knead for 4 to 5 minutes, until smooth. Let the dough rest for 5 minutes.

Divide the dough into 4 pieces and flatten each sufficiently to go through a pasta machine. Roll each piece through the machine to make 4 flat sheets of pasta. Cut the sheets into 3-by-4-inch rectangles and let them dry for up to 1 hour before cooking.

Meanwhile, make the filling. Heat the oil in a large skillet

over moderate heat. Add the onion and cook, stirring occasionally, for 5 minutes until softened. Add the garlic and cook for 1 to 2 minutes more. Stir in the meat, salt and pepper and cook for 8 to 10 minutes until the meat is browned. Add the basil and parsley and continue to cook for 15 minutes, stirring occasionally. Keep the filling warm while you make the béchamel.

Heat the milk in the small saucepan but do not allow it to boil. Heat the butter in another saucepan over moderate heat. When the butter starts to bubble, add the flour and cook, stirring, for 3 to 4 minutes.

Gradually add the milk, a little at a time, stirring until smooth. Stir in the salt. Cook the sauce over low heat for 12 to 15 minutes, stirring occasionally, until thick and smooth.

Bring a large saucepan of salted water to the boil over high heat. Drop the pasta strips into the water a few at a time. When the water returns to the boil, cook the pasta for about 15 seconds. Lift out the pasta with a slotted spoon and drain on paper towels. Cook the remaining pasta in the same way.

Heat the oven to 325 degrees. Butter a rectangular baking dish.

Spread 2 to 3 tablespoons of the filling evenly on each cooked pasta strip and roll up, starting from one of the longer sides, to form a neat cylinder. Lay the rolls, seam side down, in the baking dish so that they fit snugly without overlapping.

Spoon the béchamel sauce over the pasta and sprinkle with Parmesan cheese. Bake for 15 to 20 minutes, uncovered, until the sauce is bubbly and the cheese is melted and lightly browned.

much as you can in advance. They were definitely not everyday fare in our household; we only had cannelloni a couple of times a year, on occasions when Mama wanted to impress. A few times she made them without the sauce, just baked with a drizzle of butter and grated Parmesan; to tell the truth, I'm not sure which version was more delectable."—Robert Giaquinto, Boulder, Colorado

ZITI WITH BROCCOLI ≋ AND GARLIC CREAM ≋ SAUCE

Serves 4

1 pound broccoli, cut into 1½-inch florets (about 3 cups)
8 cups water
1 tablespoon olive oil
8 to 10 ounces ziti
2 tablespoons butter
3 cloves garlic, finely chopped
¼ cup white wine
1½ cups heavy cream
3 scallions, white and green parts, cut into strips
½ red pepper, cut into strips (optional)
3 tablespoons grated Parmesan cheese
Freshly ground black pepper

Steam the broccoli or blanch it in boiling water until it is bright green and just tender. Drain well and set aside.

Put the water and olive oil in a large saucepan and bring to the boil. Add the ziti and cook for 10 minutes. Drain in a colander and set aside.

Heat the butter in a large skillet over moderate heat. Add the garlic and cook for about 2 minutes, until softened but not brown. Add the wine and cook for 1 minute until reduced to 1 tablespoon. Add the cream. Increase the heat to moderately high and bring to the boil. Boil for 2 to 3 minutes, until the cream thickens and is reduced by about a third.

Put the ziti and broccoli in a large bowl. Add the sauce, scallions, red pepper and Parmesan cheese and toss together. Season with freshly ground black pepper and serve at once.

My Grandmother's Red Beans and Rice

Serves 4

Beans:
10 to 12 thin slices bacon (about 6 ounces)
3 cups chopped onion
2 teaspoons chopped garlic
2 15½-ounce cans red beans with liquid
1½ teaspoons Dijon mustard
¼ teaspoon Tabasco sauce
1 tablespoon tarragon wine vinegar or red wine vinegar
Salt and pepper
4 tablespoons freshly chopped parsley, for garnish
Rice:
3 quarts (12 cups) water
1 teaspoon salt
3 cups long-grain rice

Fry the bacon over medium-high heat until crisp in a large heavy frying pan (a well-seasoned cast-iron one works well). Take the slices from the pan and drain on paper towels. When the bacon is cool, crumble it and set it aside.

Pour off all but 2 tablespoons of bacon fat from the pan. Heat the fat over moderate heat and when it is hot, add the onion and garlic and cook, stirring, for 3 to 4 minutes until softened. Add the beans and liquid, mustard, Tabasco and vinegar. Stir well and bring the mixture to a simmer. Lower the heat to a gentle simmer and cook, uncovered, for about 15 minutes, stirring frequently. If the beans start to cook down and all the liquid evaporates, stir in 1/2 to 1 cup of water, as needed.

Meanwhile, cook the rice. bring the water to the boil in a large heavy pot over high heat. Add the salt and rice and cook, uncovered, for about 12 minutes until the rice is light and fluffy. Drain in a colander. This will make 9 cups of rice.

"My earliest culinary remembrance is of my grandmother, a talented Southern lady, and her feisty, dear cook, Ada. Both Mama and Ada cooked together, side by side, every day of the week in my grandmother's kitchen. They turned out a bounty of Dixieland favorites— fresh cream of coconut cake, plates of red beans and rice, hot pecan pies and stately golden biscuits. They were famous in Southern Mississippi for their fig preserves, which they made out of figs from the towering fig tree shading the backyard. After gathering several aprons full each, they went back to the kitchen, started huge pots of sugar and water boiling and set about making the preserves.

"As fate would have it, neither of these women wrote down any of their recipes. My cousins and I have tried unsuccessfully to reproduce the preserves for 30 years. I make red beans and rice often for my own family. The memories of these two women comprise some of my fondest childhood recollections."— Betty Rosbottom, Columbus, Ohio

Divide the rice evenly among 4 individual serving plates and top with the beans. Sprinkle the crumbled bacon and parsley on top of the beans and serve at once.

EMPANADAS

Makes about 18 empanadas

Tuna filling (Relleno de atun):
6 ½-ounce can tuna, shredded
½ cup heavy cream
3 tablespoons olive oil
1 tablespoon finely chopped onion
2 hard-cooked eggs, chopped
Salt and freshly ground black pepper
Mexican hash filling (Relleno de picadillo):
1 pound lean ground beef
1 small onion, finely chopped
1 clove garlic, finely chopped
2 teaspoons finely chopped parsley
¼ cup raisins, plumped in water and drained
1 cup tomato sauce
¼ cup slivered almonds, toasted
¼ cup dry sherry
Crab meat filling (Relleno de cangrejo):
1 tablespoon butter
1 small Spanish onion, finely chopped
1 tomato, peeled and chopped
¾ pound cooked crab meat
1 tablespoon finely chopped parsley
¼ cup capers or chopped green olives
1 teaspoon vinegar
½ teaspoon dried thyme
Salt and freshly ground black pepper

Dough:
1 teaspoon sugar
1 teaspoon salt
2 ½ cups flour
8 tablespoons butter, cut into small pieces
1 egg, beaten
½ cup ice-cold milk

To make the tuna filling, put all the ingredients in a bowl and mix well.

To make the Mexican hash, cook the meat in a skillet over medium-high heat for 30 minutes, stirring occasionally. Add the onion, garlic, parsley, raisins, tomato sauce and almonds. Cook until thickened, stirring constantly. Remove from the heat and stir in the sherry.

To make the crab meat filling, heat the butter in a heavy skillet over moderate heat. Add the onion and cook, stirring, until softened and transparent. Add the tomato, crab meat, parsley, capers, vinegar, thyme, and salt and pepper to taste. Increase the heat to medium-high and cook for 10 minutes to blend the flavors.

To make the dough, combine the sugar, salt and flour in a large mixing bowl. Work the butter into the flour with your fingertips until the mixture is the consistency of coarse bread crumbs. Mix the beaten egg with the milk and add enough of this liquid to the flour mixture to form a dough that holds together.

Roll the dough out on a lightly floured work surface to a thickness of about 1/2 inch. Using a cookie cutter or inverted glass, cut the dough into 4-inch rounds.

Heat the oven to 350 degrees.

Place a spoonful of the desired filling on each dough round. Moisten the edges with water, fold over into a semicircle and seal the edges well with a fork.

Arrange the empanadas on a baking sheet and bake for 18 to 20 minutes or until browned.

old dilemma, and, in this city of immigrants, a very common one—how to maintain the customs of the old country while adopting those of the new. My 19-year-old daughter spent her formative years in Buenos Aires and remembers it very clearly, but my 7-year-old son is rapidly becoming an all-American boy. One way in which I hope to keep up his interest in his Argentinian heritage is by preparing the marvelous dishes of my homeland." —
Christina Gremigni,
Los Angeles, California

89

≡ ENCHILADAS VERDES ≡
(GREEN ENCHILADAS)

Serves 4 to 6

½ *pound tomatillos, husked (see note)*
¼ *cup fresh coriander (cilantro)*
¼ *cup chopped Spanish onion*
2 *cloves garlic, crushed*
¼ *cup chicken broth*
⅔ *cup vegetable oil*
Salt and freshly ground black pepper
12 *tortillas*
2 *cups shredded cooked chicken (see note)*
Salt and pepper
Grated mozzarella cheese
Chopped scallions
Sour cream

To make the sauce, wash the tomatillos in warm water and pat dry with paper towels. Put the tomatillos in a large heavy skillet and toast over medium-high heat, stirring constantly, for 10 to 15 minutes, until brown spots appear all over them. Remove from the heat and allow to cool slightly.

Put the tomatillos in a blender or food processor. Add the coriander, chopped onion, garlic and chicken broth and process until pureed.

Heat 2 tablespoons of the oil in a saucepan over low heat. Add the puree, season to taste, and simmer for 25 minutes or until slightly thickened.

Heat the remaining oil in a large heavy skillet. Dip each tortilla in the hot oil for 30 seconds on each side – they should be pliable, not crisp – and drain on paper towels.

90

Dip each tortilla in the sauce. Spoon some shredded chicken onto each one and top with more sauce. Fold the tortillas and transfer to serving plates, 2 or 3 to a plate. Sprinkle each enchilada with grated mozzarella and chopped scallions and top with a spoonful of sour cream. Serve immediately.

Note: These are called "green" enchiladas because they use the slightly tart-tasting green tomato-like fruit known in Mexico as tomatillos. Fresh tomatillos are sold in Spanish markets and specialty shops and can usually be found, canned, in supermarkets with other Mexican foods.

To cook the chicken for the filling, poach a whole chicken breast in a quart of water with 1 small onion, 1 clove garlic, 1 teaspoon salt and a few sprigs of parsley. Cook for about 20 minutes or until tender. Alternatively, any cooked chicken meat may be used.

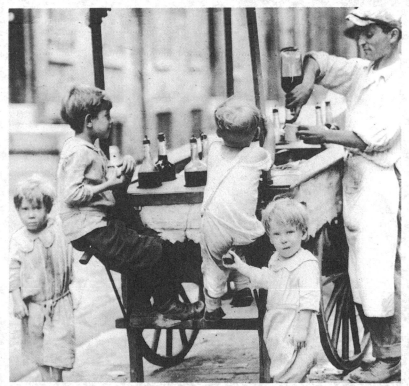

art. Tortillas, like paintings, carry the signature of the creator. Mom's tortillas reflect the woman she is. They are made of the softest flour, the purest shortening; they are tender and melt in the mouth with a dab of butter, but are strong enough to fold into a fat, juicy burrito. They are small and delicate because her hands are small and delicate. They are not perfectly shaped or toasted, but one's mouth waters looking at them, smelling them. To receive a dozen of her finest, wrapped in a checkered napkin, is to experience a great lady."—Shelby Paxton Soto, San Jose, California.

TAMALE PIE

Serves 4 to 6

1½ pounds lean ground beef
1 cup frozen whole-kernel corn
¼ cup cornmeal
16-ounce can tomato sauce
2 scallions, chopped
½ teaspoon dried oregano
½ teaspoon chili powder
½ teaspoon cumin
½ teaspoon salt
Crust:
3 tablespoons cornmeal
1 scant cup all-purpose flour
5 tablespoons butter or margarine, cut into small pieces
4 tablespoons cold water
Topping:
¼ cup milk
1 egg
1¼ cups grated Monterey Jack cheese
1 cup grated cheddar cheese
Sour cream

"My brother had many friends in Mexico and he would often return from visits with them with new recipes for my mother to try. She was very good-natured about experimenting and one of her greatest successes was tamale pie. It was such a success, in fact, that it became a staple on her list of 'company food,' and she often prepared it for Saturday evening suppers or Sunday brunch.

"After he married, my brother liked to try his hand at cooking and our mother gave him many of her favorite recipes. Among them, of course, was the recipe for tamale pie, which he had first given to her. He still makes it and it has become a favorite of the whole family."—
Joanne Delbert,
San Jose, California

Brown the beef in a large heavy skillet over medium-high heat. Remove from the heat and drain off the fat. Add the corn, cornmeal, tomato sauce, scallions, oregano, chili powder, cumin, and salt and stir until well mixed.

To make the crust, combine the cornmeal with the flour in a mixing bowl. Work in the butter or margarine with your fingertips until the mixture resembles coarse bread crumbs. Add the water, a little at a time, until the dough holds together. Lightly flour a work surface. Roll the dough out into a 13- to 14-inch round.

Heat the oven to 425 degrees. Line a 9-inch deep-dish pie pan with the rolled dough. Fill with the meat mixture and bake for 30 minutes.

While the pie is baking, combine the milk, egg and grated cheeses in a bowl. Spread the mixture evenly over the baked pie and return to the oven for 5 to 8 minutes, or until the cheese has melted. Let the pie stand for a few minutes so that the cheese can set, then serve immediately, with spoonfuls of sour cream on top.

"In 1958 my father was transferred from West Virginia to Southern California, and we made the exodus across country in a spirit of high adventure. Everything Californian was exotic to us— palm trees, surfboards, golden hills dropping down to ocean beaches—and my mother, sister, and I spent at least our first year here as virtually full-time tourists. Not least among the area's charms was its food, and Cal-Mex staples like burritos and enchiladas became a mainstay of our diet. My mother does not delve seriously into Mexican cooking, but from local newspapers and magazines she has assembled quite a repertoire of Mexican-inspired dishes, of which tamale pie is a perfect example. Nowadays I'm sure this wouldn't raise an eyebrow back in Charleston, but when Mom first started making tamale pie, most West Virginians would have considered ingredients like cumin and Monterey Jack very strange indeed."— June Allen, Northridge, California

STUFFED CABBAGE LEAVES

Serves 4 to 6

1 large head cabbage
Stuffing:
¼ cup rice
½ pound ground pork
1 pound ground beef
1 egg
1 teaspoon salt
1 teaspoon pepper
1 teaspoon dried marjoram
1 cup finely chopped onion
5 large cloves garlic, finely chopped
Sauerkraut:
2 pounds sauerkraut
½ cup finely chopped onion
2 cups white wine
4 tablespoons tomato paste
8 ounces tomato sauce
8 ounces canned tomatoes, with juice
½ pound smoked pork chop, cut into ¼-inch cubes,
   or ¼ pound Hungarian bacon (also called speck), cut into cubes
1 teaspoon caraway seeds
½ teaspoon dried marjoram
1 bay leaf
1 teaspoon sweet Hungarian paprika
1 teaspoon freshly ground pepper

Core the head of cabbage and plunge it in boiling salted water. Let it cook for 15 minutes, lift it from the water and drain. When cool, separate the leaves and lay them aside.

Make the stuffing by cooking the rice in about 1/2 cup boiling water for 10 minutes until tender but still firm. Drain the rice

and combine it with the ground pork and beef in a bowl. Add the egg, salt, pepper, marjoram, onion and garlic. Stir well. Set the stuffing aside while preparing the sauerkraut.

Drain the sauerkraut and rinse it well under running water. Drain again and then combine it with the onion, wine, tomato paste, tomato sauce and tomatoes. Add the cubed pork chop, caraway, marjoram and bay leaf. Spread the sauerkraut mixture in a large, shallow baking dish.

Lay a cabbage leaf on a flat work surface and put 2 to 3 tablespoons of filling in the center of the leaf. Roll the leaf up and tuck in the sides. Lay the rolled cabbage leaf on top of the sauerkraut. Secure it closed with a toothpick, if necessary. Stuff the rest of the cabbage leaves in the same manner and lay them on the sauerkraut.

Cover the baking dish with a lid or foil and cook over low heat for 2 hours. Baste the cabbage leaves several times with the juices from the bottom of the casserole but do not stir the food. Sprinkle the paprika and pepper over the cabbage and serve.

"Stuffed cabbage was always a special treat in our home when I was young. It was an all-day affair for my mother and aunt to prepare the stuffed cabbage leaves and sometimes, as I grew older, I was permitted to help. I always burned my fingers because I was too impatient to let the cabbage leaves cool sufficiently before I tried to stuff them, but I couldn't wait to taste them after they had baked for what seemed to me an eternity. If I helped them, my mother and my aunt always rewarded me with the first piece out of the oven, and they would watch me carefully, pretending to be worried about my reaction. Of course, the cabbage was always just right but, as the official taster, I took my job seriously and I always hesitated a bit before beaming and pronouncing them perfect."— Elena Carr, Cincinnati, Ohio

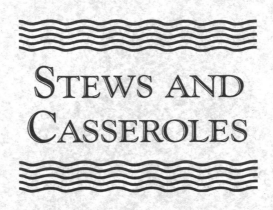

STEWS AND CASSEROLES

Opposite: Eggplant Parmigiana (page 121)
Page following: Kedgeree (page 78)

POLLO EN PEPITORIA
(CHICKEN WITH ALMONDS AND GARLIC)

Serves 4 to 6

3½- to 4-pound chicken, cut into serving pieces
¼ cup olive oil
2 cloves garlic, finely chopped
1 large onion, sliced
2 tablespoons all-purpose flour
1½ cups white wine
1 cup chicken broth
Salt and freshly ground black pepper
1 bay leaf
1 sprig fresh thyme or ½ teaspoon dried
24 blanched whole almonds, finely chopped
½ teaspoon ground saffron
2 hard-cooked eggs, chopped
¾ cup toasted bread crumbs
1 tablespoon finely chopped parsley

Pat the chicken pieces dry with paper towels. Heat the oil in a large, heavy skillet and cook the chicken over moderate heat, turning frequently, until golden brown on all sides Remove the chicken from the pan and set aside. Pour off most of the fat from the pan, leaving about 2 tablespoons.

Add the garlic and onion to the skillet and cook for 3 to 4 minutes, until softened. Return the chicken to the pan and stir in the flour. Stir in the wine and the chicken broth. Season with salt and pepper to taste and add the bay leaf and thyme. Bring to the boil, reduce the heat to low and simmer, covered, for 20 minutes.

Add the almonds and saffron and cook for about 20 minutes more or until the chicken is tender. Sprinkle with the chopped eggs, bread crumbs and parsley just before serving.

> "My grandfather always said he had delicate taste and could not tolerate the use of either onion or garlic in his food. My grandmother was a very hearty cook and eater, and when I was about 10, I discovered that over the years she had been adding onion and garlic to Grandpa's food in increasing amounts. By the time I found out, she was using both with a heavy hand. Grandpa never knew, because he almost never entered the kitchen— a woman's domain." —
> Niki Singer Sheets,
> New York, New York

Opposite: Chicken Pot Pie (page 56)
Page preceding: Boston Baked Beans (page 199)

PAELLA

"I loved the old stone house near the water's edge, outside Buenos Aires, where my brother and I used to spend our long summer vacations. No question, my favorite spot was the enormous terrace, with its view over the ocean. There I could spend untold hours looking out over the landscape and breathing in the cool, moist sea air. At midday we would set the table in the shade of an orange tree, and at the stroke of noon my grandmother would serve lunch. Because we preferred seafood over anything else, every Sunday she would delight us with a lavish paella Valenciana— a family tradition, since Grandma herself had grown up in Valencia. Armed with a wicker basket, she would go down to the port first thing in the morning, knowing that there she could buy the best and freshest seafood available. Grandma took unbelievable pains to use only the best ingredients in her cooking; I try to follow her lead in mine."— Cristina Gremigni, Los Angeles, California

Serves 6

12 mussels
2- to 2½-pound chicken, cut into pieces
2 to 3 teaspoons salt
1 teaspoon black pepper
½ cup olive oil
½ pound garlic sausage, cut into ¼-inch slices
12 jumbo shrimp, shelled
4 ounces boneless pork, trimmed and cut into small pieces
1 medium-size onion, finely chopped
2 cloves garlic, finely chopped
1 large red pepper, seeded and thinly sliced
2 tomatoes, peeled, seeded and chopped
3 cups short or medium-grain rice
¼ teaspoon ground saffron
6 cups hot chicken broth
¾ cup fresh or frozen peas
2 tablespoons finely chopped parsley
2 lemons, cut into wedges

Scrub the mussels well under cold running water and remove their beards. Heat the oven to 400 degrees.

Pat the chicken pieces dry with paper towels and season them with 1 teaspoon of salt and the pepper. Heat half the oil in a 14- to 15-inch paella pan or large skillet, add the chicken pieces and the sausage and cook until they are golden brown on all sides. Remove the chicken and sausage from the pan to a warm plate. Add the shrimp to the pan and cook briefly until they are just pink. Remove them from the pan to the plate with the chicken and sausage.

Pour the remaining 1/4 cup of olive oil into the pan. When it is hot, add the pork and cook, stirring, until browned. Add

the onion, garlic, red pepper and chopped tomatoes and cook for 5 to 6 minutes until the mixture thickens.

Return the chicken, sausage and shrimp to the pan. Add the rice, 1 to 2 teaspoons of salt and the saffron. Add the hot chicken broth and bring to the boil, stirring constantly.

Remove the paella from the heat and check the seasoning. Stir in the peas and add the mussels. Put the paella on the lowest shelf of the oven and cook, uncovered, for 30 to 35 minutes or until the liquid is absorbed and the rice is tender. Remove from the oven, sprinkle with the chopped parsley and garnish with lemon wedges.

"When I was a young girl in the Bronx, visits to Aunt Sofia's apartment were a gourmet's delight. As we walked up the flight of stairs, we immediately smelled the savory scents of her famous paella. If we arrived early, we would don colorful aprons and participate in the preparation of this tasty dish. In the Old World tradition, the men in the family retired to the living room where they smoked their cigars and talked about politics. When we all sat down at the oversized table and Aunt Sofia entered with the huge pot of paella, the Ah's and Oh's reverberated throughout the apartment."—
Mara Fernandez,
Riverdale, New York

≋ Arroz con Pollo ≋
(Chicken with Rice)

Serves 4

3- to 3½-pound chicken, cut into serving pieces
Salt and freshly ground black pepper
¼ cup plus 1 tablespoon olive oil
1 medium-size onion, coarsely chopped
2 cloves garlic, finely chopped
1½ cups chicken broth
½ cup water
½ cup white wine
¼ teaspoon red pepper flakes
¼ teaspoon ground saffron
1 bay leaf
1-pound can plum tomatoes
1 cup rice
½ red pepper
½ yellow pepper
½ green pepper

Season the chicken pieces with salt and pepper. Heat the oil in a large heavy skillet over moderate heat. Add the chicken in batches to avoid overcrowding and cook, turning once, until golden brown, about 5 minutes on each side. Remove the chicken to a large ovenproof casserole. Heat the oven to 350 degrees.

Add the onion and garlic to the skillet and cook until softened, about 3 minutes. Add the broth, water, wine, red pepper flakes, saffron, bay leaf, tomatoes and rice. Season with salt and pepper to taste and bring to the boil.

Pour the liquid over the chicken, cover and bake in the oven until the rice is tender and the chicken is done, about 25 minutes.

Meanwhile, cut the peppers into strips. Heat the remaining tablespoon of olive oil in a small skillet. Add the peppers and cook for about 4 minutes, until they are just tender. Add the peppers to the casserole and serve at once.

Coq au Vin

Serves 4 to 6

4 ounces bacon, cut into 1-inch pieces
3-pound chicken, cut into serving pieces
Salt and freshly ground black pepper
2 tablespoons olive oil
3 cups red wine
2 cloves garlic, finely chopped
1 bay leaf
1½ teaspoons chopped fresh thyme or ½ teaspoon dried
1 pound (about 12) small white onions
½ pound mushrooms, sliced
2 tablespoons butter, softened
2 tablespoons all-purpose flour
2 tablespoons chopped parsley

Heat the oven to 375 degrees.

Heat a large ovenproof casserole and cook the bacon over moderate heat until crisp and brown. Remove the bacon pieces with a slotted spoon.

Season the chicken with salt and pepper. Add the oil to the casserole and heat until very hot but not smoking. Add the chicken pieces to the pan and cook in 2 batches until golden brown on all sides, about 10 minutes per batch. Pour off and reserve the remaining oil.

Return the chicken and bacon to the casserole. Add the wine, garlic, bay leaf and thyme to the pan. Cook over moderate heat for about 5 minutes. Cover and cook in the oven for 20 minutes.

Meanwhile, heat the reserved oil in a small skillet over moderate heat. Add the onions and cook them until browned, about 10 minutes.

When the chicken has been in the oven for 20 minutes, add the onions and mushrooms to the casserole. Cover and cook for another 40 minutes, until the chicken is tender.

"Chef Chambrette of La Varenne Cooking School in Paris is a veteran of pre-World War II kitchens and has strong ideas on how to prepare coq au vin. He insists that only an old barnyard rooster will do. He's quite right that a rooster tastes quite different. It takes three hours to cook and emerges mellow and full-bodied, more like a game bird than a chicken. If we're lucky, he'll have wheedled a carafe of pig's blood from his friend the charcutier for thickening the sauce." — Anne Willan, Washington, D.C.

Discard the bay leaf. Remove the chicken, mushrooms and onions from the casserole with a slotted spoon and put them in a warmed serving dish. Blend the butter with the flour and gradually whisk it into the liquid in the casserole over moderate heat. When the sauce thickens and just coats the back of a spoon, pour it over the chicken. Garnish with parsley and serve with the vegetables.

CHICKEN WITH DUMPLINGS

Serves 6

3½-pound chicken, cut into serving pieces
1 medium-size onion, cut into quarters
1 stalk celery, cut into 1-inch pieces
1 large carrot, cut into 1-inch pieces
½ teaspoon salt
½ teaspoon freshly ground black pepper
Dumplings:
1½ cups all-purpose flour
2 teaspoons baking powder
½ teaspoon salt
1 egg
½ cup milk
1½ tablespoons chopped fresh sage or 1¼ teaspoons dried (optional)

Put the chicken pieces into a large, flameproof casserole and add the onion, celery and carrot. Add enough water to cover and add the salt and pepper. Cover and bring to the boil. Reduce the heat to low and simmer for about 1 hour until the chicken is tender.

To make the dumplings, combine the flour, baking powder and salt in a medium-sized bowl. Whisk the egg and the milk together and stir the mixture into the dry ingredients. Stir in the sage if you are using it.

When the chicken is tender, remove it from the pan and strain the broth. Measure 3 cups of the broth, return them to the pan and reheat. Return the chicken to the pot. Gently drop heaping tablespoons of the dumpling dough over the chicken. Cover and simmer over low heat for about 20 minutes until the dumplings are cooked through.

≋ POT-ROASTED ≋ CHICKEN

Serves 6

5- to 6-pound roasting chicken
2 tablespoons unsalted butter, or 3 slices bacon
Salt and pepper
1 large carrot, cut into 4-inch lengths
1 large stalk celery, cut into 4-inch lengths
1 medium-size Spanish onion, peeled and quartered
1 medium-size turnip, peeled and quartered
½ cup water
1 tablespoons chopped fresh tarragon or basil
1 tablespoon chopped fresh thyme

Heat the oven to 325 degrees.

Rub the outside of the chicken with the butter, or cover the breast with the bacon slices and secure with string. Season the bird inside and out with salt and pepper. Place the chicken on its side in a heavy, shallow roasting pan and put it in the oven. Scatter the vegetables around the bird, pour the water over the vegetables and sprinkle the herbs over the top.

.After 5 minutes of cooking, lift the bird onto the vegetables and cook for 30 minutes more. Baste the chicken and turn it onto its other side. Continue cooking for another 30 minutes

"Amid all the talk of 'American cuisine,' certain preparations continue to survive for generation after generation. Somewhere in the lists of food 'ins and outs,' we may have sidelined the idea of a simply cooked fowl. Picture it for a minute. No, not one of those Hollywood sun-glassed birds ready for photography. More like the tasty rooster strutting in the way of the police car rounding the corner in hot pursuit of Cary Grant and Grace Kelly in To Catch a Thief. Now that's a chicken! Plump, proud, barnyard fed and ready for a good cook." —
Michael Foley,
Chicago, Illinois

and turn the bird onto its chest. Baste again and cook for 30 minutes more. Turn the chicken breast side up and baste again. Cook for 30 minutes more.

Increase the heat to 450 degrees and cook the chicken for another 10 minutes to crisp the skin. The juices should run clear when the chicken is pierced with a skewer.

Remove the chicken from the pan and let it stand for 10 minutes in a warm place. Remove the bacon. Carve the chicken and garnish each serving with the roasting vegetables. Spoon some of the roasting juices over each portion.

POT ROAST

Serves 6

4-pound rump roast of beef
1 teaspoon salt
½ teaspoon freshly ground black pepper
¼ cup vegetable oil
1½ pounds carrots, sliced thick
8 celery stalks, trimmed and coarsely chopped
4 medium-size onions, thinly sliced
3¾ cups beef broth
3 tablespoons cider vinegar
4 sprigs parsley
1 bay leaf
1 teaspoon dried thyme

Rub the meat with the salt and pepper. Heat the oil in a large, heavy flameproof casserole and brown the meat over moderately high heat, turning frequently to brown on all sides and

prevent burning. Add half the carrots, celery and onions to the pan and continue to cook, stirring occasionally, until the onions are golden brown. Be careful not to burn the onions as this will give the roast a bitter taste.

Add the broth, vinegar and the herbs to the pot and bring to the boil. Lower the heat and simmer, partly covered, for 2 to 2 1/2 hours until the meat is tender.

Add the remaining vegetables, cover, and simmer for another 50 to 60 minutes until the vegetables are done and the meat is very tender. Remove the bay leaf from the pot and serve.

CASSOULET

Serves 12 to 14

2 ½ pounds boned pork loin
2 pounds navy beans
½ pound fresh or salt pork rind
4 bay leaves
2 ½ teaspoons dried thyme
8 to 10 parsley stems
1 pound pork belly or lean rindless salt pork,
  simmered in water to cover for 10 minutes
3 cups finely chopped onion
Salt and freshly ground black pepper
6 tablespoons rendered pork fat or lard
2 to 2 ½ pounds boned shoulder or breast of lamb
1 pound cracked lamb bones
4 cloves garlic, finely chopped
6 tablespoons tomato puree
3 cups dry white wine

Great dishes of the world seem
to come and go. They are, for
an instant in culinary time,
revered like great heroes and
then are tossed aside.
Cassoulet enjoyed its moment
in the sun for a while but has
since been cast into the
shadow. But not for me.
For me, cassoulet is one of the
most glorious of all the
country dishes of France. It is
made by a series of steps, all
of them easy, most of them
time-consuming and
ultimately worth every
moment of care that results in
one of man's finest creations.

3 8½-ounce cans chicken broth
1 cup water
1 pound garlic sausage, sliced
2 cups dry white bread crumbs
½ cup finely chopped parsley

Heat the oven to 350 degrees.

Roast the pork loin, uncovered, for 1 1/2 to 2 hours, until a roasting thermometer registers an internal temperature of 155 degrees. Reserve the cooking juices, let the meat cool and cut it into 2-inch cubes. Set the pork aside.

Bring 5 quarts of water to a boil in a large casserole. Add the beans, return to the boil and cook for 2 minutes. Remove from the heat and let the beans soak, covered, for 1 hour.

Put the pork rind in a pan and add water to cover. Bring to the boil and cook for 1 minute. Take the rind out of the water, allow it to cool slightly, then cut it into small squares. Cover these with cold water, bring just to a simmer and cook gently for 30 minutes. Drain the pork rind; discard the cooking liquid.

Make a bouquet garni with 2 bay leaves, 2 teaspoons of thyme and the parsley stems on a 4-by-4-inch piece of doubled cheesecloth, fold up the corners and tie tightly with kitchen twine.

Add the pork belly or salt pork to the beans in the casserole. Add 1 cup of chopped onion, the pork rind squares and the bouquet garni. Bring to a simmer, skim away any scum that rises to the surface and simmer gently, uncovered, for 1 1/2 hours or until the beans are just tender. (Add more boiling water if necessary to keep the beans covered.) Season with salt and pepper at the end of the cooking time.

Drain the beans, reserving the cooking liquid. Remove the piece of pork and set aside. Remove and discard the bouquet garni.

Heat the rendered pork fat or lard in a large heavy casserole over medium-high heat. Cut the lamb into 2-inch pieces, dry them carefully and cook in the hot fat until browned on all sides. Remove the meat with a slotted spoon and set aside. Add the lamb bones and brown them thoroughly. Remove the bones and lower the heat to moderate. Add the remaining chopped onion and the garlic and cook, stirring, until lightly browned. (Take great care not to let the fat burn. If, alas, it does, discard it and replace with fresh.)

Return the lamb meat and the bones to the casserole. Add the tomato puree, the remaining bay leaves and thyme, and the wine and broth. Season with salt and pepper to taste. Cover and simmer gently for 1 1/2 hours. (If you prefer, you can put the casserole in the oven, preheated to 325 degrees, for 1 1/2 hours.) Add up to 1 cup of water during the cooking time, if necessary, to keep all the ingredients covered.

Remove the lamb meat from the casserole and set aside Remove and discard the bones and the bay leaves. Spoon off most of the fat and reserve. Add the drained beans to the casserole, along with the cooking juices reserved from the pork loin, and add sufficient bean cooking liquid to cover the beans. Bring to a simmer and cook for 5 minutes. Remove from the heat and allow to stand for 10 minutes, then drain the beans again, reserving the liquid to add to the cassoulet.

Heat the oven to 375 degrees.

Slice the piece of belly or salt pork 1/4 inch thick. Spread half the beans in the bottom of an 8- to 10-quart casserole. Cover the beans with layers of lamb, pork loin, belly pork and garlic sausage, in that order. Top with the remaining beans. Pour enough of the liquid you just reserved over the cassoulet to cover the beans. (If there is not enough, augment it with some of the reserved liquid in which you originally cooked the beans.) Sprinkle the bread crumbs and chopped parsley over the top. Drizzle the reserved lamb fat all over the top.

Bring the cassoulet to a simmer on top of the stove and then set it, uncovered, in the upper third of the preheated oven.

"My grandmother's younger sister, great aunt Fernande, is so archetypically French that even she laughs about it. Fernande lives in the suburbs of Toulouse, where le vrai cassoulet Toulousain is king. Every three or four years she makes the Transatlantic trip to visit her sister and the rest of the family, and she comes equipped with what she considers the two indispensable ingredients for a cassoulet— dried white beans from the Toulouse market, and a container of goose confit which she manages to slip past the customs inspectors. She spends several weeks with us each time, and after a few days' settling in, the first project she takes on is preparing the cassoulet. It's always a little different, depending on the vagaries of our supermarket on her shopping day, yet somehow it's also, from one time to the next, reassuringly the same."— Jeanne Martin, Syracuse, New York

Cook for 20 minutes or until a crust has formed on the top. Break the crust with a spoon and baste with liquid from beneath. Cook for 15 to 20 minutes more, until the crust forms again. Continue this process for a total cooking time of 1 hour, adding more bean cooking liquid or water, if needed.

As you see, this involves dozens of steps and acres of time – and with every mouthful you will be satisfied that it was worth it!

≋ BOEUF EN DAUBE ≋

Serves 6 to 8

Marinade:
2 cups red wine
2 tablespoons olive oil
3 large carrots, sliced
2 medium-size onions, sliced
2 cloves garlic, finely chopped
2 bay leaves
1 teaspoon salt
1 teaspoon freshly ground black pepper
½ teaspoon dried sage
Stew:
3 pounds top round of beef, cut into 1-inch pieces
½ cup all-purpose flour
¼ pound bacon, cut into small pieces
4 medium-size tomatoes, quartered
2 cups mushrooms, quartered
1½ cups beef broth

Combine the marinade ingredients in a large glass bowl. Add the beef, cover with transparent wrap and marinate in the

"I grew up relishing a stew that, until I was pratically a teenager, I knew as 'beef dough.' No, it wasn't steak and kidney pie. I t was boeuf en daube, which my mother made often; the name was one of those favorite childish mispronunciations, like 'pasghetti' or 'tatoes,' that my folks found too cute to correct. I knew the minute I walked in the door that we'd be having 'beef dough' for dinner because of the wonderful aromas it spread throughout the house, and to this day I always associate it with apple cobbler and wintry evenings. When I first learned the real name boeuf en daube I was angry at my parents for having encouraged the misnomer, but now, with children of my own, I know that sometimes you just can't help yourself."—
Martine Toussaint,
St. Louis, Missouri

refrigerator for 8 hours or overnight, turning the meat 3 or 4 times.

Heat the oven to 300 degrees.

Strain the meat through a sieve, reserving the liquid and the vegetables from the marinade. Pat the meat dry with paper towels and dredge each piece with the flour.

Put the bacon in a large heavy skillet and cook over moderate heat until it is browned and the fat is rendered. Remove the bacon with a slotted spoon. Add the reserved onions and carrots to the skillet and cook for about 5 minutes until the onions are translucent. Remove the vegetables with a slotted spoon. Increase the heat to high and add the beef to the skillet, a few pieces at a time, turning them until browned on all sides. Take each batch of meat from the skillet before adding the next and drain on paper towels. Add a little oil if necessary.

Put the bacon in the bottom of a 4- to 5-quart casserole and cover with the browned beef and vegetables. Add the tomatoes and mushrooms and pour in the beef broth.

Pour the reserved marinade into the skillet and cook over high heat for 5 to 6 minutes until reduced by half, scraping the sides and bottom of the pan to loosen any browned particles. Add the reduced marinade to the casserole, cover and cook in the oven for 4 hours, adding more stock after 1 or 2 hours if the stew looks dry. This is a rich, thick stew.

"My mother learned to prepare boeuf en daube *from her own mother, who was the cook for a well-to-do family in Lyon—until she eloped with their oldest son and emigrated. Like* boeuf bourguignonne *(which Mom also makes very well),* boeuf an daube *sounds like a name to conjure with but it's really a simple, hearty stew, perfect on cold nights with a hunk of French bread and a bottle of red wine. When I make this stew for my own kids I like to think I'm giving them a taste of their heritage, and a subliminal lesson that food can be delicious and easy to prepare without coming from a microwave box."—Suzanne Chevret, Chicago, Illinois*

CARBONNADE FLAMANDE

For a while, every time I had a party, this traditional Flemish dish is what I would serve. Simply stated, it is a beef stew, but when properly made, the beef is simmered in that dark bock beer that hides at the bottom of the barrel, gathering character and strength and resolve while the lighter stuff giggles merrily on the surface. The stew takes on the moral resolve of the grandfather of beers and when it has mellowed into maturity, the casserole is covered with a layer of crisp, mustard-covered rounds of French bread. With a tossed salad—no vegetables, thank you—this is a fine choice for a buffet.

Serves 6

½ cup all-purpose flour
1 teaspoon salt
½ teaspoon freshly ground black pepper
3 pounds chuck steak, cut into 1-inch pieces
¼ pound bacon, cut into small pieces
3 large onions, thinly sliced
3 cloves garlic, finely chopped
Vegetable oil
2½ cups dark beer (flat or carbonated)
1½ tablespoons dark brown sugar
1 bay leaf
4 slices whole wheat bread, crusts removed
Dijon mustard

Combine the flour, salt and pepper in a medium-sized bowl. Toss the meat in the flour mixture, a few pieces at a time, until well coated.

Put the bacon pieces in a large heavy casserole and cook over high heat until they are browned and the fat is rendered. Remove the bacon with a slotted spoon and set aside.

Add the onions and garlic to the casserole and cook in the bacon fat for about 5 minutes until softened and translucent. Remove with a slotted spoon and set aside. Increase the heat to high and add the meat to the pan, a few pieces at a time. Sear the meat on all sides, adding a little vegetable oil if necessary to avoid sticking. Return the bacon, onions and garlic to the casserole.

Add the beer, sugar and bay leaf to the casserole, stirring well. Cover the pan and cook over low heat for 1 1/2 hours or until the meat is tender.

Spread both sides of the bread slices with mustard and place them on top of the meat, spooning some of the juices over the bread. Cover the pan and cook for a further 30 minutes. Remove the bay leaf before serving.

Beef Stew with Dumplings

Serves 6

Stew:
6 tablespoons all-purpose flour
2 teaspoons salt
1 teaspoon freshly ground black pepper
3 pounds stewing beef, trimmed and cut into 1-inch pieces
3 tablespoons butter
2 tablespoons vegetable oil
2 medium-size onions, coarsely chopped
7 cups beef broth
2 bay leaves
Dumplings:
3½ cups fresh bread crumbs
3 tablespoons water
2 eggs, lightly beaten
¼ teaspoon salt
¼ teaspoon freshly ground black pepper
1 tablespoon finely chopped parsley
1 medium-size onion, finely chopped
½ teaspoon mace
½ pound mushrooms

Heat the oven to 325 degrees.

Combine the flour, salt and pepper in a medium-sized bowl. Toss the beef pieces in the flour mixture, a few at a time, until they are well coated.

Heat 1 tablespoon of butter with 1 tablespoon of oil in a large heavy skillet over moderate heat. Add the onions and cook, stirring occasionally, until they are softened and translucent. Remove the onions from the pan with a slotted spoon and put them in a large, ovenproof casserole.

"German-style dumplings were standard fare on our winter table, not just in beef stew but with chicken or even vegetable soup.
"Richly seasoned, they are not the fluffy air balls of Southern legend. Rather they have a bit of bite, a texture from the breadcrumbs which gives them some substance. Mother used to say that they were substantial like our ancestors.
"All I know is that this stew with the mushrooms, tender beef, pungent onions and the aroma and flavor of bay leaves made for the wonderful winter meal. Often, she'd serve pickled beets with it which she'd put up that summer. It was a great meal.
"I make it in the winter, too. I use it as an excuse to talk about family history and our heritage. I don't know if it makes it taste any better, but it sure makes for interesting dinner conversasion."—
Robert Koch,
Cleveland, Ohio

111

Add the remaining butter and oil to the skillet and increase the heat to high. Cook the beef in the hot butter and oil, a few pieces at a time, until well browned on all sides. Once the pieces are browned, remove them from the skillet and add to the onions in the casserole.

Pour the beef broth into the skillet and stir over moderate heat, scraping the bottom and sides of the pan to loosen any browned particles. Add the broth to the casserole along with the bay leaves. Cover and cook in the heated oven for 2 hours.

While the casserole is cooking, make the dumplings. Put the bread crumbs in a medium-sized bowl and add just enough water to moisten them. Add the beaten eggs along with the remaining ingredients and mix well. Check the seasoning and add more salt and pepper if desired. Roll the mixture between the palms of your hands into balls about 2 inches in diameter.

Remove the casserole from the oven and stir in the mushrooms. Scatter the dumplings evenly over the surface of the stew so that they are partially submerged. Return the stew to the oven and cook, covered, for an additional 30 minutes. Remove the bay leaves before serving.

Opposite: Braised Sweet and Sour Spareribs (page 145)
Page following: New England Boiled Dinner (page 135)

Irish Stew

Serves 4 to 6

3 pounds boneless lamb stew meat
3 pounds potatoes, peeled and sliced ¼ inch thick
1 pound onions, sliced ¼ inch thick
1 teaspoon salt
½ teaspoon freshly ground black pepper
1 teaspoon dried thyme
2 cups cold water

Trim the fat from the lamb and cut the meat into 1-inch pieces.

Arrange a layer of potato slices in the bottom of a heavy 4-quart casserole. Cover with a layer of onions and then a layer of meat. Sprinkle with some of the salt, pepper and thyme. Continue the layers in this way until all the ingredients have been used, ending with a layer of potatoes. Add the water.

Bring the stew to the boil over moderate heat. Reduce the heat to low and cover with a tight-fitting lid. Simmer gently for 2 to 2 1/2 hours or until the lamb is tender. Shake the pan occasionally to make sure the potatoes do not stick to the bottom. When the lamb is tender, remove the casserole from the heat and serve immediately.

"My father did most of the cooking in our house My mother had no interest in it. Father was born in Ireland and spent a good part of his childhood there and he cooked plain, simple Irish food, such as lamb stew. I still remember how the kitchen smelled when I came in from playing ball or skating on a Saturday afternoon when he was making Irish stew."— *Maurice Fitzgerald, Ridgewood, New Jersey*

Opposite: Stifado (page 115)
Page preceding: Spaghetti and Meatballs (page 83)

VENISON STEW

Serves 6 to 8

4 to 5 tablespoons vegetable oil
4 pounds venison, trimmed of fat and cut into cubes
2 large onions, chopped
3 cloves garlic, finely chopped
2 stalks celery, chopped
3 carrots, chopped
2 cups beef broth
1 cup tomato sauce
½ cup cider vinegar
2 tablespoons chopped parsley
1 teaspoon dried thyme
1 teaspoon dried sage
2 to 3 bay leaves
6 medium-size potatoes, quartered
1 tablespoon salt
Freshly ground black pepper

Heat the oven to 300 degrees.

Heat the oil in a large frying pan or flameproof casserole. Brown the meat over moderately high heat, a few pieces at a time, setting each batch aside to drain before adding the next. Add more oil if necessary and cook the onions for about 5 minutes, stirring until softened. Add the garlic, celery and carrots and cook, stirring, for 7 or 8 minutes until the vegetables are tender. Be careful not to burn the garlic.

If you are using a frying pan, transfer the vegetables to a large lidded casserole and add the meat. If you are using a casserole on the stovetop, take it from the heat and add the meat. Stir in the broth, tomato sauce and vinegar. Add the herbs, potatoes, salt and pepper, cover the casserole and cook it in the oven for 1 1/4 to 1 1/2 hours, until the meat and potatoes are tender.

"My mother taught me how to cook venison with a little tomato and sage and onion to take out the wild taste. When I was growing up in Texas we made a lot of things with venison, including stew and chili."— Florence Dedman, Killingworth, Connecticut

STIFADO
(Beef Stew with Onions and Cheese)

Serves 4 to 6

⅓ cup olive oil
2 ½ pounds beef rump roast or boneless round, cut into 1-inch cubes
2 cups red wine
1 cup tomato juice
2 cloves garlic, finely chopped
3 tablespoons tomato paste
3 tablespoons red wine vinegar
1 stick cinnamon
2 bay leaves
Freshly ground black pepper
1¼ pounds pearl onions, peeled
   and blanched for 5 minutes in boiling water
½ cup crumbled feta cheese
½ cup walnuts

Heat the olive oil in a deep heavy skillet over high heat. Add the beef to the hot oil in batches and cook, stirring occasionally, until browned on all sides. Set the meat aside and drain the fat from the pan.

Add the wine, tomato juice, garlic, tomato paste, vinegar, cinnamon and bay leaves to the skillet. Season with pepper to taste and bring to the boil, stirring frequently. Lower the heat to a simmer and return the meat to the pan. Cook for 1 1/2 to 2 hours over very low heat.

Add the blanched onions to the stew and cook for about 20 minutes or until tender. Add the cheese and walnuts and cook just until the cheese is soft.

"My grandparents emigrated to New York from a village in Macedonia, arriving at Ellis Island in 1924. At the ripe age of 84, my grandmother hasn't slowed down one iota; she still cooks at least one meal daily for her extended family, and her style of cooking is almost as purely Greek as if she had never left home. Stifado is one of her specialties— actually several of her specialties, since she cooks beef, veal, lamb and fish stifado-style (that is, with wine and pearl onions). Except for the cheese and walnuts, she always makes beef stifado a day or two ahead because the flavor mellows and ripens on standing. When she reheats the stew she stirs in the feta and nuts, which combine to make a fantastically rich and complex dish. I've never known another Greek to make stifado with this combination of ingredients. Grandmother doesn't know whether it's peculiarly Macedonian or not, just that she's 'always made it like this.'"— Tricia Liacouras, Houston, Texas

MENUDO
(TRIPE STEW)

Serves 6 to 8

1 pound honeycomb tripe
1 calf's foot, cut into 2 to 4 pieces
2 cloves garlic, finely chopped
½ teaspoon salt
6 cups water
1 cup posole or canned hominy
½ cup chopped green chilis or red chili puree
½ teaspoon dried oregano
Freshly ground black pepper
Chopped green chilis, for garnish
Lime wedges, for garnish
Chopped onion, for garnish

"Menudo is synonymous with New Year's Day in our family. I'm sure this has something to do with its reputation as a hangover cure, even though we don't usually get too crazy the night before. My Aunt Alma is offically in charge of the menudo, and a good part of New Year's Eve day is taken up with preparing and cooking the tripe. I suppose some of its ingredients would be considered exotic in many parts of the country, but here in New Mexico it's so common to cook menudo for New Year's that nearly every market has tripe and calves' feet at that time of year. Tia Alma makes the menudo in a big clay pot— always the same one, featuring an extra chip or two each year— and we have it with mountians of steaming hot tortillas and a big bowl of fresh tomato salsa."—
Alicia Ceballos,
Albuquerque, New Mexico

If the tripe is not thoroughly cleaned, put it in a bowl with 1/3 cup vinegar. Add enough cold water to cover and let it soak for 3 hours. Rinse well and cut it into 1-inch squares.

Put the tripe, calf's foot, garlic, onion and salt in a heavy saucepan. Add 6 cups of water and bring to the boil. Reduce the heat to low and cook for 2 to 3 hours, skimming off any foam that rises to the surface.

Add the hominy, chilis, oregano and pepper, to taste, and simmer for 10 to 15 minutes more. Adjust the seasoning, if necessary.

Serve the stew with chopped chilis, lime wedges and chopped onion.

116

 # BIGOS

Serves 6

¼ cup dried mushrooms, preferably European
1 pound fresh or canned sauerkraut
¼ pound bacon, cut into pieces
½ pound boneless lamb, trimmed and cut into 1-inch pieces
½ pound boneless pork, trimmed and cut into 1-inch pieces
1 pound boneless round eye beef, cut into 1-inch pieces
2 large tomatoes, peeled, seeded and coarsely chopped
2½ cups shredded white cabbage
1½ cups coarsely chopped onion
1 large Granny Smith apple, peeled, cored and coarsely chopped
1 cup beef broth
1 cup red wine or Madeira
1 teaspoon salt
Freshly ground black pepper
¼ teaspoon ground allspice
½ pound kielbasa, cut into 1-inch slices
2 tablespoons chopped parsley

Put the mushrooms in a small bowl and cover them with boiling water. Leave them to soak until soft, about 2 hours. Drain the mushrooms, reserving the liquid, and slice them very thin.

Put the sauerkraut in a colander and rinse thoroughly under cold running water. Drain well and then squeeze it dry, a handful at a time.

Put the bacon in a heavy 4-quart casserole over moderate heat and cook until crisp and brown. Remove the bacon with a slotted spoon. Add the lamb, pork and beef to the pan and cook, stirring, until browned on all sides. Do this in batches to prevent crowding the pot. Lift each batch of browned meat from the casserole and set aside while browning the next one. When all the meat is browned, return it to the pot.

"I remember my grand-mother telling me about making bigos in Poland. When the men went hunting, the women would make a big pot of stew and take it out to the fields where they would heat it over an open fire, ready for the the tired hunters at the end of the day. I can just imagine how good it must have tasted in the cold fall evening.

"Naturally, the stew varied from one time to the next depending on what the cook had at hand. But although the other ingredients were flexible, my grandmother wouldn't have dreamed of making bigos without dried mushrooms, bacon, kielbasa and a combination of sauerkraut and fresh cabbage."—
Krysia Osinki,
Evanston, Illinois

Add the sauerkraut, tomatoes, cabbage, onion and apple to the meat. Return the bacon to the pan and stir well. Cook for 15 minutes, stirring frequently to prevent the meat from sticking.

Pour the beef broth, wine and reserved mushroom juice into the pan. Stir in the seasonings, cover and cook the bigos over low heat for 1 1/4 hours or until the meat is tender. Add the kielbasa and cook, covered, for another 30 minutes. Sprinkle the parsley over the stew before serving.

GOULASH

Serves 4

½ pound bacon, cut into small pieces
1 large onion, finely chopped
2 ¾ pounds beef bottom round, cut into cubes
5 cloves garlic, finely chopped
1 large tomato, peeled and coarsely chopped
1 teaspoon caraway seeds
1 teaspoon dried marjoram
1 teaspoon freshly ground pepper
1 cup white wine
2 teaspoons sweet Hungarian paprika
2 teaspoons hot Hungarian paprika

Cook the bacon and onion over moderate heat in a large heavy pot or casserole for about 5 minutes, stirring, until the onion has softened. Add the beef and garlic and cook over moderately high heat until the beef cubes are nicely browned. Add the tomato, caraway, marjoram and pepper and stir well. Pour 1/2 cup of the wine into the pot and add 1 teaspoon each of the sweet and hot paprikas. Cover, reduce the heat to low, and cook for 45 minutes, stirring occasionally.

Add the rest of the wine and the paprika, stir and continue cooking, covered, for 30 minutes more.

CHOLENT

Serves 4

1 cup dried lima beans
2 tablespoons vegetable oil
1 pound beef brisket
1 onion, halved lengthwise and sliced thin
2 carrots, cut into ½-inch slices
2 cloves garlic
½ cup pearl barley
2 cups water
2 cups beef broth
2 bay leaves
1 teaspoon salt
1 teaspoon paprika
½ teaspoon freshly ground black pepper

Cover the beans with cold water and soak them overnight.

Heat the oven to 225 degrees.

Heat the oil in a large ovenproof casserole over high heat until hot but not smoking. Sear the meat on both sides, about 5 minutes in all. Remove the meat from the casserole and lower the heat to moderate. Add the onion, carrots and garlic to the casserole and cook for about 5 minutes or until the onions are softened. Return the meat to the casserole. Drain the lima beans and add them to the meat together with the barley, water, broth, bay leaves, salt, paprika and pepper. Increase the heat to high and bring the liquid to the boil. Cover the casserole and put it in the oven.

Cook the casserole for 8 hours, stirring occasionally and adding extra water, if necessary.

"Because Orthodox Jews do not cook after sundown on the Sabbath, cholent, with its long cooking time, was a perfect dish for the midday meal on Saturday. The women put it in a very heavy pot in a very low oven before sundown and let it simmer very slowly all night. After synagogue on Saturday, they would then have their hot meal all ready.

"I remember staying at my grandparents' house for the weekend when I was small and waking up in the morning to the wonderful, rich smell of the cholent cooking in the oven. My grandparents and I would walk to the small synagogue not far from the house and I would daydream through the services as I thought about the meal that waited for us when we returned to the house. The meat that melted in my mouth, and the vegetables and seasonings were a mouthwatering treat."—
Mollie Spitzer,
Miami, Florida

119

 CHILI

"My father was a rancher in the Rio Grande Valley and a wholesale meat man as well, so we always had lots of beef. We grew up eating chicken-fried steak, Swiss steak and chili. Real Texas chili can be made with nearly any kind of red meat, I guess, but it cannot be made with beans."
— Florence Dedman, Killingworth, Connecticut

Serves 4 to 6

1 tablespoon vegetable oil
1 large onion, chopped
1 pound lean ground beef
1 pound lean ground pork
28-ounce can tomatoes, including juice
15-ounce can tomato puree
3 tablespoons Worcestershire sauce
1½ cups beef broth
3 cloves garlic, crushed
1 teaspoon crushed red pepper flakes
1 tablespoon chili powder
1 teaspoon cumin
1 teaspoon dried thyme
1 teaspoon dried oregano
1 teaspoon dried basil
Grated cheddar cheese
Sliced scallions

Heat the oil in a heavy 5- to 6-quart pan. Add the onion and cook over moderate heat, stirring occasionally, until softened. Add the beef and pork and cook over medium-high heat, stirring constantly, until browned, 15 to 20 minutes. Discard the fatty juices that have formed in the pan.

Stir in the tomatoes and their juice, breaking them up with the spoon. Add the tomato puree, Worcestershire sauce, beef broth, garlic, red pepper flakes, chili powder, cumin, thyme, oregano and basil. Bring to the boil, then lower the heat and simmer, uncovered, for about 3 hours, stirring occasionally, until the chili is thick and the flavors are well blended. Skim the surface and discard the fat.

Ladle the chili into individual serving bowls and sprinkle with the grated cheddar and sliced scallions before serving.

EGGPLANT PARMIGIANA

Serves 6

1½ pounds eggplant, cut into ½-inch slices
¼ cup plus 1 teaspoon salt
2 tablespoons butter
1 medium-size onion, finely chopped
1 clove garlic, finely chopped
1 pound ground beef
3 cups canned whole tomatoes, with juice
⅓ cup tomato paste
1½ teaspoons dried basil
1½ teaspoons dried oregano
½ teaspoon freshly ground black pepper
2 eggs, lightly beaten
1 cup grated Parmesan cheese
½ cup bread crumbs
⅓ cup olive oil
8 ounces mozzarella cheese, thinly sliced

Spread the eggplant slices on paper towels and sprinkle them liberally with salt. Let them drain for 15 to 20 minutes, turn them over and repeat the process. Heat the oven to 350 degrees.

Heat the butter in a large heavy skillet over moderate heat. Add the onion and garlic and cook, stirring occasionally, for about 5 minutes until the onion is softened but not browned. Add the ground beef and cook, stirring, until the meat is browned.

Add the tomatoes, tomato paste, basil, oregano, the teaspoon of salt and the pepper to the skillet and mix well. Bring to the boil, stirring constantly. Lower the heat and let the mixture simmer, uncovered, for 30 minutes or until thickened.

Put the beaten eggs into a shallow bowl. Combine the Parmesan with the bread crumbs in another shallow bowl. Pat the

eggplant slices dry and dip them first in the beaten egg and then in the bread crumb mixture until evenly coated.

Heat a third of the olive oil in a second large skillet. Add a third of the coated eggplant slices and cook on both sides until golden brown. Lift from the pan and drain on paper towels. Repeat the process with the remaining oil and eggplant until it is all cooked.

Spread half the eggplant slices over the bottom of an ovenproof casserole and cover with half the meat sauce. Add the remaining eggplant slices in a layer, top with the remaining sauce and sprinkle any leftover Parmesan mixture over the top. Cover the casserole and cook in the oven for 20 minutes. Remove the lid from the casserole and spread the mozzarella slices on top of the meat sauce. Return the casserole to the oven and cook for another 20 minutes or until the cheese is melted and just beginning to brown.

LASAGNE

Serves 8

2 tablespoons olive oil
1 medium-size onion, chopped (about ½ cup)
2 cloves garlic, finely chopped
28-ounce can crushed tomatoes
16 ounces tomato sauce
6 ounces tomato paste
¾ cup chicken broth
¾ cup water
3 teaspoons dried basil
2½ teaspoons dried oregano
1 teaspoon sugar
¼ teaspoon celery seed
Pinch of ground red pepper
2 teaspoons salt
½ pound ground beef, browned and drained
½ pound pork sausage meat, browned and drained
1 egg
2 pounds ricotta cheese
1 tablespoon finely chopped parsley
2 tablespoons freshly grated Parmesan cheese,
   plus extra for sprinkling (optional)
Freshly ground black pepper
1 pound lasagne noodles
1 pound mozzarella cheese, grated

    Heat the olive oil in a large saucepan over medium-high heat. Add the onion and garlic and cook until the onion is softened, stirring constantly Add the crushed tomatoes, tomato sauce, tomato paste, broth and water, stirring with a wooden spoon until combined. Add the basil, oregano, sugar, celery seed, red pepper and 1 teaspoon of the salt. Cover and simmer for 30 minutes, stirring occasionally. Add the browned and drained ground beef and sausage to the pan, cover and simmer for 30 minutes more.

"There must be as many recipes for lasagne as there are cooks who make it. I've had it filled with pesto, with vegetables, with little meatballs, with lamb, in 'all-white' versions, you name it. But naturally the version you grow up with is the best, and I grew up with my father's. This was definitely an aberration; though Dad was the official family barbecuer and occasional weekend breakfast maker, he was hardly the cook in the family. But for some reason that was never made clear to me, he was in charge of lasagne. He would fix it every couple of months, always with great fanfare and preening of feathers, because he knew that his lasagne was unsurpassable. Just as we all fought over the golden skin on a roast chicken and the crusty heels of Italian bread, there was invariably competition for the crisp-edged noodles in the lasagne's top layer. Dad made a show of dividing them equitably, but I know the truth: My sister always got a little more."—
Richard LaRosa,
Pittsburgh, Pennsylvania

Lightly beat the egg in a medium-sized bowl. Add the ricotta cheese, parsley, Parmesan cheese, pepper and the remaining teaspoon of salt. Stir until well combined.

Bring 5 quarts of salted water to the boil in a large pan. Drop the lasagne noodles into the water one at a time. Cook the lasagne for 12 to 15 minutes, until al dente, stirring occasionally. Drain the pasta and rinse in cold water.

Heat the oven to 350 degrees.

Spread a thin layer of the meat sauce over the bottom of a 12-by-9-by-2 1/2-inch baking dish. Cover the sauce with a layer of noodles and then spread 10 heaping tablespoons of the ricotta mixture evenly over the noodles. Cover the ricotta with a light sprinkling of grated mozzarella and then with another thin layer of meat sauce (the sauce need not cover the noodles completely). Repeat the layers as before until all the ingredients are incorporated, ending with a thin layer of sauce. Sprinkle the top with additional grated Parmesan, if desired.

Bake the lasagne for 40 to 50 minutes, until the edges of the top layer are crispy. Remove from the oven and allow to stand for 8 to 10 minutes before serving.

Roasts, Braises, Sautés and Pan-Cooked Meats

Roast Chicken
with Cornbread
Stuffing

Serves 4 to 6

Cornbread:
1 tablespoon vegetable oil
1 cup cornmeal
1 teaspoon baking soda
½ teaspoon salt
1 cup frozen corn, thawed
1 egg
½ cup buttermilk
5 tablespoons butter, melted
Stuffing:
1 recipe cornbread, above
3 slices firm white or whole wheat bread
2 tablespoons butter
1 onion, coarsely chopped
1 stalk celery, coarsely chopped
1 egg, lightly beaten
¼ to ½ cup chicken broth
3-pound chicken
Salt and freshly ground black pepper

Heat the oven to 375 degrees.

Oil an 8- to 9-inch baking dish with the vegetable oil and put it in the oven to heat up. Mix together the cornmeal, baking soda and salt and then stir in the corn kernels. Whisk the egg with the buttermilk and stir the liquid into the dry ingredients until just combined. Stir in the melted butter. Pour the batter into the hot dish and bake for about 30 minutes, until firm and golden brown. Remove from the oven and cool.

To make the stuffing, crumble the cornbread. Toast the bread slices and cut into cubes—you should have about 2 cups. Heat the butter in a skillet over moderate heat. Add the onion and celery and cook for about 5 minutes or until softened.

Heat the oven to 350 degrees.

In a large bowl, combine the crumbled cornbread, bread cubes, onion and celery. Stir in the egg and enough broth to moisten the stuffing without making it too liquid.

Season the chicken inside and out with salt and pepper. Fill the chicken cavity with the stuffing and truss it or tie the legs together tightly. Roast for about 1 3/4 hours or until a meat thermometer registers 165 degrees.

"We always had chicken on Sunday and I loved the way she fixed it, roasted with cornbread stuffing. It wasn't until I had been there for about a month that I found out where the fresh chickens came from. I will never forget the sight of my 90-pound grandmother holding a squawking chicken in one hand and wielding a hatchet in the other."—
Nancy C. Harris,
Lake Bluff, Illinois

SOUTHERN-FRIED CHICKEN

"Growing up on a cotton plantation in the Mississippi Delta, I am a true 'child of the South' and have rich memories of the kitchen of my childhood. I remember large, simmering pots and the array of wonderful raw materials—just-picked tomatoes, sweet potatoes, buttermilk, eggs fresh from the chicken house, a chicken which, moments before, had been flapping around the backyard.
"My memory also encompasses the days before air conditioning, with 100-degree July heat, floor fans whirling and open window.
"A wonderful lady named Rosabelle, whose talent was matched only by her smile and girth, could take a black iron skillet and produce food never since matched. If you stayed out of her way and only moved to fetch her what she needed, you might be lucky enough to taste the first piece of fried chicken out of her skillet—hopefully, a drumstick. Crispy yet flaky, golden brown with flecks of black pepper, and sweet, salty and juicy inside—unsurpassed!"—
Sissy Sullivan,
Indianola, Mississippi.

Serves 4

1 cup flour
½ cup corn flour
1 teaspoon salt
½ teaspoon pepper
1½ cups milk
3-pound chicken, cut into serving pieces
Solid vegetable shortening

Combine the flour, corn flour, salt and pepper in a brown paper bag and shake until well mixed, holding the top closed. Pour the milk into a shallow bowl and add the chicken pieces, turning each one so that it is thoroughly soaked.

Put enough shortening into a deep heavy pan to reach a depth of 3 inches when melted. Heat to 375 degrees over high heat.

When the shortening is almost ready, remove 3 to 4 pieces of chicken from the milk and put them in the bag with the flour mixture. Shake the bag until the pieces are well coated and shake off the excess.

Add the chicken to the hot fat and brown well on all sides. Lower the heat to moderate, cover the pan and cook the chicken for 20 minutes. Remove the lid and cook for 10 minutes more. Remove the chicken from the pan with a slotted spoon, drain on paper towels and keep warm. Add more shortening to the pan if necessary and heat to 375 degrees to cook the remaining chicken pieces.

Opposite: Roast Beef (page 137)
Page following: Roast Chicken with Cornbread Stuffing (page 126)

CHICKEN-FRIED SKIRT STEAK WITH BEER AND ONIONS

Serves 6

2 ½ pounds skirt steak, trimmed
1 cup red wine vinegar
1 ¼ cups vegetable oil
3 tablespoons mustard
1 tablespoon finely chopped fresh marjoram
1 tablespoon finely chopped fresh basil
1 tablespoon finely chopped fresh oregano
1 ½ tablespoons black pepper
2 tablespoons salt
3 tablespoons butter
2 medium-size onions, cut into thin strips
¼ cup maple syrup
¼ cup dark soy sauce
½ cup beer
1 cup heavy cream
1 ½ cups all-purpose flour
1 ½ teaspoons onion powder
2 teaspoons garlic powder
¼ teaspoon cayenne pepper
1 teaspoon salt

"The fond memories I have of kitchens and great cooking experiences are those times I spent with my dad, Stan Zuromski, and uncle, John Zuromski, at the Modern Diner. Every day after school, I went to the diner. Because my mother worked nights, the diner kitchen is really where I remember growing up. The diner was owned by the family for over 30 years and its kitchen holds my first memories of what cooking is all about. Everything was prepared from scratch and made from fresh ingredients. Of course, there were daily blue plate specials—and this skirt steak is one of them."— Walter Zuromski, Boston, Massachusetts

Cut the steak into 6 serving portions. Mix together the vinegar, oil and mustard in a shallow glass dish large enough to hold the steak pieces in a single layer. Combine the herbs and seasonings in a small bowl. Coat each piece of steak with the herb mixture, place it in the glass dish and marinate for 1 hour, turning occasionally.

Remove the steak from the marinade and set it on a baking rack to drain thoroughly. Pat with paper towels to dry.

Opposite: Roast Leg of Lamb (page 141)
Page preceding: Glazed Ham (page 146)

Heat the butter in a large, heavy skillet over high heat. Add the onions and cook until they begin to turn brown. Lower the heat to moderately low and continue cooking until the onions are very soft. Increase the heat to high, add the maple syrup and soy sauce and cook for 1 minute. Add the beer and cook until the liquid is reduced by half, stirring constantly. Add the cream and cook until slightly thickened.

Blend the flour with the onion powder, garlic powder, cayenne and salt. Remove the steak from the pan with a slotted spoon and dredge with the flour mixture until well coated. Keep the sauce warm while you cook the steak.

Heat the oil in another skillet until just below the smoking point. Fry the steak evenly on both sides until golden brown. Serve with the onion-cream sauce.

≋ ROASTED SQUAB ≋

Serves 6 to 8

3 cloves garlic
1 tablespoon coarse salt
⅛ teaspoon cayenne pepper
2 teaspoons ground coriander seeds
1 teaspoon ground cumin seeds
2 tablespoons Aguardiente, Pisco or light rum
⅓ cup olive oil
6 to 8 fresh squabs

Combine the garlic, salt, cayenne, coriander and cumin in a mortar and pound to a paste with a pestle. Add the liquor, stir to dissolve the paste and let sit for 15 minutes. Stir in the olive oil and set aside.

Wipe the squabs clean with a damp cloth inside and out. Rub them inside and out with the garlic paste and allow to marinate at room temperature for 4 hours, or overnight in the refrigerator.

Heat the oven to 475 degrees.

Place the birds on a rack and roast for about 20 minutes or until they are golden on the outside but medium-rare on the inside. Remove from the oven to a serving platter.

OSSO BUCCO

Serves 6

¾ cup all-purpose flour
2 teaspoons salt
1 teaspoon freshly ground black pepper
3 pounds veal shank or knuckle
4 tablespoons butter
1 large onion, thinly sliced
1 large carrot, finely chopped
1 stalk celery, finely chopped
1 bay leaf
15-ounce can whole tomatoes, coarsely chopped, juice reserved
2 tablespoons tomato paste
1 cup dry white wine
½ cup finely chopped parsley
Grated rind of 1 lemon

Combine the flour with 1 teaspoon salt and 1/2 teaspoon pepper in a paper bag. Pat the veal pieces dry with paper towels, put them in the bag and shake until they are coated with the seasoned flour. Shake off any excess.

I like to have Osso bucco on a bed of golden saffron rice with a plenitude of crisp, cold white wine. I never get to the salad. The veal is all I want. Full and satisfying, it later gives the gift of a night of contented sleep. As with all Italian food, there is an exultant joy here. Italians love to eat and their food is a celebration of living that is different from that of other countries. Osso bucco, crafted from sweet, white veal shanks, served with the marrow still in the bone, gentled to tenderness in a long-simmered sauce, is a triumph among the many great dishes of Milan.

Heat the butter in a large casserole over high heat, add the veal and cook, turning, until browned on all sides. Remove the meat from the pan. Add the onion, carrot, celery and bay leaf to the pan and cook over moderate heat until the onions are softened and translucent. Add the tomatoes with their juice, the tomato paste and the wine and bring the mixture to the boil. Reduce the heat to low and return the meat to the pan. Put a circle of wax paper directly onto the surface of the stew. Cover the casserole and cook for 2 hours or until the meat is very tender.

Combine the parsley and the lemon rind in a small bowl. When the veal is cooked, stir the parsley-lemon mixture into the stew and simmer for another 1 minute. Using a slotted spoon, transfer the veal to a heated serving platter. Spoon the sauce over the meat and serve at once.

≋ Veal Parmigiana ≋

Serves 4 to 6

1 pound veal cutlets, cut into ¼-inch slices
2 tablespoons olive oil
1 cup chopped onion
2 tablespoons finely chopped garlic
28-ounce can tomatoes, drained
½ teaspoon dried oregano
½ teaspoon dried basil
½ cup red wine
Salt and freshly ground black pepper
2 eggs, beaten
1 cup fresh bread crumbs
1 cup vegetable oil
1 cup grated mozzarella cheese
1 cup grated Parmesan cheese

Gently pound the veal slices between two sheets of wax paper until they are approximately 1/8 inch thick and set aside.

Heat the olive oil in a medium-sized pan, add the onion and garlic and cook, stirring, for about 5 minutes. Add the drained tomatoes along with the herbs and wine. Season with salt and pepper to taste and simmer, partially covered, for 15 minutes.

Heat the oven to 350 degrees.

Dip the veal slices first in the beaten egg and then in the bread crumbs so they are coated on both sides. Heat the vegetable oil in a large heavy skillet over moderate heat. Cook the veal slices in batches for 1 to 2 minutes on each side. Do not overcook. Remove the cooked veal slices to a wide, shallow baking dish, spreading them evenly over the bottom of the dish.

Pour the sauce over the meat and sprinkle the two cheeses over the top. Bake the veal, uncovered, for 20 to 30 minutes.

"Veal Parmigiana was an expensive luxury in our house, a dish to be taken seriously. Though my mother was only 12 when she arrived in this country, she had been brought up with thrifty ways from an early age; a poor childhood in Lazio had schooled her well in stretching a bit of flour and oil, and perhaps a scrap of meat, into a tasty if not opulent meal. After she and my father married and their financial situation gradually became less precarious, she loosened up her budget a bit, allowing occasional splurges on fancy cuts of meat— but she didn't let us take them for granted. Actually, I think she never quite relinquished that Depression-era fear that everything would be pulled out from under her in the blink of an eye. Anyway, getting back to veal Parmigiana, it was one of those treats that would turn up on the occasional birthday or holiday, and whenever she served it my mother seemed to be reveling in the bounty of her adopted country."— Margaret Iannucci, Philadelphia, Pennsylvania

≋ Wiener Schnitzel ≋

Serves 4

4 veal cutlets, about 5 ounces each
½ cup all-purpose flour
2 eggs, lightly beaten
1 cup fresh bread crumbs
8 tablespoons butter
Salt and freshly ground black pepper
1 tablespoon vegetable oil
1 lemon, cut into wedges
1 tablespoon capers

Place the cutlets between 2 sheets of wax paper and pound them lightly to flatten. Dredge the slices with the flour and shake to remove the excess.

Put the eggs in a shallow dish. Put the bread crumbs on another plate or a sheet of wax paper and season with salt and pepper. Dip the veal slices in the egg and then the bread crumbs so that they are coated on both sides. Press lightly so the crumbs adhere to the meat.

Heat the butter and the oil in a large heavy skillet over moderate heat.

Cook the cutlets in the hot butter and oil for 3 to 5 minutes on each side, until golden brown. Serve at once, garnished with lemon wedges and sprinkled with the capers.

"Wiener schnitzel *was quite simply my father's idea of the perfect meal. Simple, with a nice glass of wine, he'd say. He preferred spaetzle to accompany it but would settle for potatoes. Carrots or green beans were a nice addition on the plate, he'd say, but the veal was what counted. It must be tender and young.*

"*He'd complain vociferously if he thought my mother had been compromised at the butcher shop by veal that was less than perfect.*

"*She'd let him go on, knowing that in the end he'd always tell her it was the best meal he'd ever had and she was the most wonderful cook in the world. Food was a love poem for them and veal cutlets were their favorite verse.*"—
Tania Cantwell,
New Haven, Connecticut

NEW ENGLAND BOILED DINNER

Serves 6 to 8

3 pounds corned beef
1 tablespoon black pepper
1 teaspoon dried thyme
1 bay leaf
6 medium-size carrots, roughly sliced
2 onions, sliced
2 celery stalks, sliced
4 beets (optional)
6 medium-size potatoes, cut into pieces
3 parsnips, cut into pieces
1 small turnip, cut into pieces
1 medium-size head cabbage, quartered

Put the beef in a large, heavy flameproof casserole and cover with boiling water. Add the pepper, thyme, bay leaf, 2 of the carrots, the onions and the celery. Cover the casserole and simmer over moderate heat for 2 1/2 hours or until the beef is tender. Alternatively, you may put the casserole in a heated 350 degree oven for the same amount of time.

Put the beets in a pot with enough water to cover and gently boil for 20 to 25 minutes until fork tender. Drain the beets and when they are cool enough to handle, rub off the skins. Cut the beets in half.

Remove the beef from the casserole and keep warm. Drain the cooking liquid through a colander into a large saucepan. Discard the bay leaf and the cooked vegetables. Add the remaining carrots, the potatoes, parsnips and turnips to the saucepan and cook over moderately high heat for 15 minutes. Add the cabbage wedges and cook for 7 to 10 minutes before adding the halved beets. Cook for about 8 more minutes or until all the vegetables are tender.

"This was the kind of dinner I used to love to come home to. I can remember the rich beefy smells that wafted through the back door, almost before I turned the knob and stepped inside. I remember sitting impatiently at the table while my father carved the roast, cutting it into thin slices. He loved the ceremony of it all.

"Waiting for him to fill and pass my plate always seemed like an eternity. Of course, I'd always try to get him to forget the beets and parsnips on my plate. With a laugh, he'd always say, 'Don't worry, honey, there's enough for everyone, including you.' I couldn't believe he and Mom actually liked the beets. It's a trip back home in the fall every time I serve a boiled beef dinner."—
Debbie Reagan,
Dallas, Texas

Arrange the vegetables around the meat on a serving platter. For convenience, you may want to slice the meat across the grain in the kitchen before putting it on the platter. Spoon a little of the cooking liquid over the meat and pass the rest separately.

≋ CORNED BEEF AND ≋ CABBAGE

Serves 6

5-pound piece corned beef, brisket or round
1 clove garlic
1 teaspoon peppercorns
6 medium-size onions
6 medium-size potatoes, scrubbed
6 medium-size carrots, peeled and trimmed
1 green cabbage, trimmed and cut into 6 wedges

Put the beef in a large, heavy saucepan with sufficient cold water to cover it by 1 inch. Add the garlic and peppercorns, bring to the boil and reduce the heat to low. Cover and cook gently for about 3 hours until the meat is tender but not falling apart.

About 30 minutes before the meat is done, add the onions, potatoes, carrots and cabbage and continue cooking for about 20 minutes until they are just tender.

Remove the beef and transfer it to a serving platter. Cover and keep warm.

Increase the heat under the saucepan to moderately high and cook for about 10 minutes until the root vegetables are tender. Arrange the vegetables on the platter around the beef. Serve immediately with pickles, horseradish and mustard.

 # ROAST BEEF

Serves 6 to 8

4 to 4½-pound sirloin roast
Salt and freshly ground black pepper
2 carrots, coarsely chopped
1 onion, coarsely chopped
1 beef stock cube
2 cups boiling water
1 tablespoon all-purpose flour (optional)
1 tablespoon butter (optional)

Heat the oven to 425 degrees.

Pat the meat dry with paper towels. Season it with salt and pepper and put it on a rack in a roasting pan. Place the meat in the oven for 15 minutes, basting it two or three times. Remove from the oven and arrange the vegetables around the meat. Lower the oven temperature to 350 degrees. Baste the meat again and return it to the oven. Roast the meat for 1 to 1 1/2 hours, basting occasionally, until a meat thermometer registers 120 degrees for rare or 145 degrees for well done. Remove the meat from the oven, cover it with foil and let it rest in a warm place for 15 to 20 minutes before carving.

Meanwhile, remove the rack from the roasting pan. Strain the pan juices through a fine sieve, pressing the vegetables to extract as much liquid as possible. Dissolve the stock cube in the boiling water. Return the strained juices to the pan, pour in the stock and stir over moderate heat, scraping the bottom of the pan to loosen any browned particles.

To thicken the sauce, blend the flour with the butter to make a smooth paste. Whisk the flour mixture into the sauce a little at a time until it is all incorporated and the gravy is smooth and thickened. Allow the sauce to boil for 2 minutes and then strain before pouring it into a warmed sauceboat.

"At the height of wartime rationing, only restaurants and hotels were able to serve food in any quantity. So when my parents and I found ourselves dining at a London railway hotel before catching the night train to Scotland, I naturally ordered up roast beef.

"A gigantic plate arrived, positively heaped with slices of beef, crispy roast potatoes and mashed (all wartime meals featured potatoes in a big way), and I seem to remember Yorkshire pudding and cabbage too. By the time I had eaten my fill, fully half the contents of the plate were still sitting there.

"It was considered unpatriotic ever to leave food at a meal. So, I asked permission to leave the table— and ran right around Euston Station at all the speed I was capable of, dodging porters with their baggage carts, soldiers lugging kitbags and other travelers, like us, with bicycles in tow. Ten minutes later, I slipped back into my seat at the table— and I genuinely did eat the whole thing."—
Alice Buchanan
Warwick, New York

Carve the meat and arrange the slices on a warmed serving platter. Pour a little of the sauce over the meat and pass the rest separately.

SAUERBRATEN

Serves 6 to 8

Marinade:
1 large onion, thinly sliced
1 large carrot, thinly sliced
1 stalk celery, thinly sliced
¼ teaspoon allspice
2 cloves
8 peppercorns
1 clove garlic, finely chopped
2 bay leaves
1 cup red wine vinegar
2 cups red wine
1 cup water
4-pound boneless rump roast
Salt and freshly ground black pepper
2 tablespoons all-purpose flour
2 tablespoons butter
2 tablespoons vegetable oil
½ cup crumbled gingersnaps

Combine all the marinade ingredients in a glass dish large enough to hold the meat. Season the beef with salt and pepper to taste, put it into the dish and spoon the marinade over it. Cover the dish with transparent wrap and let the meat marinate in the refrigerator for 3 days, turning it once or twice a day.

Remove the beef from the dish, reserving the marinade, and pat it dry with paper towels. Dredge the beef with the flour.

Heat the butter and oil in a large casserole over high heat. Add the beef and sear it on all sides. Lower the heat and pour in the marinade. Cover the pan and cook the meat over low heat for 3 hours or until the beef is very tender. Fifteen minutes before the end of the cooking time, heat the oven to 200 degrees.

Remove the meat from the casserole and keep it warm in the heated oven. Stir the gingersnaps into the cooking juices and continue stirring over high heat until the crumbs have dissolved and the sauce has thickened. Adjust the seasoning and keep the sauce warm while you carve the meat.

Arrange the sliced meat on a warm serving platter, pour a little of the sauce over it and pass the rest separately.

"Both of my grandparents, immigrants from Luxembourg, made everything from jams and apple kuchen *(which was my grandfather's specialty) to sausage and head cheese, both of these from the pigs they raised on their farm. I remember being cooled on hot summer days with a bowl of fresh raspberries and chilled cream... .*

"For special occasions, I remember sauerbraten, *the dish prepared with love for every birthday, Christmas and even Easter dinner. The ritual of marinating the roast was begun days in advance and culminated in a warm kitchen filled with the pungent fragrance of beef braising in the spicy, vinegary marinade. The kitchen was also filled with the steam rising from the rolling, boiling water used to cook the* kartoffelöse, *dumplings that would bounce to the top of the kettle, announcing that they were within minutes of being done and ready to be covered with rich, dark gravy. No matter how many servings we ate, Mum always encouraged us to eat more."—* Eileen Barthelmy, Alexandria, Virginia

LIVER AND ONIONS

Serves 6

⅓ cup olive oil
2 tablespoons butter
6 medium-size onions, thinly sliced
¼ cup flour
Salt and pepper
1¼ pounds calves' liver, trimmed and thinly sliced
3 tablespoons finely chopped parsley

Heat the olive oil and butter in a large skillet over moderately low heat. Add the onions and cook, stirring occasionally, for 15 to 20 minutes until they are very soft. Remove the onions to a serving platter with a slotted spoon and keep them warm.

Season the flour with salt and pepper. Dredge the liver slices with the flour, shaking off the excess.

Increase the heat under the skillet to high, adding a little more oil if necessary. When the oil is sizzling, add the liver slices in batches and cook for 1 to 2 minutes on each side, until lightly browned on the outside but still slightly pink in the center. Remove the pieces to the serving platter on top of the onions as they are cooked. Sprinkle with parsley and serve immediately.

≋ ROAST LEG OF LAMB ≋

Serves 6

4- to 4 ½-pound leg of lamb
3 sprigs fresh rosemary or 1 tablespoon dried
Salt and freshly ground black pepper
1 cup full-bodied red wine
Juice of half a lemon
¼ cup red currant jelly

Heat the oven to 425 degrees.

Pat the meat dry with paper towels and season it all over with the rosemary leaves, salt and pepper. Put it on a rack in a roasting pan and roast, uncovered, for 15 minutes, basting frequently. Lower the oven temperature to 350 degrees and continue to roast for 1 1/2 hours or until a meat thermometer registers 145 degrees. The meat should be pale pink inside. Remove the meat from the pan, cover it with foil and let it rest for 15 to 20 minutes in a warm place.

Meanwhile, remove the rack from the roasting pan. Spoon off most of the fat from the pan. Add the red wine and lemon juice and stir over moderate heat, scraping the bottom of the pan to loosen any browned particles. Stir in the red currant jelly. Bring the sauce to the boil, stirring continuously, and season with salt and pepper to taste. Strain the sauce into a warmed sauce boat.

"It isn't fashionable anymore to be a confirmed meat eater, but for my parents, Sunday dinner means a roast and that's all there is to it. Even as a small child I appreciated Sunday's special rhythm; every other day of the week brought the usual quick breakfast, lightish lunch and hearty dinner, but the routine changed on Sunday. Only then would we have a long, leisurely hot breakfast— with pancakes, French toast, maybe eggs and hash browns. There would be a big dinner around three o'clock, and late supper would be something fun to eat like waffles or hot open-face sandwiches. I think my mother's treatment of leg of lamb is a little unusual, combining as it does rosemary, wine and currant jelly. I don't know how she hit on this formula, but it's one of her trademark dishes and we all adore it."—
Brenda Cartwight,
Louisville, Kentucky

"*My father invented his lamb dish after having something like it in 1949. He loves to tell the story: It was the last night of their honeymoon, and he and his 'bride' (as he always refers to my mother, though in this case it's literally true) were splurging on dinner at a chic little restaurant on Manhattan's East side. Dad went crazy for the saddle of lamb and, having no luck in wrestling the recipe from the chef, he set about to recreate it. There was always a certain something missing— until, years later, he started dabbling in Chinese cooking and realized that the mystery ingredient in the lamb was fresh ginger. Of course, how closely this recipe resembles the one from the now long-defunct restaurant is anyone's guess, but Dad's* Roast Saddle of Lamb *has become a family heirloom nonetheless.*"— Martin Hunter, Manhasset, New York

Serves 6 to 8

Marinade:
¼ cup red wine vinegar
¼ cup olive oil
1 tablespoon tomato puree
1-inch piece fresh ginger
6-pound saddle of lamb
1 teaspoon salt
1 teaspoon freshly ground black pepper
2 cloves garlic, cut into 8 slivers
8 sprigs fresh rosemary
¼ cup red wine
¾ cup beef broth
1 tablespoon all-purpose flour
1 tablespoon butter

Combine the marinade ingredients in a large shallow dish. Rub the meat all over with the salt and pepper and place it in the marinade. Let the meat marinate at room temperature for 3 hours or in the refrigerator for 8 hours, turning every 30 minutes.

Heat the oven to 425 degrees.

Remove the meat from the marinade and pat it dry with paper towels. Make 8 small incisions in the meat and insert a sliver of garlic and a sprig of rosemary in each. Put the meat on a rack in a roasting pan and place in the oven for 1 hour, basting frequently. Lower the oven temperature to 300 degrees and cook for another hour, basting occasionally. When the meat is cooked, the juices should be just slightly pink. Take the meat from the pan, cover with foil and let it rest in a warm place for 15 to 20 minutes before carving.

Remove the rack from the pan and spoon off as much fat as possible. Add the red wine and stir over moderate heat, scraping the bottom of the pan to remove any browned particles. Stir in the beef broth. Mix the flour with the butter to form a smooth paste and

whisk the mixture into the sauce, a little at a time. Simmer the sauce for 2 to 3 minutes more and strain it into a warm sauceboat.

Carve the lamb and arrange the slices on a warm serving platter. Pour a little of the sauce over the meat and pass the rest separately.

ROAST LOIN
OF PORK

Serves 6

3 ½- to 4-pound loin of pork
1 carrot, cut into ¼-inch slices
1 onion, cut into ¼-inch slices
1 stalk celery, cut into ¼-inch slices
1 cup chicken broth
1 cup water
Salt and freshly ground black pepper

Heat the oven to 425 degrees.

Put the pork, fat side up, on a rack in a roasting pan. Roast the meat for 15 minutes. Remove the meat from the oven, baste it with the cooking juices and add the vegetables to the pan. Lower the oven temperature to 350 degrees. Return the meat to the oven and roast for 2 to 2 1/4 hours or until a meat thermometer registers 160 degrees.

Remove the meat from the pan, cover it with foil and let it rest in a warm place for 15 to 20 minutes.

Meanwhile, remove the rack from the roasting pan. Spoon off most of the fat and strain the remaining juices and vegetables through a fine sieve, pressing on the vegetables to extract as much juice as possible. Return the juices to the roasting pan and add the

"As far as the Deans are concerned, pork is the very apotheosis of meat. There's no denying that we are carnivores: A garlicky leg of lamb, a rare beef tenderloin, a slow-braised veal roast are all highly esteemed in my family. But roast pork— well, roast pork is as good as it gets. In the belief that a fine hunk of pork cannot be improved upon, my mother treats it simply, adding just a few vegetables to the roasting pan and stirring up a light brown gravy to anoint the slices of meat. A few times she's gotten a little more experimental, and though we all greeted the results politely, I think she got the message; it's like experimenting with the Thanksgiving turkey stuffing, which is tantamount to heresy."—
Virginia Dean O'Connor, Annapolis, Maryland

chicken broth and water. Bring the liquid to the boil over moderate heat, stirring and scraping the bottom of the pan to loosen any browned particles. Season with salt and pepper to taste and strain the sauce into a warm sauceboat.

Carve the pork and arrange the slices on a warm serving platter. Pour a little of the sauce over the meat and pass the rest separately.

≋ PORK CHOPS BONNE ≋ FEMME

6 pork chops, cut ¾-inch thick
Salt and pepper
Flour, for dredging
4 slices bacon, pancetta or salt pork, cut into ½-inch pieces
12 to 18 small red potatoes
2 cups peeled pearl onions
½ cup dry white wine
Parsley sprigs, for garnish

Rub the pork chops with salt and pepper. Dredge them with flour, shake off the excess and set aside.

Cook the bacon in a large skillet over moderately low heat until the fat is rendered and the bacon is browned. Remove the bacon with a slotted spoon and set it aside. Add the pork chops to the fat remaining in the pan and cook slowly for about 10 minutes on each side until browned.

Meanwhile, cook the potatoes in enough boiling water to cover by a few inches and remove them while they are still slightly undercooked, after 20 to 25 minutes. Cook the onions in the same way.

Opposite: Osso Bucco (page 131)
Page following: Pot Roast (page 104)

Remove the chops from the skillet and pour off the fat. Add the wine and cook, stirring to dissolve the browned particles. Return the meat to the pan. Add the onions and potatoes, partially cover the pan and cook, stirring occasionally, for about 15 minutes until the vegetables are tender and the meat is cooked through.

Set the pork chops on a serving platter and arrange the potatoes and onions around the meat. Garnish with sprigs of parsley.

BRAISED SWEET AND SOUR SPARERIBS

Serves 4 to 6

3 ½ pounds meaty spareribs, separated,
  each rib chopped into 2 or 3 pieces
3 tablespoons rice wine or dry sherry
4 tablespoons dark soy sauce
6 tablespoons rice wine vinegar or cider vinegar
4 tablespoons sugar
½ cup water
3 cups steamed rice (optional)

Put the ribs into a large heavy saucepan over high heat. Add the remaining ingredients, except the rice, and stir to combine. Bring the mixture to the boil. Reduce the heat to low, cover the pan and cook gently over moderately low heat, stirring from time to time, for about 45 minutes, until the meat is tender. Uncover the pan and raise the heat to high. Turn the meat in the sauce as it thickens to a glaze. Serve hot with freshly cooked rice.

"My earliest recollections of Chinese food center around a small restaurant in my home town. Exotic windows with dragons and pork ribs in gummy, number 2 red dye, sweet-sour sauce constitute the total sum of my memories. The sticky sweet ribs were delicious—at least to an unknowing eight-year-old of 50 years ago. Evidently my mother wasn't of the same opinion. She happened to make the acquaintance of a kindly Chinese lady who generously shared her favorite recipe for sweet and sour spareribs. She said the recipe came from her mother's old recipe notebook, one of her most prized possessions. Mother made the ribs often. They weren't as pretty as the gaudy colored restaurant ribs, but even to my childish palate, they tasted infinitely better."— Maggie Durston, New York, New York

Opposite: Risotto (page 197)
Page preceding: Kugel (page 279)

GLAZED HAM

Serves 8 to 10

4- to 5-pound ham, bone in
10 cloves
½ cup honey
¼ cup Dijon mustard
2 tablespoons cider vinegar

Put the ham in a large dish and cover with water. Let the ham soak overnight to remove some of the saltiness.

Put the ham in a large pan and add enough cold water to cover. Bring to the boil, lower the heat and simmer, covered, for 2 hours. Allow the ham to cool in the cooking liquid. Remove the skin, leaving the fat on, and pat dry. Heat the oven to 400 degrees.

Put the ham in a roasting pan and score the fat diagonally in both directions to make a diamond pattern. Stud each diamond with a clove.

Combine the honey, mustard and vinegar in a small bowl and mix well. Spoon the mixture over the ham. Bake the ham for 20 minutes. Remove from the oven and baste the ham with the glaze in the pan until it is well coated. Transfer the ham to a warm platter to serve.

Ham with Red Eye Gravy

Serves 6

1 tablespoon butter
1 tablespoon vegetable oil
6 thick slices cooked ham, preferably country ham
2 cups strong coffee
1 cup heavy cream
Salt and freshly ground black pepper

Heat the oven to 200 degrees.

Heat the butter and oil together in a large, heavy skillet. Add the ham slices in two batches and cook for 2 to 3 minutes on each side until lightly browned. Keep the ham warm in the oven while you make the gravy.

Pour the coffee into the skillet and bring to the boil, stirring and scraping the bottom and sides of the pan to loosen any browned particles. Cook over high heat for 4 to 5 minutes until the coffee is reduced by about a third. Stir in the cream and season with salt and pepper to taste. Continue to cook, stirring, for 3 to 4 minutes more until the gravy is again reduced by about a third. Pour the gravy over the ham and serve at once.

"When you make red eye gravy, you fry the ham slowly (remember, you're using country ham and it's already been cooked once) so there are drippings in the pan. You then take out the ham and pour coffee in the pan and stir it around to make gravy. It tastes good spooned over the biscuits we always had as well as ham. We usually had it for breakfast when I was growing up and even though I'm from Kentucky, I like Virginia country ham best."—
Hildreth Rosendahl, Newtown, Connecticut

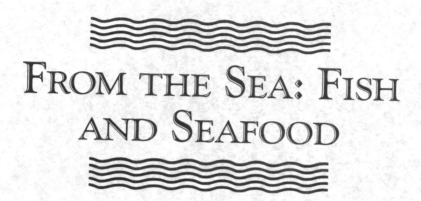

FROM THE SEA: FISH AND SEAFOOD

HERRING SALAD

Serves 4 to 6

1½ pounds pickled herring, cut into ¼-inch strips
1 large potato, peeled, cooked and cut into ½-inch pieces
1 cup chopped tart apple, such as Granny Smith
1 cup chopped red onion
2 stalks celery, finely chopped
4 hard-cooked eggs, roughly chopped
2 medium-size beets, cooked, peeled and cut into 1-inch strips
2 tablespoons chopped fresh chives
Dressing:
1 teaspoon Dijon mustard
1 teaspoon horseradish
¼ cup red wine vinegar
⅔ cup cup vegetable oil
Salt and freshly ground pepper

Combine all the salad ingredients except the chives in a large bowl and mix together gently.

For the dressing, mix the mustard with the horseradish and vinegar in a small bowl to make the dressing. Slowly whisk in the oil. Season with salt and pepper to taste.

Pour the dressing over the salad and toss together lightly. Sprinkle the chives over the top.

"When my wife and I were first married, we used to drive to my parents' every Sunday for brunch. Mom would have bagels, bialys, lox, cream cheese, and— my favorite— herring salad. She would often call me at home before I left and ask me to pick up the fish at the local appetizing store on my way, but, if we were lucky, she made her own herring salad. The spicy, delicious salad, with fresh bagels and cream cheese was a special delight. Fortunately, my wife got the recipe from my mother and now she makes it for me and my sons as well."— Dick Kahn, Woodmere, New York

"Saturday was the only day all week my dad didn't eat lunch from a sack. Instead, my mom made him a big plate of sardines and the current releases from her GE vegetable bin. She makes the same salad to this day and although she still calls it the cold platter, it was actually a composed salad. On the plate were small silvery sardines from Norway— the whole can— sitting on a bed of ruffly lettuce and scattered with chopped onions. My mom built around the sardines, starting at the 12 o'clock position. First, she overlapped cool, transparent slices of cucumbers, then came whole radishes, carrots, slices of beefsteak tomato, yellow-white halves of hard-boiled eggs and, always, bell peppers, sliced in rings so that they resembled hollow shamrocks. On top, a spray of leggy green onions. She emptied the oil from the sardine can and poured it over the salad . My dad ate it all, with crackers and his weekly can of Budweiser."— Elaine Corn, Sacramento, California

Sardine Cold Platter

Serves 1 generously

Curly endive
Leaf lettuce
4 ⅜-ounce can sardines, in oil
4 thin slices scored cucumber
2 thick slices tomato
1 to 2 carrots, cut in matchsticks
1 to 2 stalks celery, cut in matchsticks
¼ cup chopped onion
2 radishes, trimmed
1 hard-boiled egg, halved
1 green or red pepper, sliced in rings
2 scallions

Arrange the endive and lettuce on a large plate so that it covers the plate. Arrange the sardines in a circle in the center of the plate. Layer the cucumbers and tomato slices around them and then arrange the carrot and celery around them in a pretty pattern. Scatter the chopped onion on top of the sardines. Decorate the plate with the radishes, egg halves and pepper rings. Lay the scallions on top of the salad and then pour the oil from the sardine can over the whole platter. Serve the salad with crackers.

 # CRABCAKES

Makes 6 crabcakes

1 pound lump crabmeat, picked over
3 eggs
1 cup fine white bread crumbs
¼ cup finely chopped parsley
2 scallions, finely chopped
1 tablespoon butter, melted
1 tablespoon lemon juice
Worcestershire sauce
Salt and freshly ground black pepper
½ cup cornmeal
2 tablespoons butter
1 tablespoon vegetable oil
Lemon wedges, for garnish

Put the crabmeat in a medium-sized bowl. Lightly beat one of the eggs and add it to the crabmeat along with 1/2 cup of the bread crumbs, the celery, parsley, scallions, melted butter and lemon juice. Mix well, taking care not to to break up the crab chunks too much. Add Worcestershire sauce, salt and pepper to taste. Form the mixture into 6 patties about 3 inches in diameter and 1 to 1 1/2 inches thick.

Beat the remaining 2 eggs in a shallow bowl with 2 teaspoons water. In another shallow bowl, toss the remaining bread crumbs with the cornmeal. Dip each crabcake first in the eggs and then in the bread crumbs so that both sides are coated. Shake off any excess and set the crabcakes on a rack to dry a little.

Heat the butter and the oil in a large skillet over moderate heat until foamy. Add the crabcakes and cook for 3 to 4 minutes on each side or until a golden crust forms and they are heated through. Serve with the lemon wedges.

"My uncle kept a boat on the Chesapeake Bay when I was growing up, and we caught crabs by tying baited lines all around the boat. Sometimes we hauled in three bushels or more of crabs which we boiled almost as soon as we caught them. When we had our fill of plain boiled crabs, my mother took the rest of them and made the best crabcakes I have ever had. I never could decide which I liked better: the boiled crabs or the crabcakes."— Kathy Knapp, Westport, Connecticut

CODFISH CAKES

Serves 6

¾ pound salt cod
1 small onion, chopped
1 small carrot, chopped
1 bay leaf
3 sprigs parsley
½ teaspoon dried thyme
6 medium-size potatoes
2 tablespoons butter
1 egg, beaten
Freshly ground black pepper
½ cup vegetable oil

Soak the fish in enough cold water to cover for 24 hours, changing the water several times.

Put the onion, carrot and herbs in a casserole large enough to hold the fish in one layer. Add the fish and enough water to just cover. Bring to a simmer and cook for 10 minutes.

Meanwhile, cook the potatoes in boiling salted water until tender. Drain in a colander and put them in a large mixing bowl. Add the butter, egg and pepper to taste. Mash the potatoes until they are smooth. Lift the fish from the casserole and let it cool. Discard the vegetables and herbs. Break the fish into pieces and combine them with the potatoes. Mix together well, check the seasoning and chill in the refrigerator for at least 1 hour.

Remove the mixture from the refrigerator and form into cakes, using about 1/4 to 1/3 cup of the mixture for each one.

Heat the oil in a large skillet until hot and cook the cakes, a few at a time, until well browned on both sides. Keep the cooked cakes warm in a low oven while you cook the remainder.

"I don't recall my mother making codfish cakes but I do remember the ones my aunt, my father's sister, made—just 'fishy' enough and with plenty of potatoes. She told me, over and over, that she learned how to cook codfish cakes and most other things from my grandmother, who died before I was born. The cod cakes were a weekend tradition in Aunt Ellen's house and I sometimes rode my bike over there on Saturday morning to have fresh cod cakes with her and Uncle Ed. Aunt Ellen was a wonderful New England cook and listening to her tell stories about my grandmother as she cooked, somehow made me feel as though I knew my grandmother a little after all."—Lisa MacMillan, East Dennis, Massachusetts

≋ Scalloped Oysters ≋

Serves 4 to 6

6 tablespoons butter
1½ cups crushed saltine crackers
1 tablespoon chopped parsley
1 quart oysters, shucked and drained, liquor reserved
Salt and freshly ground black pepper
1 cup heavy cream

Heat the oven to 400 degrees.

Butter the bottom of a 1 1/2-quart casserole, using 2 tablespoons of the butter. Sprinkle 1/2 cup of the crushed crackers and half the parsley into the casserole. Spread half the drained oysters in the casserole. Season with salt and pepper to taste and dot with 2 tablespoons of butter. Sprinkle another 1/2 cup of crushed crackers over the oysters.

Continue layering in the same manner with the remaining oysters, butter and cracker crumbs. Pour the oyster liquor and cream into the casserole and bake for 25 minutes. Sprinkle with the remaining parsley before serving.

"I spent a good part of each childhood summer at my grandmother's big old Victorian house, wedged between Chesapeake Bay and a salt marsh near Lewes, Delaware. Part of the time my parents were there, but then they'd take a week or two of vacation by themselves and it would be just Grandma and me. I loved everything about those times—riding my bike on the flat roads, running after gulls along the sand, swimming and kite-flying and nestling in one of the window seats on rainy days. But still, many of my favorite memories of summers with Grandma have to do with food; we would bake pies and cookies, brew up gallons of iced tea and lemonade, and gorge on crab and clams and oysters at the seafood shacks that lined the coast roads. We never paid any attention to that old rule about only eating oysters in "R" months, because we were too crazy about oysters to forgo them all summer."— Lorraine Selby, Richmond, Virginia

≋ STEAMED MUSSELS ≋

Serves 4

32 mussels
2 tablespoons unsalted butter
1¼ cups finely chopped onion
2 cloves garlic, finely chopped
2 cups white wine
Salt and freshly ground black pepper
2 tablespoons chopped parsley

Soak the mussels in cold water and scrub clean.

Melt the butter in a large saucepan. Add the onion and garlic and cook over moderate heat for 5 minutes, stirring, until they are softened. Add the wine and bring the liquid to the boil. Add the mussels. Cover and steam over moderate heat for about 5 minutes, until all the mussels have opened. Transfer the mussels to a serving dish with a slotted spoon, discarding any that have not opened. Cover the dish and keep warm.

Return the cooking liquid to the boil over high heat and cook for 10 minutes. Season with salt and pepper to taste and stir in the parsley. Pour the liquid over the mussels and serve at once.

BOUILLABAISSE

Serves 4 to 6

Broth:
2 cups water
2 cups dry white wine
Fish trimmings (bones, heads, shrimp shells)
2 medium-size carrots, chopped
4 stalks celery, chopped
Rind of 1 orange
Parsley stems
2 bay leaves
1½ teaspoons dried thyme
1½ teaspoons salt
1 teaspoon white pepper
Stew:
3 tablespoons olive oil
1 medium-size onion, finely chopped
2 cloves garlic, finely chopped
1 pound plum tomatoes, peeled, seeded and finely chopped
2 tablespoons lemon juice
½ teaspoon hot red pepper flakes
Salt and freshly ground pepper
1½ pounds non-oily, firm-fleshed, salt water white fish, such as halibut, tilefish, red snapper or sea bass, trimmed of skin and bones and cut into 1½-inch pieces
½ littleneck clams, scrubbed
½ pound sea scallops, rinsed and drained
½ pound shelled, cleaned large shrimp
2 tablespoons finely chopped parsley

Combine all the ingredients for the broth in a large saucepan. Bring to the boil, lower the heat and simmer for 30 minutes. Remove the broth from the heat and strain through a large, fine sieve, pressing the solids to extract as much liquid as possible.

"Who can forget his first trip to Europe? For me, it was the year I graduated college. I had saved summer earnings for six years to make this trip and was beside myself with excitement. With backpack strapped on and Eurailpass in hand I zigzagged from one side of the continent to the other, blissfully ignorant of itineraries or 'must-sees.' Midway through the trip I landed in Antibes, tired of roughing it and ready for a splurge. I found a small, cheerful bistro, where I settled down with a glass of Beaujolais and wished for a companion to share the meal— when, to my delight, a dapper old man— in fact, an American expatriate who had been living in Antibes for years— asked if he could join me for a bit of English conversation. The dinner, at his suggestion, was bouillabaisse; the evening was the most memorable of my trip. When bouillabaisse is offered on a restaurant menu I always order it, reminded of that charming man— whom I never saw again."— Sam Wagner, Newark, New Jersey

Measure out 2 cups of broth and reserve the rest for another use (it may be frozen).

Heat the oil in a large, deep skillet or casserole. Add the onion and cook, stirring, over moderate heat until softened. Add the garlic and cook for another 1 to 2 minutes. Add the tomatoes and cook for 2 minutes or until slightly softened. Pour in the broth and lemon juice and season with the red pepper flakes and salt and pepper to taste. Bring to the boil, cover and simmer for 5 minutes.

Keeping the broth at a bare simmer, add the white fish and clams and cook for 5 minutes or until the fish just turns opaque. Add the scallops and shrimp and cook for 2 to 3 minutes, until the shrimp are pink. During this time, all the clams should open. If not, discard any which still have not opened. Serve the bouillabaisse in warm bowls, distributing the broth and fish evenly.

CIOPPINO

Serves 4 as a main course, 6 as an appetizer

8 littleneck clams
4 mussels
2 tablespoons olive oil
2 medium-size onions, coarsely chopped (about 2 cups)
2 cloves garlic, finely chopped
2 medium-size red peppers, cut into 1-inch strips
1 tablespoon red pepper flakes
2 cups white wine
½ ounce dried porcini mushrooms
4 medium-size tomatoes, chopped
3 tablespoons tomato paste
½ cup chopped fresh basil
1 pound large shrimp, peeled and deveined
1 pound crab claws, cooked
Salt and freshly ground black pepper

Soak the clams and the mussels in cold water and scrub the shells clean.

Heat the oil in a large saucepan over moderate heat. Add the onions and garlic to the pan and cook for about 5 minutes until the onions have softened. Add the red peppers and pepper flakes and continue to cook, stirring occasionally.

Meanwhile, put 1/2 cup of the wine in a small saucepan and bring to the boil. Remove the pan from the heat and add the dried mushrooms. Set aside to give the mushrooms time to plump up.

Stir the chopped tomatoes into the onion and pepper mixture. Mix the remaining 1 1/2 cups of wine with the tomato paste and stir into the vegetables with the chopped basil. Allow the sauce to simmer for 10 to 15 minutes until all the vegetables are softened.

Add the mussels and clams to the sauce, cover and simmer for 5 minutes. Check to make sure all the clams and mussels open as they cook. Discard any that stay closed. Add the shrimp and crab claws, cover again and cook for 5 to 10 minutes more. Season with salt and pepper to taste.

Oyster Stew

Serves 6

4 tablespoons butter
¾ teaspoon salt
¼ teaspoon paprika
½ teaspoon celery salt
Freshly ground black pepper
1 quart oysters, shucked, liquor reserved
4 cups light cream
Paprika, for garnish

Heat the butter in a large saucepan over moderate heat. Add the salt, paprika, celery salt and pepper to taste. Add the shucked oysters and their liquor to the pan and cook just until their edges start to curl. Reduce the heat to a simmer.

Put the cream in the top of a double boiler and heat gently. When it is hot, add the oysters along with their cooking liquid. Cook over low heat for 15 minutes.

Ladle the stew into individual bowls, garnish each with a pinch of paprika and serve immediately with oyster crackers.

BRODETTO DI PESCE
(FISH STEW, PESCARA STYLE)

Serves 8

Sauce:
6 tablespoons olive oil
2 cloves garlic, chopped
32-ounce can peeled tomatoes
1½ teaspoons tomato paste
2 sprigs parsley
Pinch of dried basil, or chopped fresh basil leaves
Pepper
Diavoletto (hot chili pepper), coarsely chopped (optional)

Fish:
1 pound squid, cleaned and cut into circles
3 pounds assorted light fish, such as scrod, cod, whiting, bass or red
    snapper, cut into serving-sized pieces, unless small enough to be
    left whole
½ pound shelled and deveined shrimp
½ pound scallops
20 mussels, scrubbed and bearded
Freshly chopped parsley

Combine the ingredients for the sauce in a skillet large enough to hold all the fish in one layer. Bring to the boil, stirring occasionally, and then reduce the heat and simmer for 10 minutes.

Add the squid to the pan and cook for another 10 minutes. Add the fish and cook for 20 to 25 minutes until the fish begins to flake. Add the shrimp and cook for a few minutes, just until they turn pink. Finally, add the scallops and mussels. Cook the stew for 5 to 8 minutes longer until the mussels open. As soon as they do, sprinkle the stew with parsley and serve at once.

"Years ago in Italy, men didn't cook. They just talked about it as experts. But my dashing father couldn't wait for an opportunity to get in the kitchen to prepare a meal. My mother (a good cook by osmosis but not passion) loved it when he did. But my twin brother Mimmo and I, teenagers who stuck to the norm, found this peculiarity a little disturbing. A father who cooks? Whoever heard of such a thing? But when some of our young friends started to get married and called my father for recipes— and then spent hours discussing them— it dawned on Mimmo and me that we had an exceptional father.

"His Brodetto di Pesce, an Italian fish stew, became famous among family and friends. Father would go to the port to wait for the fishing boats to be certain of getting the best of the catch of the day from his favorite fishermen. Today, I make his brodetto often and everybody loves it. But I always say, 'You should have tasted my father's.'"— Anna Teresa Callen, New York, New York

SHRIMP CREOLE

Serves 4 to 6

2 tablespoons olive oil
1 cup chopped onion
3 tablespoons chopped garlic
2 green peppers, seeded and chopped
1 cup chopped celery
28-ounce can tomatoes, with juice
1½ pounds shrimp, shelled and deveined, shells reserved
1 cup white wine
2 tablespoons tomato paste
¼ teaspoon red pepper flakes
½ teaspoon filé powder
Salt and freshly ground black pepper
1 tablespoon lemon juice
2 cups steamed rice

Heat the oil in a large skillet over moderate heat. Add the onion, garlic, peppers and celery and cook, stirring, for about 5 minutes until softened. Add the tomatoes and bring to a simmer.

Put the reserved shrimp shells in a pan and add the wine. Bring to the boil, simmer for 3 minutes and strain the liquid into a small bowl. Stir in the tomato paste, pepper flakes, filé powder, salt and pepper to taste, and the lemon juice.

Add this seasoned liquid to the vegetables in the skillet. Cover and simmer for 40 minutes. Remove the cover and continue to simmer, stirring occasionally, for another 5 minutes.

Add the shrimp to the skillet and cook for about 5 minutes. Serve at once over rice.

"My family has a lot of culinary offshoots. My father's parents are from Alsace and Luxembourg; my mother's are German and English. Somehow they all got together here in New Orleans, where my mother learned to cook and now habitually gives a Southern and Creole twist to many mainstream American or European dishes. I never really know whether most of the family's favorite combinations are authentic New Orleans specialties or just my mom's flights of fancy, but they've always seemed just right to me."— Renee Hanf, New Orleans, Louisiana

Opposite: Steamed Fish with Black Bean Sauce (page 165)
Page following: Shrimp Creole (page 160)

SHRIMP SAUTÉED WITH GARLIC

Serves 4

2 pounds large shrimp, in the shell
2 tablespoons butter
2 tablespoons olive oil
2 to 3 cloves garlic, finely chopped
Freshly ground pepper

Peel the shrimp and discard the shells. Clean the shrimp by removing the black intestine running down the middle.

Heat the butter and olive oil in a large, heavy skillet over moderately high heat until foaming and fragrant. Lower the heat to moderate and add the garlic to the pan, stirring for about 30 seconds to release its flavor. Do not let it burn.

Add the shrimp to the pan and raise the heat a little. Cook for 2 to 3 minutes, stirring gently, until all the shrimp are pink. It is important not to cook the shrimp over heat that is too high or the garlic may burn. Season with 2 or 3 turns of freshly ground pepper. Serve at once over steamed or boiled rice.

Opposite: Clams Oreganata (page 44)
Page preceding: Fried Fish (page 172)

"My father's brother Tony is a big, jovial, mustachioed teddy bear of a man who loves to cook. He's not the least bit interested in sweets or in fussy, 'composed' dishes; this is a guy who likes his food simple, savory and in generous quantities. Uncle Tony learned a lot of the basics as an Army cook in Korea; after coming home, he picked up most of what he knows about Italian cooking from my mother. I remember one Saturday night, when I was about ten, Uncle Tony came home from an all-day poker game with an enormous box of fresh shrimp that someone had ante'd up in place of cash. He enlisted everybody in the house to help him shell and devein them, and then he cooked them up with butter, olive oil, and lots of garlic. They would have cost a fortune if you'd ordered them as scampi in a restaurant— so, knowing that lightning would probably not strike twice, we ate shrimp until we practically exploded."— Ed Gennaro, Brooklyn, New York

161

Bean Curd with Shrimp and Scallions

Serves 4

½ *pound shrimp, shelled*
1 tablespoon finely chopped peeled fresh ginger
2 scallions, chopped
2 tablespoons vegetable oil
2 tablespoons rice wine or dry sherry
2 tablespoons light soy sauce
Pinch sugar
1 cup chicken broth
1 pound fresh tofu (bean curd), cut into ½-inch cubes
1 tablespoon cornstarch dissolved in 2 tablespoons water
1 to 2 teaspoons sesame oil
1 scallion, thinly sliced for garnish (optional)

Rinse the shrimp and pat dry. Place in a bowl with the ginger and scallions.

Heat a wok or large skillet over high heat. Add the vegetable oil and heat until it is very hot but not smoking. Add the shrimp, ginger and scallions and stir-fry for about 15 seconds. Add the rice wine or sherry, soy sauce, and a pinch of sugar and stir until the shrimp begin to turn pink. Add the chicken broth and tofu. Stir gently and simmer for 2 minutes. Add the dissolved cornstarch to the simmering liquid. Stir gently until the sauce thickens. Add the sesame oil.

Spoon the mixture onto a platter and sprinkle with the sliced scallions.

Sautéed Soft-Shell Crabs

Serves 4

8 soft-shell crabs, cleaned
1 cup all-purpose flour
½ teaspoon salt
½ teaspoon pepper
8 tablespoons unsalted butter
3 tablespoons lemon juice

Rinse the cleaned crabs under cold running water and pat them dry with paper towels. Season the flour with the salt and pepper. Dredge the crabs with the flour, shaking off the excess.

Heat the butter in a large, heavy skillet over moderately high heat. Cook the crabs, four at a time, for 3 minutes on each side. Transfer them to a warm platter and cook the remaining crabs. Transfer them to the same platter.

Lower the heat to moderate. Add the lemon juice to the skillet and stir. Pour the lemon-butter mixture over the crabs and serve at once.

Note: Make sure the crabs are alive when you buy them, before you or the fish merchant clean them.

I've had soft-shell crabs dressed up in all kinds of finery in grand restaurants. I've had them at the beach, deep fried and dumped on paper plates with hush puppies and coleslaw, and I've had them cloaked in a mustard-flavored marmalade sauce. But to my mind, they are best quickly cooked and served utterly plain, touched only with the merest hint of lemon juice. The trick is to give them space enough in the pan and fry them for only a few minutes. Then the sweet crab meat will wear a mantle of crunchy crispness. Soft-shell crabs are as surely part of the ritual of spring and asparagus, the blooming of the dogwood, and the appearance of the first daffodils.

≋ BROILED LOBSTER ≋

Some people root themselves in history by engraving on their mind the exact moment at which they heard of some usually cataclysmic event. I can remember my first lobster. I was in Boston, in love. I had never before had a lobster, though I didn't immediately volunteer this information. My naïveté though, quickly became apparent. Sheepishly, I confessed. The initiation was a conversion into an affection for lobster that long outlasted that for my companion. I learned how to draw the meat from the tail with just the same curing movement that brings a baby into the world. I discovered the silken smoothness of the green tomally and the hard sac of coral. I discovered the tenderness that lay hidden inside the formidable barrier of the red claws, and I learned how to bite each little finger to extract the last tiny morsels of meat. It was an evening to savor.

Serves 4

4 1½-pound lobsters, split and cleaned
1¼ cups melted butter, or more, for brushing the lobsters
Salt and freshly ground black pepper
Melted butter, for dipping
Lemon wedges

Have the fishmonger split and clean the lobster, leaving any roe (also called coral) in the lobster.

Heat the broiler.

Brush the split-open section (the meat) of each lobster with 2 to 3 tablespoons of melted butter and place under the boiler, about 3 to 4 inches from the heat source. Broil for 10 to 14 minutes and brush the lobsters with more butter every few minutes to keep them moist. Serve immediately with melted butter and lemon wedges.

STEAMED FISH WITH BLACK BEAN SAUCE

Serves 4 to 6

1 whole 3-pound firm, white fish, such as sea bass, trout or red
  snapper, cleaned and scaled, or 3 pounds of firm white fillets,
  such as flounder or sole
½ teaspoon salt
1 tablespoon fermented black beans
2 cloves garlic, finely chopped
1 teaspoon finely chopped fresh ginger
2 tablespoons light soy sauce
1 tablespoon rice wine or dry sherry
Pinch sugar
2 tablespoons finely sliced scallions
1 tablespoon vegetable oil
1 tablespoon sesame oil

Rinse and dry the fish thoroughly. Make 2 or 3 diagonal slashes on each side of the fish about 1 1/2 inches apart. Rub the fish with the salt.

Rinse the black beans in water, drain and chop coarsely. Combine with the garlic, ginger, soy sauce, rice wine and sugar. Spread this mixture evenly on both sides of the fish and put it on a heatproof plate large enough to hold it comfortably. Fit a rack into a large pot, steamer or roasting pan with a tight-fitting lid. Add enough water to come up to within 2 inches of the rack. Bring the water to the boil over high heat. Put the plate with the fish on it on the rack and cover tightly. Steam the fish for about 15 minutes until the eyes turn white and the flesh flakes when tested with the tip of a knife. If cooking fish fillets, steam the fish for 7 to 8 minutes.

When the fish is done, slide it carefully onto a warm platter. Scatter the scallions on top. Keep the fish warm.

Heat the oils in a small pan over moderate heat. When they are very hot, pour over the fish and serve immediately.

"I was born in Canton, China, 75 years ago. In my parents' home, we always kept a kitchen boy to help mother and grandmother with the chopping and scrubbing chores. Mother personally undertook the job of cooking, especially the cleaning and preparation of fresh fish. I can remember that she prepared it for us almost daily. She knew many ways of cooking fish to enhance its fresh taste and appearance. Steaming was her favorite cooking method because she thought the moist heat retained all the fish's natural flavors. Two of my father's favorite seasonings for steamed fish were sliced scallions and salted, fermented black soybeans. I always become very hungry every time I think of our happy family meals and especially those when mother prepared our favorite dish, Steamed Fish with Black Bean Sauce." — Mai Wong, Newport Beach, California

≋ POACHED SALMON ≋

If I were voting, I think I would elect striped bass as the Queen of Fish; though maybe it would be halibut… it is a difficult decision— not nearly as easy as declaring salmon to be King of the Seas. There has never, of course, been any doubt about the regal stature of salmon and this is as true in Britain as in Europe, and North America.

My first memory of salmon was as a mere child in Scotland on a freezing, overcast day. A large, bearded man draped in black oilcloth and high hip boots arrived at our house, whether expected or not I know not, bringing with him a freshly netted salmon for my mother. I remember the way she smiled at him and I knew at once that this fine specimen of a man with his fine specimen of a salmon had brought a gift of considerable consequence. It was poached, probably before as well as after…

Serves 4

1-inch piece lemon peel
1 bay leaf
4 sprigs parsley
1 teaspoon dried thyme
2 ½ cups water
1 ½ cups dry white wine
1 medium-size onion, coarsely chopped
1 stalk celery, coarsely chopped
2 medium-size carrots, coarsely chopped
2 teaspoons salt
4 salmon steaks, 1 inch thick
Finely chopped parsley, for garnish
Lemon wedges

Place the lemon rind, bay leaf, parsley sprigs and thyme on a 4-by-4-inch piece of muslin or doubled cheesecloth. Bring the muslin up around the herbs and tie with kitchen twine to make a bouquet garni.

Combine all the remaining ingredients except the salmon in a heavy pan, large enough to hold the steaks in a single layer. Add the bouquet garni, bring to the boil and simmer, covered, for 30 minutes.

Strain the liquid through a sieve, pressing the vegetables to extract as much liquid as possible. Return the strained liquid to the pan and discard the vegetables.

Bring the liquid to a simmer, add the salmon and poach for 8 to 10 minutes. Check the salmon after 8 minutes—the flesh at the thickest part should be just opaque and separate easily from the bone. Do not overcook.

Transfer the salmon steaks to a warm serving platter. Sprinkle with parsley and garnish with lemon wedges.

"When my daughter, Ellen, was young, we took her with us on a trip to France. She was, of course, thrilled and delighted to be in Europe, but found the food a bit too exotic and spicy, and choosing a meal in a restaurant every evening became somewhat of a trial. One evening, however, my husband persuaded her to try the poached salmon. The French have a way with fish, as every one knows, and the fish was prepared simply and just right. Ellen was delighted and finished every morsel of fish on her plate. After the meal, however, she asked for saumon in every restaurant wherever we went. If she (and we) were lucky, the restaurant would serve her salmon; if not… . At any rate, we still tease Ellen about her 'salmon spree' in France, and she has continued it to this day in the U.S.— she still orders salmon whenever she can."—
Judy Marks,
Wilmington, Delaware

167

BAKED SHAD WITH ROE

Serves 4 to 6

1 whole shad (about 3 pounds), *boned and cleaned*
3 tablespoons butter
2 tablespoons finely chopped garlic
1 cup sliced onion
½ teaspoon dried thyme
1 cup sliced mushrooms
Salt and freshly ground black pepper
1 pair shad roe
2 tablespoons lemon juice
½ cup white wine

Heat the oven to 400 degrees. Pat the fish dry with paper towels.

Heat the butter in a medium-sized skillet. Add the garlic and onion and cook, stirring occasionally, for about 3 minutes or until the onions are softened and translucent. Stir in the thyme and mushrooms and cook for another 3 to 5 minutes over moderate heat. Season with salt and pepper to taste.

Open the cavity of the fish, extending it carefully at both ends if necessary to make stuffing it easier. Spread half the onion mixture in the cavity. Lay the roe on top and then cover them with the remaining onion mixture.

Place the fish on a sheet of foil large enough to wrap the fish. Lift up the edges of the foil slightly and pour the lemon juice and wine over the fish. Bring the sides of the foil together over the fish and fold them together to seal the package completely.

Put the package in a roasting pan and bake for 30 to 40 minutes (about 10 minutes per pound). Unwrap the package and serve the fish with its juices.

Baked Bluefish

Serves 4

4 bluefish fillets
2 tablespoons butter
Salt and freshly ground black pepper
2 tablespoons chopped parsley
1 tablespoon chopped fennel
2 tablespoons lemon juice
¼ cup white wine

Heat the oven to 350 degrees.

Put the fish fillets in a shallow, ovenproof dish and dot with the butter. Sprinkle the fish with salt and pepper to taste and the chopped fennel and parsley. Pour the lemon juice and wine over the fillets.

Cover the dish with foil and seal the edges. Bake for about 15 minutes or until the fish flakes easily with a fork.

"When I was a girl we had fish for dinner every Monday night, since Monday morning the fish peddler came around. As soon as she heard his call, 'fish for sale, fish for sale,' my mother took her change purse and ran down the steps from our apartment to meet him. She bought whatever was fresh and good and in the summertime it often was bluefish from local waters. In those days, our Brooklyn neighborhood had lots of peddlers selling, besides fish, onions, apples, bananas—oh, all sorts of vegetables and fruit."— Sophie Reiner, Queens, New York

≋ STEAMED STRIPED ≋ BASS

Serves 6

2 ½-pound striped bass, cleaned
2 teaspoons salt
2 tablespoons peanut oil
2 teaspoons sesame oil
2 tablespoons thin soy sauce
1 tablespoon white wine
4 large slices fresh ginger, shredded
4 dried mushrooms, stems trimmed and discarded,
    soaked in water to reconstitute and soften
¼ pound fresh pork, finely shredded
2 tablespoons boiled peanut oil
3 scallions, finely chopped

Trim the fish of extra fat, wash it well, inside and out, and pat it dry.

Combine the salt, peanut oil, 1 1/2 teaspoons of the sesame oil, the soy sauce, white wine and ginger. Rub this mixture inside the cavity of the fish and over the outside. Let the fish stand at room temperature for 2 hours.

Slice the soaked mushrooms thinly and combine them with the pork along with the remaining 1/2 teaspoon of sesame oil. Scatter the pork over the fish.

Put 2 sets of chopsticks or a rack in a wok. Pour water in the bottom of the wok, but not enough to touch the chopsticks or rack. Bring the water to the boil and then lay the fish on the chopsticks or rack. Cover the wok and steam the fish for 30 to 45 minutes, or until a chopstick can easily be inserted into the flesh.

Lift the fish from the wok and pour the boiled oil over it. Sprinkle with chopped scallions and serve immediately.

"In the Canton household of my grandmother, the small, autocratic woman I always knew as Ah Paw (which means 'my mother's mother'), the second and sixteenth day of every month were special. Being a Buddhist, my grandmother ate only vegetables on the first and fifteenth of the month and then retired to her couch to finger her wooden beads and pray to her ancestors. But on the days following these fasts, she assembled the servants and my uncle's two wives to set out her menu. She liked fresh pork in soup aromatic with Chinese parsley; chicken steamed with tiger lily buds, cloud's ear fungus and black mushrooms; and steamed fish with spring onions, ginger and occasionally black beans. But not too many beans or garlic, because my grandmother said they put 'too much wet heat' in her system. I never saw my grandmother go into the huge kitchen with its red brick wood-burning stove, but she always knew exactly how everything should be prepared to taste good."—
Eileen Yin-Fei Lo,
Montclair, New Jersey

Note: The peanut oil may be boiled the day before. It need not be hot when it is poured over the fish. To boil, heat it just until wisps of smoke are visible above it. Let it cool and then keep it at room temperature until you cook the fish. If the fish is too large for the wok, cut it in half.

 FINNAN HADDIE

Serves 4

3 tablespoons butter
2 pounds smoked haddock, cut into 4 pieces
Milk
6 peppercorns

Heat the oven to 350 degrees.

Butter a shallow, ovenproof dish, using 1 tablespoon of the butter. Place the haddock fillets in the dish and pour in enough milk to cover. Add the peppercorns and dot with the remaining butter.

Cover the dish with foil and bake for 15 minutes or until the fish flakes easily with fork.

Alternatively, place the fish in a heavy skillet. Cover with milk, add the peppercorns and dot with butter. Cover and simmer for 10 to 12 minutes, or until the fish flakes easily with a fork.

Transfer the fish to serving plates with a slotted spoon, discarding the milk.

"I never liked fish much when I was a child— probably because we lived many miles from the sea and in those days fish didn't really travel well. But everything changed when I was 13 and went for the first of many visits with my mother's elder sister in her flat high above the old city of Edinburgh.

"The fish there was so fresh it seemed to have only just stopped swimming, and as it was also very cheap my aunt had it regularly for supper. She used to steam fillets of whatever was freshest on an old cracked plate over a saucepan of boiling water with just a little salt and a sprinkling of pepper and a dot or two of fresh butter to give it savor. Haddock, cod, sole, finnan haddie— everything tasted so sweet and good that way. I don't remember what we ate with it, but there was always a good strong cup of tea.

"And afterwards Auntie Jean would sit back in her old green armchair and light up a cigarette and just sit and smoke and smile to herself in the gloaming as the lights winked on in the city below. I smile, too, just thinking of that 40-year-old memory."—
Alice Buchanan,
Warwick, New York

≋ MIXED FRIED FISH ≋

Serves 6

Batter:
2 cups all-purpose flour
1 teaspoon salt
3 eggs, separated
3 tablespoons olive oil
¼ cup dry white wine
1 cup cold water
1 pound squid, cleaned
18 (about ½ pound) medium-size shrimp, peeled and deveined
12 large sea scallops
6 small soft-shell crabs, cleaned
24 whole fresh smelts, or other small whole fish, cleaned
Vegetable shortening or vegetable oil for frying
Lemon wedges
Parsley

To make the batter, combine the flour and salt in a mixing bowl. Make a well in the center. Add the egg yolks, olive oil, wine and water and stir with a whisk until the batter is smooth. Let the batter stand at room temperature for at least 1 hour. Add tablespoonfuls of cold water as needed to make the batter the consistency of heavy cream.

When you are ready to cook the seafood, slice the squid bodies into rings and the tentacles into 2 or 3 pieces. Soak the squid in cold water for 10 minutes, then drain and pat dry with paper towels. Put the squid in a bowl and sprinkle with salt and pepper. Similarly, dry the shrimp, scallops, crabs and smelts with paper towels. Put them in separate bowls and sprinkle with salt and pepper.

Whisk the egg whites for the batter in a large bowl until stiff. Fold the whites into the batter.

"When I was a girl, we lived in a three-family house in Brooklyn. My parents moved here from Norway when I was two years old and my mother always cooked the way she had learned at home. An Italian family lived below us and I remember my mother being appalled by the smell of garlic coming from their kitchen—Norwegians didn't use many spices. My mother cooked with a lot of fish and would buy fish heads and bones to make soup with celery, carrots and onions. My mother also fried fish a lot. When we had company, she took very small mackerel and filled them with parsley, nothing else, and fried them in butter. In Norway, mackerel is very popular. I remember visiting my mother's sister once in Norway who refused to go out to dinner with us because she had fresh mackerel at home."—
Ruth Stern,
New York, New York

Heat the vegetable shortening in a deep-fat fryer or deep heavy frying pan until very hot, about 370 degrees. Heat the oven to 150 degrees.

Dip the seafood pieces in the batter to coat them. Drop them gently into the hot fat, a few at a time, and cook for about 4 minutes, until golden brown. As each batch is cooked, remove with a slotted spoon and drain on several thicknesses of paper towel. Keep warm in the oven while cooking the remaining seafood. Make sure the fat returns to the correct temperature before you cook each fresh batch.

Arrange the seafood on a serving platter and garnish with lemon wedges and parsley. Serve immediately.

Note: If desired, the parsley may be dipped in the batter and fried just before serving.

> *"There's something about eating fried fish and corn on the cob that means 'summer' to me. When I was young, our family would go to the Jersey shore for the summer and one of our favorite meals was fried fish and corn. Mom would go to the fish market and buy any fresh fish she thought was not too expensive. When she felt like splurging, she would buy shellfish; if not, sole or trout, or any less expensive fish (in those days!) would do. Then she would fry up a whole 'mess' of fish, steam the corn on the cob, and off we would go to the beach for a late afternoon/early evening supper that left us groaning in pleasure."—*
> *Martin Davidoff, Trenton, New Jersey*

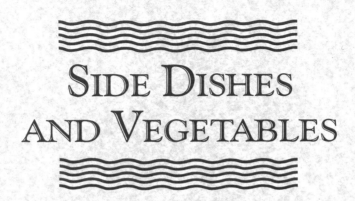

SIDE DISHES AND VEGETABLES

RATATOUILLE

Serves 6 to 8

1 teaspoon salt
1 large eggplant, cut into ½-inch pieces (about 4 cups)
2 tablespoons olive oil
1 cup coarsely chopped onion
2 large cloves garlic, finely chopped
1 large green zucchini, cut into ½-inch pieces (2 to 2⅔ cups)
1 large yellow zucchini, cut into ½-inch pieces (2 to 2⅔ cups)
⅓ cup finely chopped green pepper
2 cups coarsely chopped fresh tomatoes
14½-ounce can whole peeled tomatoes
2 tablespoons tomato paste
1 tablespoon fresh basil leaves or 1 teaspoon dried
½ teaspoon crushed red pepper flakes
1½ teaspoons fresh oregano or ½ teaspoon dried
Salt

Sprinkle the teaspoon of salt over the eggplant pieces and let sit for 8 to 10 minutes. Rinse the salt from the eggplant and pat dry with paper towels.

Heat the olive oil in a large skillet over moderate heat. Add the onion and garlic and cook, stirring occasionally, for 3 to 4 minutes, until the onions are softened and translucent.

Add the eggplant, green and yellow zucchini, green pepper and fresh tomatoes and toss to combine. Pour the canned tomatoes and their liquid over the vegetables, crushing the whole tomatoes with a spoon to break them up. Stir in the tomato paste, basil, red pepper flakes, oregano and salt to taste. Cook the mixture, uncovered, over moderate heat for 20 to 25 minutes, until the liquid reduces slightly and the vegetables are tender.

One of the many joys of summer is the exuberance of shopping at the Farmers Market. Cascades of tomatoes are an explosion of brilliant redness next to purple-black, round-bellied eggplants. Crackling brown-skinned onions are presented in family grouping with their heroic garlic cousins, fat leeks, delicate scallions and baby shallots. From this abundance it is my custom many times during the summer to select the freshest and most colorful vegetables and with a generous benediction of fine olive oil, transform a group of the vegetables into an exhilarating ratatouille. I love to eat it with a roast leg of lamb or breast of cold chicken. I fold it into an omelette and spoon it over spaghetti.
Oddest of all, you may think until you have tried it, is a ratatouille sandwich on whole wheat crusty fresh baked bread. This last idea was handed to me as I sat reading in a sunny walled garden in the south of France. There was too, I recall, a bottle of wine. I sampled the wine to the last drop, ate the ratatouille sandwich to the last bite and afterwards slept wonderfully.

BRAISED ENDIVES

Serves 4

8 endives
Salt and freshly ground black pepper
4 tablespoons butter
1 cup beef broth

Trim the endives and season to taste with salt and pepper. Heat the butter in a skillet over moderate heat. Add the endives and cook until slightly browned on both sides, about 4 minutes in all. Add the beef broth and cook, uncovered, over low heat for about 35 minutes, until the endives are tender.

SUCCOTASH

Serves 4

2 slices bacon
1 small onion, finely chopped
10 ounces frozen corn (about 2 cups) or 4 ears fresh corn,
   kernels cut from cob
10 ounces frozen lima beans (about 2 cups), cooked
½ cup light cream
2 tablespoons butter
Salt and freshly ground black pepper

Cook the bacon in a large heavy skillet over moderately high heat until crisp. Add the onion and cook for 2 to 3 minutes, stirring, until softened. Stir in the corn, cooked lima beans and cream and cook for about 10 minutes, until the flavors have blended and the cream has thickened slightly. Stir in the butter and season with salt and pepper to taste. Serve at once.

176

Opposite: Corn Fritters (page 191)
Page following: Ratatouille (page 175)

≋ STIR-FRIED CHINESE ≋
CABBAGE

Serves 4 to 6

1½ pounds Chinese cabbage (bok choy)
3 tablespoons vegetable oil
3 ⅛-inch slices peeled fresh ginger
½ teaspoon sugar
½ teaspoon salt
2 teaspoons sesame oil

Trim the leaves from the stalks of the cabbage and cut into 2-inch pieces. Cut the stalks diagonally into 1 1/2-inch pieces.

Heat a wok or a large skillet over high heat. Add the oil and heat until very hot but not smoking. Add the ginger and stir, pressing the pieces in the pan. Add the cabbage, sugar and salt and stir-fry, tossing the pieces in the oil for about 3 minutes until the leaves turn bright green and the stalks begin to soften and turn translucent. Add the sesame oil, stir a few times more and serve immediately.

"During the fifties, I had an intense dislike for cabbage because all the cooks I knew had a tendency to overcook it, resulting in a limp mass of fiber with a strong smell and taste. I remember drastically altering my opinion about cabbage a few years later at a dinner party I attended at a friend's home. A Chinese houseguest surprised us with an extraordinary meal which included a cooking demonstration of a simple dish of stir-fried cabbage. I was really impressed watching the chef quickly cook the cabbage, continually tossing the small cut-up pieces in hot oil. It was then that I fell head-over-heels in love with the extraordinary fresh taste and appearance of stir-fried cabbage."—
Marvin Bloome,
Morristown, New Jersey

Opposite: Roesti (page 185)
Page preceding: Home-Fried Potatoes (page 188)

GRANDMA MOLLIE'S VEGETABLE STUFFING

Makes enough to stuff a 20-pound turkey

½ cup raisins
¼ cup safflower or vegetable oil
3 medium-size onions, finely chopped
3 garlic cloves, finely chopped
4 stalks celery, finely chopped
1 bunch carrots, peeled and grated
1 parsnip, peeled and grated
2 large zucchini, grated
½ cup finely chopped parsley
8 to 10 mushrooms, chopped
2 to 3 tablespoons oatmeal
2 to 3 tablespoons all-purpose flour
2 to 3 tablespoons dry bread crumbs
¼ cup dry red wine
Salt and freshly ground black pepper

Put the raisins in a bowl, cover them with water and soak for about 20 minutes until plumped.

Heat the oil in a large, heavy skillet. Add the onions and garlic and cook, stirring occasionally, for about 5 minutes until softened and transparent. Add the celery, carrots, parsnip and zucchini and toss well. Cook for 5 minutes, until the vegetables begin to soften. Drain the raisins and add them to the vegetables with the parsley and mushrooms. Stir in 1 tablespoon each of the oatmeal, flour and bread crumbs. Add the wine and mix well. Stir in the remaining dry ingredients, a little at a time, until the stuffing is moist and soft, but firm in texture. Season to taste with salt and pepper.

Use the stuffing for turkey, chicken or veal breast.

"My mother's vegetable stuffing is European in origin and was inherited from her mother-in-law, my grandmother. The large amount of fresh vegetables used makes it entirely different from most of the starchy stuffings we are used to. Raisins give it a touch of sweetness, and it tastes just as good reheated. This recipe is now a Thanksgiving tradition in my family and is also used all year round for family get-togethers. And now it has become my children's 'Grandma Mollie's Stuffing.' Clearly, an heirloom isn't just a piano, a Persian rug or family silverware. It can be a favorite recipe, too, that is treasured for its delicious self, besides the happy memories it evokes of family celebrations."— Judy Zeidler, Los Angeles, California

COLESLAW

Serves 10 to 12

1 small head cabbage, shredded
2 carrots, grated
1 onion, chopped
1½ teaspoons caraway seeds
2 tablespoons sugar (optional)
1¼ cups mayonnaise
½ cup cider vinegar
Salt and freshly ground black pepper

Combine the vegetables in a large bowl. Add the caraway seeds, sugar, mayonnaise and vinegar and stir until well mixed. Season to taste with salt and pepper. Cover the bowl and refrigerate until the slaw is well chilled and the flavors have blended.

SAUERKRAUT WITH ONIONS AND POTATOES

6 servings

2 tablespoons butter
½ cup chopped onion
3 pounds canned sauerkraut
¾ cup shredded potato
1½ teaspoons caraway seeds
1½ tablespoons light brown sugar
1 cup white wine
1 cup boiling water
¼ teaspoon freshly ground black pepper

"Coleslaw was one of the first dishes I got to make by myself and it truly was a dish I learned by doing. I remember my first awkward efforts at slicing the cabbage in thin shreds, with Mother patiently urging me to cut 'thinner, thinner.'

"It was a long time before I wrote it down as a recipe. In fact, it was when my son-in-law, who does most of the cooking at their house, wanted it that I put it down in recipe form. Since they live on the West Coast, I couldn't tell him to come on over and watch me make it until he got the hang of it. But that's really the best way to learn.

"I know not everyone likes caraway seeds, but they really are the secret of this slaw."—
Betty Ogle,
Kansas City, Missouri

"My father, who was born in Bohemia and came to this country when he was 14, insisted on making sauerkraut every fall the way he remembered it. He rigged up a big shredding contraption with two blades and one of us kids would sit on the top of the shredder and push heads of

Heat the butter in a large heavy-bottomed saucepan over moderate heat. Add the onion and cook for about 5 minutes, until lightly browned.

Rinse the sauerkraut under cold water and drain in a colander. Rinse and drain again. When the onions are cooked, add the sauerkraut, potato, caraway seeds, sugar, wine and water and season with black pepper.

Increase the heat and bring the mixture to the boil. Lower the heat and simmer for 15 to 20 minutes, or until all the liquid has been absorbed. Serve warm.

Potato Salad

Serves 6

1½ pounds red potatoes (about 5 medium-size potatoes)
2 tablespoons chopped parsley
2 tablespoons chopped fresh dill or ¾ teaspoon dried
2 scallions, trimmed and finely chopped
½ stalk celery, chopped
2 tablespoons vinegar
1 cup mayonnaise
Salt and freshly ground black pepper

Put the potatoes in a large saucepan and cover with cold water. Bring to the boil and cook for 20 to 30 minutes, until the potatoes are tender but still firm. Drain the potatoes and let them cool slightly. Peel, if desired, and cut them into 1/2-inch pieces.

Put the potatoes in a large bowl and add the parsley, dill, scallions, celery, vinegar and mayonnaise. Season to taste with salt and pepper and toss gently to mix. Cover and chill until the flavors have had time to blend.

GERMAN POTATO SALAD

Serves 6

1½ pounds red potatoes (about 5 medium-size potatoes)
¼ pound bacon
2 scallions, trimmed and thinly sliced
½ cup beef broth
¼ cup vinegar
1½ tablespoons sugar
Salt and freshly ground black pepper

Put the potatoes in a large saucepan and cover with cold water. Bring to the boil and cook for 20 to 30 minutes, until the potatoes are tender but still firm. Drain and, when cool enough to handle, peel the potatoes and cut them into 1/4-inch slices.

Cook the bacon in a skillet until crisp and brown. Remove from the skillet and set aside. Add the scallions to the pan and cook for 2 minutes, until tender. Add the broth, vinegar and sugar, and crumble the bacon back into the pan. Season with salt and pepper and cook for about 1 minute to heat through. Pour the hot dressing over the potatoes, toss and serve.

to argue with success and just about everything she prepared was good.

"Her potato salad always says summer to me. She always served it for cook-outs. I can taste it along with hamburgers or hot dogs fresh off the grill served with potato chips and pickles or relish.

"When potluck was in order, my mother always toted her 'famous' potato salad, whether it was to a funeral, a family reunion, or just a block party." — Anna Boriskie, Cleveland, Ohio

"German Potato Salad has a different taste from other potato salads. For one thing, it is warm; for another, the bacon and sugar add a delectable touch. When I lived in Brooklyn as a child, I loved to have Saturday evening supper with my friend Katrina, whose German grandmother would prepare all kinds of unusual (for me) meals for us. One of her specialties was German potato salad, served with bratwurst. I would eat until I thought I would burst; then, I would come back for more!"— Alice Berg, Riverdale, New York

≋ POTATO DUMPLINGS ≋

Serves 6

1 tablespoon butter
¼ cup finely chopped onion
3 large potatoes
1 egg
¼ cup milk
⅓ to ½ cup all-purpose flour
Salt and freshly ground black pepper
Nutmeg

Heat the butter in a small skillet over low heat. Add the onion and cook for about 5 minutes, until softened and translucent.

Cook the potatoes in boiling salted water until soft. Drain and peel the potatoes and mash them with the egg and the milk. Add the onions and stir in the flour, adding enough to make a very soft dough. Season to taste with salt, pepper and nutmeg.

Fill a large saucepan with salted water and bring to the boil. Form the potato dough into small 1-inch balls. Cook the dumplings, a few at a time, for 10 minutes. Drain and keep warm while you cook the remaining dumplings.

"For many reasons, potato dumplings remind me of my mother's warm, inviting kitchen and the whole family sitting around the large kitchen table waiting for one of her extrodinary meals. We didn't have much money in those Depression years but, somehow, there was always a good, filling meal on the table for my four sisters and me. Potato dumplings were filling and inexpensive and we all loved them, so Mom tried to make them often. Now that I am able to afford to prepare many different types of meals, I find that I still make potato dumplings for my own grandchildren, and they, like my sisters and I, eat them with delight."— Arlene Kase, Syracuse, New York

Pommes de Terres Dauphinois
(Scalloped Potatoes)

Serves 4 to 6

4 tablespoons butter
1½ pounds potatoes
Salt and freshly ground black pepper
1½ cups half-and-half
¼ teaspoon grated nutmeg

Heat the oven to 350 degrees. Butter an ovenproof casserole with 1 tablespoon of the butter.

Peel the potatoes and slice them very thin. Put the slices in a colander and rinse thoroughly under cold running water. Pat the potatoes dry with paper towels.

Layer a third of the potatoes in the bottom of the buttered casserole. Sprinkle with salt and pepper and dot with a tablespoon of the butter. Make two more layers with the remaining potatoes. Season each layer with salt and pepper and dot with butter in the same way. Pour the half-and-half over the potatoes and sprinkle the nutmeg over the top.

Bake the potatoes for 1 1/4 to 1 1/2 hours, until tender.

Many years ago I bought a wildly expensive, small, lidded copper pot whose only function was to cradle scalloped potatoes. In this pot, the sides of the potatoes crisped to a lightly browned crust around the edges while the center oozed unctuous creaminess. I am passionately fond of potatoes cooked this way, in the style of a long-ago distinguished dauphin. Any expense, I reasoned then, would be worth the cost and I have never regretted the decision.

The pot for this precise purpose was designed with care. The potatoes simmer in the controlled copper environs until they have reached that moment of perfection and then the idea is to invert the pot so that the lid becomes the serving dish with the potatoes standing high above the rim. (In fact, I have never dared attempt to turn it upside down.) Less daring is the substitution of heavy cream for half-and-half— but on this matter, you must let your conscience be your guide.

Brunede Kartofle
(Caramelized Potatoes)

Serves 4 to 6

1½ pounds medium-size potatoes
¾ cup sugar
10 tablespoons butter, melted

Peel the potatoes and cut them into 1 1/2-inch pieces. Cook them in boiling salted water for about 15 minutes or until just tender.

Put the sugar in a large, heavy skillet and cook over low heat for about 4 minutes, stirring constantly, until it starts to turn golden brown. Add the melted butter and stir to combine. Add the potatoes in batches so that they are not crowded. Toss gently until they are well coated and then remove them to a warm serving dish while you caramelize the remaining potatoes.

Potato Latkes

Serves 4

4 potatoes, peeled and grated
1 small onion, grated
1 egg, beaten
1 teaspoon salt
1 teaspoon baking powder
½ cup all-purpose flour
Freshly ground pepper
Vegetable oil, for frying

184

Combine the grated potatoes with the onion and egg. Stir well. Mix together the salt, baking powder and flour and slowly stir the dry ingredients into the potatoes. Season with a little pepper.

Heat the oil in a large skillet or on a griddle. Drop the batter, a tablespoon at a time, and fry for about a minute on each side, until both sides are golden brown. Serve immediately.

ROESTI
(PAN-FRIED SHREDDED POTATOES)

Serves 6

6 medium-size baking potatoes
1 teaspoon salt
8 tablespoons butter

Cook the potatoes in boiling water until they are barely tender. Drain them in a colander and allow to cool. Peel the potatoes and grate them coarsely into a bowl. Sprinkle with the salt and toss gently.

Heat 2 tablespoons of butter in a small heavy frying pan over moderate heat. Add about a sixth of the potatoes and stir until they are coated with the butter. Spread the potatoes over the bottom of the pan with a spatula, pressing them into a flat cake. Fry the cake until it is brown and crisp on the bottom. Turn and fry on the other side. Transfer the cake to a platter and keep warm while you cook the remaining potatoes, adding more butter to the pan as necessary.

"My Swiss-German grandmother came from a small village near Zurich and moved in with us in upstate Pennsylvania when I was young. She made many hearty and wonderful Swiss-German dishes: Bratwurst, Sauerbraten, and Rouladen (rolled beef spread with mustard and filled with onions, bacon, and pickles) to name a few. Our favorite dish, without a doubt, however, was her Roesti. Somehow she was always able to brown the potatoes perfectly without ever having them stick to the pan, and I will always remember their lovely golden-brown color and wonderful flavor. To this day, I have never tasted Roesti like my grandmother's, despite my many visits to Switzerland and my constant searching. I wonder now if I imagined their delicious taste and consistency or if they were really as special as they seemed to me when I was so young!" — Marie Hoffman, Pittsburgh, Pennsylvania

HASHED BROWN POTATOES

Serves 6

6 tablespoons bacon fat or vegetable oil
1 medium-size onion, coarsely chopped
5 to 6 medium-size potatoes, chopped or cut into ¼-inch dice
Salt and pepper

Heat the fat in a skillet over moderate heat. Add the onion and cook, stirring, for 2 minutes until softened. Add the potatoes, turn the mixture with a spatula and press gently into an even layer. Decrease the heat to low, cover the pan and cook for about 25 minutes.

Remove the lid from the pan, season the potatoes with salt and pepper and cook for about 10 minutes more until they are crusty and browned on the bottom. Slide the spatula under the potatoes to loosen them and serve at once.

POTATOES ANNA

Serves 6

1½ pounds russet potatoes, peeled
½ pound butter
Salt and pepper

Heat the oven to 375 degrees.

Cut the potatoes into very thin slices, about 1 1/6 inch thick. Rinse the slices in cold water, drain and pat dry with paper towels.

Melt the butter in a small pan over low heat. Skim off the froth that rises to the surface. Pour the clear fat into a bowl (this is clarified butter), and discard the milky residue in the pan.

Spread about 2 tablespoons of the clarified butter on the bottom of a 10-inch cast iron skillet. Arrange some of the potato slices in an overlapping spiral pattern on the bottom of the skillet. Sprinkle with salt and pepper and drizzle 2 more tablespoons of clarified butter over the slices. Continue layering the potatoes in the same way, reversing the direction of each layer. Drizzle clarified butter over each layer in turn.

Leave the potatoes in the skillet and bake them in the oven for about 45 minutes, pressing them flat several times with a spatula. Remove the skillet from the oven when the potatoes are soft and a rich golden brown on the bottom. Holding the spatula against the potatoes, pour off any excess butter. Loosen the potato cake and invert it onto a warm platter. Cut into wedges and serve immediately.

COLCANNON

Serves 4

6 tablespoons butter
½ head cabbage, shredded
1½ pounds potatoes
¾ cup heavy cream
Salt and freshly ground black pepper
1 tablespoon chopped parsley

Heat 4 tablespoons of the butter in large pan over moderately low heat. Add the shredded cabbage and toss to coat

potatoes that much richer and creamier. The smooth flavor and texture mellows the cabbage and makes it a treat even for non-cabbage people like my husband.

"I once asked his mother where she got the recipe. She said she thought it was probably Irish, but that she had come by it the way I had. Her husband hated cabbage but loved it with mashed potatoes. Like father, like son."— Catherine Wells, Salt Lake City, Utah

"Home-fried potatoes were my Dad's specialty. He'd cook the potatoes while Mom did the rest of the meal. I'm not really sure why he adopted fried potatoes as 'his' dish, but once he got going he perfected it. He certainly wasn't content to just fry up some potatoes. But then he came from New Orleans where eating is a municipal pastime and flavor is very important. Plain fried potatoes just didn't have enough of it. So he started improving on the basic dish and came up with one which was enhanced by rosemary, smoked ham, paprika, and a dash of red

with the butter. Let the cabbage cook slowly in the butter for 30 to 40 minutes, stirring occasionally.

While the cabbage is cooking, peel and quarter the potatoes. Boil them in salted water until tender. Drain the potatoes and mash them until smooth. Add the remaining butter and the cream to the potatoes and mix well.

When the cabbage is soft, stir it into the mashed potatoes. Season with salt and pepper, add the chopped parsley and serve.

HOME-FRIED POTATOES

Serves 4 to 5

6 cups water
4 medium-size white or red potatoes, cut into 1-inch pieces
1 teaspoon dried rosemary
2 to 3 tablespoons clarified butter
½ cup sliced onions
1½ ounces smoked cooked ham, cut into ½-inch pieces
1 teaspoon chopped parsley
1 teaspoon paprika
Salt and freshly ground black pepper
⅛ teaspoon ground red pepper

Put the water, potatoes and rosemary leaves in a medium-sized saucepan and bring to the boil. Cook for 5 to 7 minutes, until the potatoes are tender but still firm. Drain and rinse under cool water to stop the cooking and remove the rosemary. Pat the potatoes dry with paper towels.

Heat the clarified butter in a large cast iron skillet over moderate heat for 3 to 4 minutes, until it begins to smoke. Add the onions and cook for 2 to 3 minutes, until they begin to soften. Add the potatoes and an additional tablespoon of butter if desired. Cook the potatoes undisturbed for about 5 minutes and then toss them gently and cook for 3 to 5 minutes more to brown them on all sides.

Add the ham, parsley, paprika, salt, pepper and red pepper. Toss with the potatoes and cook for 5 to 7 minutes longer.

GRANDPA'S MAMALIGA

Serves 8

8 cups water
2 teaspoons salt
2 cups yellow cornmeal

Bring the water and salt to the boil in a large pot or saucepan. Add the cornmeal very slowly, stirring constantly. Take care, since the mixture will splatter as it is stirred.

Reduce the heat to moderate and cook, stirring constantly, for 20 to 30 minutes until very thick. Pour the mamaliga into a mold or bowl and let it sit for 2 minutes. Unmold onto a flat dish or tray and slice with a fine string. Serve with melted butter and cottage cheese, sour cream or yogurt.

pepper. Perhaps that was a Cajun touch he picked up somewhere along the way. But they're a meal in themselves."— Ray Parker, Baton Rouge, Louisiana

"The pot grandpa used solely for making mamaliga was cast iron and in it he boiled salted water and then very slowly added yellow cornmeal. He mixed the cornmeal round and round with a long wooden pole for what seemed like hours. We all believed that only he was strong enough to mix so carefully and for so long that there were no 'raw spots.

"Mamaliga, a kind of cornmeal mush and the national dish of Romania, was usually prepared on a Sunday afternoon when family members gathered for lunch. After it had cooked long enough for the wooden pole to stand up by itself, Grandpa turned it out onto a cloth-covered tabletop. With a flourish, he cut slices for us, using a thick white thread. Most often, we ate the hot mamaliga with melted butter and pot cheese. And then after lunch, I remember sitting on my beloved grandfather's lap while he drank his glass of tea."— Gail Forman, Potomac, Maryland

189

Grandma's Cornmeal Mush

"My grandmother called it
fried mush and she cooked it
for breakfasts and Sunday-
night suppers. Grandma knew
a lot about cornmeal mush
because she had come to
California from Kansas, where
her family had grown corn,
sugar beets and peaches, and
kept chickens— and where she
had ridden a horse named
Minnie. She and my
grandfather thought they had
found paradise in the sunshine
of Southern California. At
Riverside they kept chickens in
the backyard and didn't worry
about them freezing to death in
winter. My grandfather, who
as a boy had crossed the
prairies in a wagon, had lived
in sod houses and been shot at
by Indians, couldn't get
enough of the California
gardenias in December and
poinsettias in July. I couldn't
get enough of fried mush.
Grandma taught me to cut
slices 1/2 inch thick, no more,
because the crust was the best
part and if the slices were cold
and thin and the black cast-
iron frypan hot and spitting
with bacon fat, the slices would
get as crispy brown on the
outside as potato pancakes and

Serves 6 to 8

2 quarts water
1 teaspoon salt
1 pound yellow or white cornmeal (coarsely ground, if available)
Boiling water, in reserve
Bacon fat, for frying

Bring 2 quarts of water to the boil in a large saucepan. Use a heavy pan you do not need to hold—you must have both hands free. Add the salt. Pour the cornmeal very slowly into the water, stirring constantly with a long-handled wooden spoon. Stir clockwise and do not change direction.

After 30 minutes, the cornmeal should be thick and no longer cling to the sides of the pan. Continue stirring for 30 minutes, adding a little boiling water if it is too thick to stir.

Cover a work surface with a clean cloth, turn the pan upside down and allow the contents to flow onto the cloth, scraping the sides and bottom of the pan with a wooden spoon. You may leave the mush to cool in a mound on the cloth, or transfer it to a loaf pan. Cut the cold mush into slices with a sharp stainless steel knife and fry in hot bacon fat. Alternatively, the mush may be served before cooling, with melted butter and cheese.

CORN FRITTERS

Serves 4

2 tablespoons finely chopped onion
1 egg yolk
½ cup corn kernels
1 tablespoon vegetable oil plus extra for frying
½ cup all-purpose flour
½ teaspoon salt
½ teaspoon baking powder
⅛ teaspoon cayenne pepper
2 egg whites

Mix the onion with the egg yolk, corn and 1 tablespoon of oil in a bowl. Combine the flour, salt, baking powder and cayenne. Add the flour mixture to the bowl and mix well. Beat the egg whites until stiff. Stir a quarter of the egg whites into the corn mixture to loosen the batter. Fold in the remaining whites.

Heat the vegetable oil in a heavy skillet to 375 degrees. Drop the batter, two tablespoonfuls at a time, into the hot oil. Fry for about 5 minutes, turning the fritters once until golden brown. Drain the fritters on paper towels and serve immediately. Cook the remaining batter in the same way, adding more oil if necessary.

yet stay soft within.

"I still eat fried mush … the same mush my grandmother made, only now it appears on the fanciest sort of restaurant menus as polenta. My grandmother would think that a hoot."— Betty Fussell, New York, New York

"Growing up in Kentucky, we always used fresh corn in the summer. We'd have corn fritters with fried chicken or fresh fried catfish.

"Nobody could make fritters like our housekeeper. In fact, I think she was probably the best frycook I've ever known. Everything she made turned out crisp and golden. She just had the magic touch.

"These particular fritters were so light and wonderful— a perfect mouthful. I can remember her shooing us kids out of the kitchen because we'd try to eat them as soon as they came out of the hot grease. We could eat just as many as she could fry and if she hadn't chased us away, there wouldn't have been any left for the table!"— Amy Baldridge, Asheville, Kentucky

"From the time I can remember I have always cooked. I used to stand on a stool and watch my mother, which is how I learned to make most of the basic things I still make today, such as corn pudding. We would make it plain or sometimes add red or green peppers to the batter to make the pudding more of a 'vegetable'."— Hildreth Rosendahl, Newtown, Connecticut

"Whether you serve spoon bread with molasses, gravy or just lots of butter it is the most mouth-watering dish I know of. Just thinking about it reminds me of home.

"We lived on a farm and very often cornmeal was about all we had, but we kids never knew it. Heck, spoon bread wasn't a sign of lean times, it just meant a good time at dinner.

"My mother would make two or even three dishes of it, depending on how many extras there were at the table and what else she had on hand. When there was meat for the table, the spoon bread didn't have to go nearly as far. But, like I said, we

CORN PUDDING

Serves 4 to 6

3 cups fresh corn kernels
1 teaspoon sugar
1 teaspoon salt
⅛ teaspoon ground nutmeg
3 large eggs, separated
2 tablespoons butter, melted
½ cup light cream or half-and-half

Heat the oven to 350 degrees. Butter a 1 1/2-quart baking dish.

Mix together the corn, sugar, salt and nutmeg. Lightly beat the egg yolks and stir them into the corn mixture. Stir in the butter and the cream.

Beat the egg whites until stiff peaks form. Fold the whites into the corn mixture. Pour the mixture into the prepared baking dish and cook for 35 minutes, uncovered, or until a toothpick inserted in the center comes out clean.

SPOON BREAD

Serves 4

2 tablespoons butter or reserved bacon fat
½ cup yellow or white cornmeal
½ teaspoon salt
½ teaspoon baking powder
¼ teaspoon baking soda
2 eggs
1 cup buttermilk

Page following: Buttermilk Biscuits (page 202)

Heat the oven to 375 degrees.

Put the butter in a 1-quart casserole and place in the oven. While the butter is heating, combine the cornmeal, salt, baking powder and baking soda in a bowl. In another bowl, combine the eggs and buttermilk. Pour the egg mixture over the dry mixture and mix thoroughly.

When the butter is hot but not smoking, remove the casserole from the oven and pour the butter into the spoon bread mixture. Make sure that the casserole is coated with fat and place the spoon bread mixture in the casserole. Bake for 30 minutes or until the spoon bread is golden brown.

 CHEESE SOUFFLÉ

Serves 4

2 tablespoons unsalted butter
2 tablespoons all-purpose flour
1¼ cups milk, scalded
⅛ teaspoon ground nutmeg
⅛ teaspoon cayenne pepper
¼ teaspoon salt
1½ teaspoons dried dill
1½ cups grated extra-sharp cheddar cheese
3 large egg yolks at room temperature, lightly beaten
5 large egg whites at room temperature
Cream of tartar

Heat the oven to 400 degrees. Place a rack in the center of the oven. Butter a 1 1/2-quart soufflé dish.

I used to think that it was a gift granted to few, to have the skill to make a cheese soufflé. But this is not true at all. Anyone with the wit to make a cheese sauce can easily conquer a soufflé—which is after all only a cheese sauce that has swallowed a huge gulp of egg whites.
I remember the first soufflé I ever tried. I tiptoed around the kitchen and spoke softly, fearing it wouldn't rise. But it did and my spirits with it. A soufflé honors guests and pleases the cook who knows simple are the steps to produce a fine flurry of hot air.
An inspired culinary illusion, a soufflé always makes a big stir. It makes a fine lunch or spectacular but simple supper. The only thing to warn you of is that this castle in the air will not linger while you admire its architecture. So seat your guests before you carry the soufflé to the table so that you remain in control.

Opposite: Potato Latkes (page 184)
Page preceding: Cheese Blintzes (page 232)

Heat the butter in a saucepan over low heat. Add the flour and whisk until smooth and thick. Cook the flour mixture for 2 to 3 minutes, stirring. Slowly add the milk, stirring with the whisk. Increase the heat to moderately high and cook for 3 to 5 minutes, stirring constantly, until the mixture bubbles around the edge.

Remove the pan from the heat and stir in the nutmeg, cayenne, salt and dill. Add the cheese and stir until combined. Stir in the egg yolks until well combined.

Beat the egg whites with the cream of tartar in a large bowl for about 45 seconds, until they are frothy. Increase the speed to high and continue beating for 2 to 3 minutes, until stiff, but not dry, peaks form. Stir a quarter of the egg whites into the egg-cheese mixture. Fold in the remaining egg whites, using a rubber spatula. Scrape the mixture into the prepared soufflé dish and bake for 30 to 35 minutes, until the soufflé is puffed and golden brown. Serve immediately.

MACARONI AND CHEESE

Serves 4 to 6

6 cups water
1 teaspoon salt
2 cups elbow pasta
2½ tablespoons unsalted butter
2½ tablespoons all-purpose flour
2 cups milk
½ teaspoon freshly ground black pepper
¼ teaspoon whole celery seed
1½ teaspoons Dijon mustard
1½ teaspoons Worcestershire sauce
2 teaspoons chopped parsley
2 cups grated extra-sharp cheddar cheese
¼ teaspoon paprika

Heat the oven to 325 degrees.

Put the water in a saucepan with 1 teaspoon of the salt and bring to the boil. Add the pasta, stir to separate, and return the water to the boil, stirring occasionally. Cook the pasta for 5 to 7 minutes until just tender. Drain and rinse with cool water. Toss with 1/2 tablespoon of butter.

Heat the remaining butter in a medium-sized saucepan over low heat. Stir in the flour and whisk until smooth. Slowly add the milk, stirring occasionally, until it is just beginning to boil. Remove the pan from the heat. Stir in the remaining teaspoon of salt with the pepper, celery seed, mustard, Worcestershire sauce and 1 teaspoon of parsley.

Place half the cooked pasta in a 1 1/2- to 2-quart baking or soufflé dish. Sprinkle with half the grated cheese. Pour half the milk mixture over the cheese. Repeat this process with the remaining cheese and milk mixture. Bake, uncovered, for 30 to 40 minutes, until the sauce is bubbling and the top is just beginning to form a thin film. Remove from the oven. Stir the mixture with a large wooden spoon to combine all the ingredients. Sprinkle the top with the remaining teaspoon parsley and the paprika.

"The long drive every year from Michigan to Grandmother's house in Iowa was always worth it because I knew my grandmother's cooking awaited us. I don't know what it was about Grandmother's macaroni and cheese, but I could polish off a whole casserole of it myself. Luckily for me, my four sisters didn't share my obsession and I could indulge myself with square after square of the firm, oven-baked dish. Grandmother hand-grated the cheese that went into the thick filling and mixed it with old-fashioned, cooked elbow macaroni. But the best touch came last. She liberally sprinkled buttered, toasted bread crumbs on top before baking it slowly in her oven. The resulting thick, crusty top absorbed some of the casserole's bubbling juices and made the dish one I never forgot."— Carol Haddix, Chicago, Illinois.

SPAETZLE

"My grandmother was orginally from Bavaria and she prepared many wonderful German dishes for her family. We all enjoyed the somewhat heavy but delicious food, but my father's favorite was spaetzle. It was a perfect side dish for any of her meals— meat, chicken, anything— but I remember liking it all alone. My grandmother would prepare a big bowl just for me and top the spaetzle with butter and bread crumbs. I would eat the whole bowl and nothing alse. What heaven!"— Alma Berenson, Hartford, Connecticut

Serves 6 to 8

4 cups all-purpose flour
¼ teaspoon ground nutmeg
1½ teaspoons salt
1⅓ cups milk
5 large eggs
1 tablespoon oil
3 quarts water
8 tablespoons butter
1¼ cups dry bread crumbs

Combine the flour, nutmeg and half the salt in a large mixing bowl. Pour the milk into another bowl, add the eggs and beat until combined. Gradually add the liquid mixture to the dry ingredients, stirring until a soft dough forms.

Add the remaining salt and the oil to the water in a large saucepan and bring to the boil. Transfer the dough into a large-holed colander. With the colander over the saucepan, press the dough, abut 1/2 cup at a time, through the colander into the boiling water. Cook the spaetzle, stirring occasionally, for about 4 minutes or until they rise to the surface and are tender. Remove the cooked spaetzle from the water with a slotted spoon, drain thoroughly and keep warm in a heated serving dish. Cook the remaining dough in the same way.

Heat the butter in a large, heavy skillet over moderately high heat. Add the bread crumbs and cook, stirring, until golden. Scatter the bread crumbs over the spaetzle just before serving.

RISOTTO

Serves 4

¼ teaspoon ground saffron
1 cup dry white wine
5 cups chicken broth
12 tablespoons butter
1 small onion, finely chopped
2 cups long-grain rice
1 cup grated Parmesan cheese
1 tablespoon chopped parsley
Salt and white pepper

Put the saffron and wine in a small saucepan over moderate heat and stir until the saffron has dissolved and colored the liquid. In another saucepan, heat the broth to a simmer and keep simmering over low heat throughout the cooking process.

Heat 8 tablespoons of the butter in a large, heavy, deep skillet over moderate heat. Add the onion and cook for about 4 minutes or until softened, stirring occasionally. Add the rice and stir until it is coated with the melted butter. Add the wine and stir for about 2 minutes, until almost absorbed.

Add 1 cup of the simmering chicken broth to the skillet. Cook for about 3 minutes, stirring constantly, until the broth is almost absorbed. Continue to add chicken broth, 1/2 cup at a time, until the rice has absorbed all of it and is tender but firm.

Remove the pan from the heat and stir in 1/2 cup of Parmesan cheese along with the remaining butter and the parsley. Season with salt and white pepper and serve immediately. Pass the remaining cheese separately.

"When my mother made risotto she browned the onions in butter and then put the rice in the pan and stirred it for a minute or two. She had a pot of boiling beef broth (or sometimes chicken broth) on the stove and would pour in a half cup or so at a time. The broth had to be boiling very hard. Every time the liquid was absorbed by the rice, she added a little more. I remember her standing at the stove. She stood at the end stirring the risotto, adding a little broth every few minutes, for 30 or 40 minutes. She sometimes added dried Italian mushrooms or chopped-up chicken livers, if she had some."—Bianca Etkin, Flushing, Queens

≋ JAPANESE COOKED ≋ RICE

Makes about 4½ cups cooked rice

2 cups short-grain Japanese rice
2⅓ cups cold water

      Wash the rice several times until the water runs clear. Drain the rice well and put it in a heavy 1 1/2-quart saucepan.

      Add the water, cover the pan and bring to the boil over high heat. Lower the heat to moderate and cook the rice for about 10 minutes until almost all the water has been absorbed. Remove from the heat and allow the rice to sit, tightly covered, for about 20 minutes.

≋ THREE-BEAN SALAD ≋

Serves 8

¾ pound fresh green beans, trimmed and cut into 1½-inch pieces
¾ pound fresh yellow beans, trimmed and cut into 1½-inch pieces
½ cup vegetable oil
¼ cup vinegar
1 tablespoon sugar
½ teaspoon salt
¼ teaspoon freshly ground black pepper
1-pound can red kidney beans
2 scallions, trimmed and thinly sliced
2 stalks celery, chopped

Bring a large pot of water to the boil and add the beans. Boil for about 10 minutes, until the beans are firm but not fully cooked. Drain and plunge into cold water to stop the cooking process.

Put the oil, vinegar, sugar, salt and pepper in a bowl and mix well.

Put the beans in a large bowl and add the kidney beans, scallions and celery. Pour the dressing over the vegetables and toss to combine. Cover and chill for at least 4 hours until the flavors have had time to blend.

Everyone brought something—salads, cakes, pies. I know we always had three-bean salad, potato salad and coleslaw as well as ham and fried chicken."—Hildreth Rosendahl, Newtown, Connecticut

≋ Boston Baked ≋ Beans

Serves 8

1½ quarts water
2 teaspoons salt
1 pound dried navy beans, cleaned and washed
½ pound salt pork
1 small onion
4 cloves
2 cups water
¼ cup brown sugar
½ cup molasses
2 teaspoons dried mustard
Salt and freshly ground black pepper

Combine the water and salt in a large saucepan. Add the beans and leave them to soak overnight.

"You can't grow up around Boston and not eat baked beans. I have always been partial to them myself and remember in particular eating them at Sunday night suppers at the church. I seem to recall that there were usually three or four different casseroles of baked beans that the ladies in the auxiliary had made. While they were all a little different, they all tasted sort of sweet from the brown sugar and molasses and yet they had a little bite, too, from the mustard, I guess."—Charles Matthews, Dedham, Massachusetts

Bring the beans to the boil. Decrease the heat to moderate, cover and simmer for about 30 minutes. Heat the oven to 250 degrees.

Trim the rind off the salt pork and cut the pork into 1/2-inch pieces. Stud the onion with cloves.

Put 2 cups of water in a saucepan and bring to the boil. Add the brown sugar, molasses and mustard and season with salt and pepper to taste. Drain the beans.

Put the onion and salt pork in a 2-quart casserole. Add the beans and the molasses mixture. Cover and bake for 4 1/2 hours or until the beans are tender. Stir the beans every hour and add a little more water if necessary.

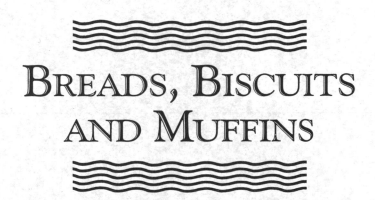

BREADS, BISCUITS AND MUFFINS

BUTTERMILK BISCUITS

Makes 8 biscuits

2 cups all-purpose flour
2 teaspoons baking powder
1 teaspoon baking soda
½ teaspoon salt
6 tablespoons unsalted butter, cut into pieces
¾ cup buttermilk
Milk or 1 egg beaten with 1 teaspoon water, for glaze

Heat the oven to 400 degrees.

Sift the flour, baking powder, baking soda and salt into a large bowl. Cut in the butter until the mixture resembles coarse meal. Make a well in the center and pour in the buttermilk. Stir with a fork until the dough starts to hold together.

Turn the dough out onto a lightly floured surface. Knead lightly and briefly until the dough holds together. Roll out the dough or pat it lightly into a circle about 3/4 inch thick. Cut into rounds with a 3-inch cookie cutter or an upturned glass.

Put the rounds on a lightly buttered baking sheet, about 2 inches apart. Brush the tops with the glaze and bake for 12 to 15 minutes or until the biscuits are golden brown on the bottom. Cool on wire racks.

# CORNBREAD

Makes 9 3-inch or 16 2-inch squares

1 cup all-purpose flour
4 teaspoons baking powder
½ teaspoon salt
½ teaspoon cayenne pepper (optional)
1 cup cornmeal
1 cup sour milk or buttermilk
2 eggs, well beaten
⅓ cup vegetable oil

Heat the oven to 425 degrees. Butter an 8-inch-square baking pan.

Sift together the flour, baking powder, salt and cayenne. Add the cornmeal, stirring well to combine. Mix together the milk, eggs and vegetable oil in a separate bowl. Pour the liquid mixture into the dry ingredients and beat until fairly smooth. Do not overbeat—it does not matter if there are a few small lumps in the batter.

Put the pan in the hot oven and let it get nice and hot before pouring the batter into it. Bake for 20 minutes or until a toothpick inserted in the center comes out clean.

"Cornbread was nothing particularly special when I was growing up. It was just what everyone had and I think everyone had their own way of making it, too. You never thought much about it— but you sure missed it if it wasn't there for a day or two!"— Millie Masterson, Austin, Texas

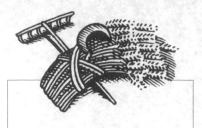

≋ MAGGIE STEFFEN'S ≋ PAN ROLLS

"I remember with special delight the Christmas food at my grandmother's farm. Granny was a wonderful cook who believed everything she served during the holidays should be like Christmas itself, rich and sumptuous.

"She would start preparing right after Thanksgiving. By Christmas Eve, when we arrived for our family reunion, her house bulged with Christmas treats. Christmas Eve supper was a joy. The table seemed vast, the good dishes endless and I usually ate until I felt as stuffed as the plump turkey that crowned the table.

"For me, though, the best dishes came at noon on Christmas Day, after the presents and before the journey home. We would sit in the parlor around the fire and feast on hot yeasty pan rolls, ice-cold cranberry relish and succulent, freshly made turkey pot pie. The pie bubbled with chunks of sweet, home-grown vegetables and generous mouthfuls of tender turkey."—
Susan Manlin Katzman, Clayton, Missouri

Makes two 9-inch round loaves of pan rolls

1 package active dry yeast
1 teaspoon sugar, for mixing with the yeast
¼ cup warm water
1 egg, beaten
4 tablespoons (¼ cup) butter, melted
4 tablespoons (¼ cup) margarine, melted
1½ teaspoons salt
½ cup sugar
2 cups lukewarm water
6 to 7 cups all-purpose flour
2 tablespoons butter, for "shining" the rolls

Sprinkle the yeast and teaspoon of sugar over the 1/4 cup of water in a large bowl. Stir to dissolve the yeast. Let the mixture rest for about 5 minutes until it foams.

Add the egg, melted butter and margarine, salt, 1/2 cup of sugar, lukewarm water and 2 cups of flour. Beat with an electric mixer for 2 minutes. Stir in enough flour to make a soft dough. Turn the dough out onto a lightly floured surface and knead until smooth and elastic.

Butter a large bowl. Put the dough in the bowl and rotate it to coat on all sides with the butter. Cover the bowl with a damp cloth and set the dough in a warm place to rise until doubled in bulk, about 1 hour.

Butter two 9-inch round baking pans, each 2 inches deep. Punch down the dough and then pull off small pieces and form them into rolls about the size of golf balls. Arrange the rolls in the pans so that they fill the pans snugly. Cover the pans with damp cloths and put them in a warm place to rise for 45 minutes to 1 hour until the rolls have nearly doubled in size.

Heat the oven to 375 degrees. Bake the rolls for about 40 minutes until they are golden brown and sound hollow when the bottom of the loaves are tapped. Lift the loaves of rolls from the pans and set them on wire racks. While they are still hot, rub butter over the tops to give the rolls shine.

SCONES

Makes 8 to 10

2 cups self-rising flour
3 tablespoons sugar
½ teaspoon baking soda
4 tablespoons cold unsalted butter, cut into 4 pieces
1 large egg, at room temperature, lightly beaten
½ cup buttermilk, or whole milk soured
   with 1½ teaspoons vinegar or lemon juice
¼ cup dried currants or raisins

Heat the oven to 400 degrees.

Sift the flour with the sugar and baking soda into a large bowl. Add the butter and cut it into the dry ingredients with a pastry blender or fork until the mixture resembles coarse meal.

Combine the egg with the buttermilk in a small bowl. Pour the liquid into the flour mixture and stir with a wooden spoon until a dough forms. Add the currants and stir or knead with your fingers until well distributed.

Drop the dough about 1/4 cup at a time onto an ungreased baking sheet, keeping them 2 inches apart. Pat the dough down with lightly floured fingertips to form 2 1/2-inch scones. Bake for 15 to 18 minutes until the scones are golden brown on top. Remove them from the baking sheet immediately and cool on a wire rack. Store the scones in an airtight container or serve them right away.

"The memories of teatime at my grandmother's house evoke feelings that are as strong today as they were the last time I saw her 35 years ago. My fondest feelings are stirred each time I look at the elegant Georgian silver tea service sitting on the antique 'Captain's chest' in my dining room. The silver glistens and I can still hear the rattling of the finely painted bone china teacups, and see the three-tier cake stand filled with sandwiches made from the freshest brown bread, thinly sliced, bursting with fresh shrimps from West Kirby— a hamlet at the mouth of the River Dee in Cheshire, England. My aunt made her scones for these meals, buttery and filled with what seemed like an impossible number of currants. These jostled for pride of place on the rosewood sideboard with fresh strawberry jam, a Victoria sandwich cake, and brandy snaps, filigreed, redolent with ginger and full of freshly whipped cream. 'Gabrielle, dear, run and wash your hands,' are words I can still hear. Ah yes, it's truly time to begin."— Gabrielle Saylor, Burlingame, California

YORKSHIRE PUDDING

Serves 6

1 cup all-purpose flour
½ teaspoon salt
1 large egg
½ cup milk
½ cup water
2 to 3 tablespoons beef drippings or vegetable oil

Sift the flour and salt into a large bowl. Lightly beat the egg in another bowl and stir in the milk and water with a fork. Make a well in the center of the flour mixture and gradually pour in the liquid, whisking just until the batter is smooth. Let the batter rest for 1 hour.

Heat the oven to 425 degrees.

Put 2 tablespoons of beef dripping into a rectangular, ovenproof dish or divide the drippings among 12 deep muffin cups. Put the dish or muffin cups on the top rack of the oven for 10 to 15 minutes until the fat is very hot.

Pour the batter into the pan or cups and return to the top shelf of the oven for 25 to 30 minutes for a single pan, about 15 minutes for muffin cups, until the Yorkshire pudding is puffed around the edges and golden brown.

POPOVERS

Makes 8 popovers

1 cup all-purpose flour
½ teaspoon salt
2 eggs
1 cup milk
4 tablespoons oil

Mix together the flour and salt. Whisk the eggs with the milk. Gradually whisk the liquid into the dry ingredients until smooth and well blended. Let the batter rest for 1 hour.

Heat the oven to 450 degrees. Brush 8 muffin cups with 1 tablespoon of the oil. Put the remaining oil in another ovenproof cup and let the muffin cups and the cup of oil heat in the oven for about 10 minutes.

Whisk the hot oil into the batter. Pour the batter into the hot muffin cups so that each is about two-thirds full.

Bake the popovers for about 20 minutes, until puffed and golden. Lower the heat to 325 degrees and bake for about 20 minutes more, until the popovers are firm and cooked through.

"Popovers became a Christmas tradition in a backwards sort of way. I made them for my parents at the first holiday dinner they shared with me and my husband. My dad loved them. Since then I've shared the recipe with my mother, my sisters and my sisters-in-law. When I first made them, my family thought I'd become a master baker but popovers will do that for you. They rise so high and look so magnificent that you can't be anything but a superstar when you make them.
"The key is timing. They are best eaten right out of the oven so I never put them on until everything is close to done. Since they take a while to bake and the batter should rest a while before going into the oven, I have plenty of time to get things under control before the popovers are done."—Kim Valentine, Tucson, Arizona

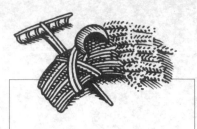

GRANDMOTHER'S BASIC WHITE BREAD

Makes 4 loaves; 40 dinner rolls; or 7 dozen bread sticks

9 to 10 cups bread flour or all-purpose flour
¼ cup sugar
2 packages active dry yeast
1 tablespoon salt
1 quart hot milk (about 125 degrees)
1 large egg (optional)

Combine 3 cups of flour with the sugar, yeast and salt in the large bowl of a heavy-duty electric mixer. Gradually add the hot milk and beat at medium speed for 2 minutes, scraping the bowl occasionally with a rubber spatula. Add the egg and 2 more cups of flour. Beat at high speed for 2 minutes, scraping the bowl occasionally. Stir in 3 to 4 cups of flour, enough to make a stiff dough.

Turn the dough out onto a floured work surface and knead for 8 to 10 minutes, until the dough is smooth and elastic. Add only as much of the remaining flour to the work surface as necessary to prevent the dough from sticking. Shape the dough into a ball and put it in a buttered bowl. Turn the dough so that the buttered side is up. Cover with a damp dish towel or transparent wrap and set in a warm (80 degrees) place to rise for about 1 1/2 hours or until the dough has doubled in size.

Butter 4 8 1/2-by-4 1/2-by-2 1/2-inch bread pans. Divide the dough into 4 pieces, shape each into a loaf and place in the prepared pans. Cover with a dry dish towel and set in a warm (80 degrees) place to rise for about 1 hour or until the dough has risen just above the rims of the pans.

Uncover the pans, put them in the oven and turn the oven to 400 degrees Bake for about 45 minutes or until the bread sounds hollow when tapped on the top and bottom. Remove the loaves from the pans and cool on wire racks.

Opposite: Boston Brown Bread (page 210)
Page following: Challah (page 213)

"My Canadian grandmother made bread from this recipe every week of her married life, which lasted over 60 years. The first time she made it, however, it was a disaster— the loaves didn't rise. To hide the failure from her husband, she buried the offending loaves in the backyard. When my grandfather came home from work that day, he walked through the front door, kissed my grandmother and walked directly out of the back door to dig in the yard to start a garden. He hit the bad bread with the first push of the shovel! Years of expert baking didn't help my grandmother live down this episode. Nevertheless, the bread is superb and has won many professional and home taste-tests."—Jennifer Harvey Lang, New York, New York

Irish Soda Bread

Makes 2 loaves

4 cups all-purpose flour
1 tablespoon baking powder
1 teaspoon baking soda
1 teaspoon salt
2 teaspoons grated orange rind
2 teaspoons caraway seeds (optional)
4 tablespoons butter, at room temperature
1 cup currants
¼ cup honey
1½ cups buttermilk, at room temperature
¼ cup Irish whisky or buttermilk
½ tablespoon milk blended with ½ tablespoon Irish whisky, for glaze

Generously butter 2 round 8-inch cake or pie pans. Set aside. Heat the oven to 350 degrees.

Combine the flour, baking powder, baking soda, salt, orange peel and caraway seeds in a large bowl. Rub the butter into the flour mixture, using your fingers or a pastry cutter. Stir in the currants.

Combine the honey with the buttermilk and the 1/4 cup whisky or buttermilk. Stir into the flour mixture just until the dry ingredients are moistened. Turn the dough out onto a generously floured work surface. The dough will be sticky. Knead for 1 minute. Cut the dough in half, shape each piece into a round loaf and place in the prepared pans. Dip a sharp knife or razor blade into flour and cut a cross on the top of each loaf. Brush each one with the glaze and let stand for 10 minutes.

Bake for 35 to 40 minutes, or until the bread sounds hollow when tapped on the bottom. Remove the loaves from the pans and cool on racks. Serve the bread thinly sliced or cut into wedges.

Note: For a lighter texture, the Irish invert deep, round cake pans over the loaves as they bake. To brown the crusts, remove the upper pans during the last 15 minutes of baking time.

Opposite: Flotbrod (page 217)
Page preceding: Popovers (page 207)

"My maternal grandmother came from Carrickmacross in Ireland. On the frostiest of winter days, as though by magic, she would somehow have a loaf of Irish soda bread waiting for me after school. I would burst through her back door, stomping clumps of snow off my shiny red boots onto the rumpled rag rug. Standing there, my cheeks tingling in the kitchen's warmth, I let her help me peel off the layers of winter clothing. She would rub my hands between hers until they were toasty and then help me onto a huge chair at the oversized oak kitchen table.
"Then, with a twinkle in her eye, she would place it before me— a huge, round loaf of soda bread, rustic and brown, with a rough-hewn cross cut into the top. The cross, she said, was to scare away the devil. Grandmother and I would start tearing off chunks of the still-warm loaf, slathering them with butter from the crock. Sitting there together in that great warm kitchen, we'd eat, talk and share secrets."—
Sharon Tyler Herbst, Greenbrae, California

≋ BOSTON BROWN ≋ BREAD

Makes 2 loaves

1 cup all-purpose flour
1 cup rye or whole wheat flour
1 cup cornmeal
1½ teaspoons baking soda
¾ teaspoon salt
¾ cup molasses
2 cups buttermilk, or whole milk soured with 2 tablespoons vinegar
1 cup raisins (optional)

Combine the flours, cornmeal, baking soda and salt in a mixing bowl. Mix the molasses and buttermilk together in a separate bowl. Toss the raisins in the flour mixture.

Generously butter two clean, empty 1-pound coffee tins. Butter 2 rounds of wax paper that have been cut to fit the tops of the cans. Tear 2 pieces of aluminum foil large enough to cover the cans and cut 2 pieces of string to tie the foil covers.

In a large saucepan or casserole that is deep enough to hold the cans, pour enough water to come halfway up the sides of the upright cans. Heat the water to a simmer.

Add the molasses mixture to the dry ingredients and stir until just blended. Do not overmix. Divide the batter evenly between the two buttered cans. Cover with buttered wax paper and tie the foil covers securely over the tops. Put the cans in the simmering water and cover the pan. Steam for 1 1/2 to 2 hours, adding more boiling water halfway through the cooking time. Let the loaves cool slightly in the cans and then push then out and let them cool completely on wire racks.

≋ SALLY LUNN BREAD ≋

Makes 1 ring-shaped loaf

⅓ cup sugar
2 packages active dry yeast
½ cup warm (110 degrees) water
¾ cup milk
8 tablespoons butter, cut into pieces
3 eggs, lightly beaten
3¾ cups all-purpose flour
1 teaspoon salt

Combine the sugar and yeast with the water and stir until dissolved. Set aside for 5 minutes until it bubbles and foams.

Heat the milk in a small pan until simmering, add the butter and stir until melted. Let the mixture cool to 110 degrees. Whisk in the eggs.

Sift the flour and salt into the bowl of a food processor. Pour in the yeast mixture and the milk-butter mixture and process, pulsing, until a dough forms. Put the dough in a large bowl, cover with transparent wrap and set in a warm place until doubled in volume, about 1 hour.

Butter a 1-quart ring mold or tube pan. Transfer the dough to the pan, cover and set aside again to rise until doubled in volume, about 30 minutes. Heat the oven to 350 degrees.

Bake the loaf for 45 minutes or until the bottom of the pan sounds hollow when tapped. Remove the loaf from the oven and let it cool in the pan for about 10 minutes. Turn it out onto a wire rack to cool completely. Serve with butter and fruit preserves.

"Sally Lunn is almost as rich as a sponge cake. It was always served at Aunt Marian's with strawberry preserves and her homemade butter. I loved the round shape of the loaf and could hardly wait until it was sliced and served steaming hot on my plate.
"She didn't have a food processor to knead it. She probably wouldn't have used it if she'd had one, but it sure makes working with that sticky, rich dough a lot easier.
"Good butter is the secret, she'd always say, as we ooh'd and aah'd over the thick slices, each time swearing this would be the last one because we couldn't possibly have another. The loaf always disappeared at one sitting."— Alexis Caudell, Orlando, Florida

SOUR DOUGH BREAD

Makes 1 large round loaf

½ cup sour dough starter, at room temperature
2 ¼ cups lukewarm water
5 ½ cups unbleached all-purpose flour
1 tablespoon sugar
1 teaspoon salt
Cornmeal, for sprinkling

Mix the starter with the water and 3 cups of the flour in a large bowl and stir until smooth. Cover loosely with transparent wrap and let sit in a warm place overnight or for 12 hours. The longer it stands, the more sour it will be.

Add the sugar and salt and work in as much more of the flour as necessary to make a dough that is cohesive and soft. Turn the dough onto a well floured surface, cover, and let rest for 15 minutes. Knead for 10 to 15 minutes, until the dough is smooth and elastic. Add more flour if necessary to make the dough stiff.

Put the dough in an oiled bowl and turn it so the oiled side is up. Cover the bowl and put it in a warm place until the dough has doubled in volume, about 2 hours. Turn the dough out onto a floured surface and gently knead again for a couple of minutes. Again, form it into a ball and return it to the greased bowl for about 2 more hours. It will almost double in volume.

Form the dough into a round loaf and put it on a baking sheet that has been sprinkled with cornmeal. Let the loaf rise in a warm place until it has doubled once more, about 2 hours. If a crust forms on the top, brush with warm water.

Heat the oven to 450 degrees.

Use a sharp knife to slash a criss cross pattern into the loaf. Put the cookie sheet into the oven, spraying the loaf with water a few times during the first 10 minutes of baking. Bake the bread a total of 50 to 60 minutes, until it is golden brown and sounds hollow when tapped on the bottom. Cool completely on a rack.

CHALLAH

Makes 1 braided loaf, about 12 inches long

Bread:
1 package active dry yeast
1¼ cups warm (110 degrees) water
1 tablespoon sugar
4 cups all-purpose flour
1 teaspoon salt
1 egg, lightly beaten
2 tablespoons butter, melted
Glaze:
1 egg
1 teaspoon water
Poppy seeds or sesame seeds

Dissolve the yeast in 1/4 cup of the water. Add the sugar and let the mixture sit for about 5 minutes, until the yeast bubbles and foams.

Combine the flour with the salt in a large mixing bowl. Make a well in the center and pour in the egg, yeast mixture, and the butter. Stir, adding enough of the remaining warm water to form a stiff dough.

Turn the dough onto a floured work surface and knead for about 8 minutes or until the dough is smooth and elastic. Form the dough into a ball and put it in a large oiled bowl, turning it so that it is lightly oiled all over. Cover the bowl with a cloth and set in a warm, draft-free place until the dough has doubled in volume, about 1 1/2 hours.

Butter a baking sheet. Punch the dough down and divide it into three equal pieces. Roll each piece into a rope about 1 inch wide and 18 inches long. Lay the ropes on the baking sheet and braid them, tucking the ends underneath. Cover with a cloth and set aside in a warm, draft-free place for about 40 minutes or until the braided dough has doubled in volume. Heat the oven to 375 degrees.

To make the egg wash glaze, beat the egg with the water. Brush the braided dough with the egg wash and sprinkle with poppy or sesame seeds. Bake for 30 minutes or until golden brown. Cool the challah on a wire rack.

"My grandmother, my 'bubby,' was a grand cook in the Jewish grandmother tradition. She lived with our family— five kids and two parents— in a tiny house in upstate New York where she and my mother shared the kitchen.

"The story I love best about my grandmother is one I wasn't there to witness. It was the day before Rosh Hashanah, the Jewish New Year. My mother awoke before dawn with labor pains; I was on my way. Bubby was already in the kitchen, cooking for the holiday. 'Well, today's the day, Mom,' said my mother. 'We're on our way to the hospital.'

*"'Oh no!' said my grand-mother, 'you can't do this to me. My challahs have just started to rise!' "—
Andrea Chesman,
New Haven, Vermont*

213

BLACK BREAD

Makes 1 16-inch round loaf

⅔ cup cold water
1 tablespoon vinegar
3 tablespoons dark molasses
1 tablespoon cocoa powder
1 teaspoon instant coffee
1 package active dry yeast
1 tablespoon sugar
⅓ cup warm (110 degrees) water
2 cups all-purpose flour
1 cup rye flour
½ cup bran
¼ cup cornmeal
1½ teaspoons salt
¼ cup oil

Combine the water, vinegar, molasses, cocoa and coffee in a saucepan over moderate heat. Bring to the boil, remove from the heat and let cool to 110 degrees.

Dissolve the yeast and the sugar in the warm water and let sit for 5 minutes, until it bubbles and foams.

Combine the flours with the bran, cornmeal and salt in the bowl of a food processor. Add the oil and process until the oil is incorporated. With the machine running, add the dissolved yeast and the molasses mixture. Process until the dough forms a ball.

Put the dough on a lightly floured work surface and knead until it is smooth and elastic. Add more flour, a tablespoon at a time, if the dough becomes too sticky to handle.

Put the dough in a buttered bowl, cover and let sit in a warm, draft-free place until it doubles in volume, about 2 hours. Punch the dough down, form it into a ball and put it on a buttered baking sheet.

214

Cover the dough and set it in a warm place until it doubles in volume again, about 1 hour. Heat the oven to 350 degrees.

Bake the bread for about 50 minutes or until it sounds hollow when the bottom is lightly tapped. Cool on a wire rack.

≋ OATMEAL MOLASSES ≋ BREAD

Makes 2 large loaves

1 package active dry yeast
2½ cups warm (110 degrees) water
1 teaspoon salt
¼ cup packed brown sugar
⅓ cup molasses
⅓ cup butter
6 cups all-purpose flour, approximately
2½ cups whole wheat flour
1½ cups plus 2 tablespoons old-fashioned oats
1 large egg, lightly beaten

Dissolve the yeast in the warm water in the large bowl of an electric mixer. Set it aside for 5 minutes until it bubbles and foams. Stir in the salt, brown sugar, molasses, butter, 2 cups of all-purpose flour and the whole wheat flour. Using a heavy-duty mixer, beat the mixture on medium speed for about 3 minutes until smooth. Beat in 1 1/2 cups of oats and as much of the remaining all-purpose flour as needed to make a dough which is soft but not sticky. The dough should start to come away from the sides of the bowl.

Turn the dough out onto a lightly floured work surface and knead for 7 to 10 minutes, until it is smooth and elastic. Put the dough in a lightly oiled bowl, turning it so that the oiled side of the dough is up. Cover with transparent wrap and set in a warm place to rise until doubled in volume, 1 to 1 1/2 hours.

Lightly butter two 9-by-5-inch or 8-by-4-inch loaf pans. Punch the dough down and turn it out onto a work surface. Divide the dough into two pieces and shape each into a loaf. Put the loaves into the pans, cover with transparent wrap and let rise for 40 to 50 minutes, until the dough starts to reach above the sides of the pans.

Heat the oven to 350 degrees.

Just before baking, brush the tops of the loaves with some of the beaten egg, making sure it does not drip down onto the pan. Sprinkle with the remaining oats. Bake the loaves for 30 to 35 minutes, until they are brown and sound hollow when the bottom of the pan is tapped. Cool on a wire rack for 5 minutes before removing from the pans.

FLOTBROD
(FLAT BREAD)

Makes 35 to 40 pieces, each about 4 inches long

5 cups all-purpose flour
1 package active dry yeast
2 ¼ teaspoons salt
¾ teaspoon sugar
1 tablespoon salt
4 tablespoons unsalted butter, melted
1¼ to 1½ cups warm water (110 degrees)
Sesame seeds

Combine the flour, yeast, salt and sugar in a large bowl. Combine the melted butter with 1 1/4 cups warm water. Stir into the dry ingredients to form a soft dough, adding another 1/4 cup of warm water if necessary. Turn the dough out onto a work surface and knead for 7 to 10 minutes, until it is smooth and elastic. Let the dough rest for 10 minutes before rolling out.

Heat the oven to 400 degrees.

Spread about 1/2 cup sesame seeds over a work surface. Divide the dough into four pieces and work with one piece at a time, keeping the rest covered with a towel. Roll the dough out thinly on top of the sesame seeds. Sprinkle the top with more seeds and press them in lightly. Using a pastry wheel or a sharp, thin-bladed knife, cut the dough into 2-by-4-inch strips. Carefully transfer the strips to baking sheets lined with parchment paper. Bake for 12 to 18 minutes, until the flat bread is crisp and golden. Continue rolling and baking until all the dough is used.

"We used to go to my paternal grandmother's house for the holidays. She was from Sweden and I remember she used to make very, very thin, very crisp flotbrod on a cooking range with a big flat steel top. The dough had to be just right so that she could roll it out very thin. She 'baked' it right on the stovetop. It was much better than what you get today."— Ardis Swanson, New York, New York

217

 # RAISIN BREAD

Makes 2 9-inch loaves

1 cup raisins
2 packages active dry yeast
1 cup warm (110 degrees) water
5 cups bread flour
3 cups all-purpose flour
½ cup sugar
5 large eggs
6 tablespoons vegetable oil

Put the raisins in a bowl, cover them with lukewarm water and set aside.

Dissolve the yeast in the warm water and set it aside until it bubbles and foams. Combine the flours, sugar and salt in a large bowl. Beat the eggs and set aside 2 tablespoons for the glaze. Combine the eggs with the oil and stir it into the dry ingredients, together with the yeast. Drain the raisins, add them to the flour mixture and stir until a dough forms.

Turn the dough out onto a lightly floured work surface and knead for 5 to 10 minutes, until smooth and elastic. Put the dough into a lightly oiled bowl, turning it so that the oiled side is up. Cover with a towel and set in a warm place to rise until doubled in volume, about 1 hour.

Punch the dough down. Turn it out onto a very lightly floured work surface, cover with the bowl and let rest for 10 minutes. Lightly butter two 9-by-5-by-3-inch loaf pans. Divide the dough into two pieces and form each into a loaf. Put the loaves in the pans, cover and let rise until doubled in volume, about 1 hour.

Heat the oven to 375 degrees.

Brush the tops of the breads with the reserved egg. Bake the bread for 25 to 35 minutes, until golden brown.

"Nanny taught me how to make raisin bread. It was her favorite and mine, too. Whenever she'd start to make it, she'd go on and on about commercial raisin bread, which she considered a pretty poor excuse for bread.

"No bread was as good as hers, mind you, but she just couldn't understand why everyone didn't make their own since homemade was so superior.

"Knowing when the dough was just right is the secret, she always said. And she could tell just by looking. Sometimes she'd have to poke it a little, but most of the time, a glance was all she needed. Watching her skillful hands knead and shape the dough was like watching a sculptor at work. She worked so quickly, so surely— by feel and instinct."— Bessie Callahan, Providence, Rhode Island

BLUEBERRY MUFFINS

Makes 12 muffins

2 cups fresh or frozen blueberries
2 cups all-purpose flour
¼ cup sugar
1 tablespoon baking powder
¼ teaspoon baking soda
¼ teaspoon salt
2 eggs, at room temperature
½ cup milk, at room temperature
4 tablespoons butter, melted
1 teaspoon vanilla extract or
    1 tablespoon maple syrup, at room temperature
Grated rind of 1 lemon

Heat the oven to 400 degrees.

If using frozen berries, put them in a bowl, sprinkle with 1 tablespoon of the flour, toss gently and return them to the freezer until ready to use. If using fresh, rinse them under cold water, pick off any stems and discard any that are not plump or ripe. Drain the blueberries.

Sift the remaining flour, sugar, baking powder, baking soda and salt into a medium-sized bowl. Beat the eggs in a separate bowl until they are light and foamy. Stir in the milk, melted butter, vanilla or maple syrup and the lemon rind.

Make a well in the center of the dry ingredients. Pour in the liquid and the blueberries and mix until just combined.

Lightly butter 12 2-inch muffin cups. Pour the batter into the cups, almost to the top. Bake for 20 to 25 minutes until the muffins are light golden brown and a toothpick inserted in the center comes out clean. Cool the muffins in the pan on a wire rack.

"I can't bite into a blueberry muffin without thinking about my grandmother. When I was a little girl I would go stay with her for a few weeks every summer at a bungalow colony in the Catskills. She always took me blueberry picking and every time, she wore the same wide-brimmed straw hat. I know she made lots of jam but what I remember best are the blueberry muffins she baked for us to eat for breakfast. And so, without fail, every time I eat a blueberry muffin I think of her wearing that hat and picking berries in the sunshine. It brings back good memories."—
Melanie Falick,
New York, New York

HOT CROSS BUNS

Makes 12

Buns:
2 packages active dry yeast
2 tablespoons sugar
1 cup warm (110 degrees) milk
3½ to 4 cups all-purpose flour
1 teaspoon salt
½ cup currants
4 tablespoons unsalted butter, melted
2 eggs, beaten
For the crosses:
2 tablespoons flour
2½ tablespoons water
Honey, for glazing

Heat the oven to 325 degrees.

Combine the yeast and the sugar in a small bowl. Add the warm milk and stir to dissolve. Let the mixture sit for 10 minutes.

Mix together the flour, salt and currants in a large bowl. Make a well in the center and add the yeast mixture with the melted butter and the eggs. Stir to form a dough and then knead for about 5 minutes. Put the dough in an oiled bowl, turning it so that it is coated all over. Cover with a cloth and set in a warm, draft-free place to rise for 1 hour.

Punch down the dough and knead for 5 minutes. Divide the dough into 12 pieces and shape each into a ball. Put the balls of dough on a buttered baking sheet, cover with a cloth and set in a warm place to rise for 30 minutes. Heat the oven to 350 degrees.

Using a sharp knife, lightly cut a cross on the top of each bun. Mix the flour with the water to make a paste and pour a little of the paste into each cross.

Bake for 20 minutes. Brush the buns with honey and bake for about 15 minutes more until the buns are nicely browned and firm. Cool slightly and serve halved, with butter.

≋ Nana's Yeast ≋ Dough

Makes enough dough for 1 recipe each of Pecan Rolls and Cinnamon Coffee Cake (recipes follow)

¼ cup warm (115 degrees) water
1 package active dry yeast
½ teaspoon sugar
1¼ cups milk
4 tablespoons butter, cut into pieces
⅓ cup sugar
5 cups (approximately) all-purpose flour
1 teaspoon salt
1 egg

Put the warm water in the large bowl of an electric mixer and sprinkle the yeast over the top. Add the 1/2 teaspoon of sugar and let stand for 10 minutes until foamy.

Meanwhile, heat the milk to a simmer in a small saucepan. Remove from the heat, add the butter and the remaining 1/3 cup of sugar. Stir until the sugar is dissolved and let the mixture cool at room temperature to 115 degrees.

Pour the milk into the yeast. Add 1 cup of the flour and mix well until smooth. Beat for 5 minutes on medium speed. Add the salt and egg and beat well.

"Most all my memories of Nana somehow involve food. She made wonderful mincemeat and chili sauce and could turn scraps from the refrigerator into marvelous soups or stews, a definite asset during the Depression. Most vividly, however, I remember Saturdays when the table would be laden with coffee cakes with sugar and cinnamon topping, pecan rolls which stuck to your fingers, cloverleaf rolls with butter melting on top, and cottage cheese kuchen with a layer of raisins on the bottom. They all came from the same

221

With the mixer on low speed, add enough of the remaining flour to make a soft dough. The dough will first come away from the sides of the bowl but then flatten out again—it should not be as heavy as bread dough.

Transfer the dough to a lightly floured work surface and knead until it is smooth and elastic. Alternatively, knead the dough for about 5 minutes with the dough hook of a heavy-duty mixer. Butter a 4-quart bowl. Put the dough into the bowl and turn so that it is buttered on all sides. Cover with a towel or transparent wrap and let stand in a warm place for 1 1/2 to 2 hours or until doubled in volume.

Turn the dough out onto a lightly floured work surface. Cut it into halves, form each half into a ball and let the dough rest for 10 minutes before using to make Pecan Rolls or Cinnamon Coffee Cake.

Note: When adding the flour, you will need to mix in the last cup or two by hand if do not have a heavy-duty electric mixer. This recipe may be doubled.

PECAN ROLLS

Makes 14 rolls

½ recipe Nana's Yeast Dough (see recipe page 221)
Topping:
4 tablespoons butter, melted
1 tablespoon light corn syrup
⅓ cup light or dark brown sugar
¾ cup pecan halves
Filling:
3 tablespoons butter, softened
⅓ cup light or dark brown sugar
1 teaspoon cinnamon
½ cup broken pecans

Make the dough, according to the recipe for Nana's Yeast Dough.

To make the topping, mix the melted butter with the corn syrup in a buttered 10-inch round or square baking pan. Add the brown sugar, mix well and spread evenly over the bottom of the pan. Arrange the pecans, rounded side down, over the brown sugar mixture.

On a lightly floured work surface, roll the yeast dough to a 12-by-8-inch rectangle. Spread the softened butter over the dough, leaving about 3/4 inch plain on one of the long sides. Sprinkle with the brown sugar, cinnamon and broken pecans Starting with the buttered long edge, roll the dough, jelly-roll fashion, pulling slightly lengthwise as you roll. Cut the rolls into 1-inch slices and place them, cut side down, on the prepared topping in the pan Cover with a cloth or transparent wrap and let stand in a warm place for about 1 hour or until doubled in volume.

"I always make wonderfully gooey Pecan Rolls for my grandchildren when they come to visit on holidays or during the summer. They want to steal pinches of the raw dough and then, once I get the rolls ready for the pan, they stand around waiting impatiently for them to bake. Once they're out of the oven, the children start hopping around, begging for a hot roll. I always tell them to let the rolls cool or they'll burn the fire out of their fingers! Those kids really love these rolls, and I don't blame them— I love them too."— Lucy Collins, Fort Smith, Arkansas

223

Heat the oven to 375 degrees. Bake the rolls for 25 minutes. Remove them from the oven, place a platter over the top of the pan and invert it, being careful of the hot syrup. Let stand for 2 to 3 minutes to let the syrup drip down over the rolls and then remove the pan. Serve the rolls warm.

≋ CINNAMON COFFEE ≋ CAKE

Makes one 9- or 10-inch square or round cake

½ recipe Nana's Yeast Dough (see recipe page 221)
1 cup sugar
1 tablespoon cinnamon
3 tablespoons butter, melted and cooled

Butter a 10-inch round cake or pie pan, or a 9- or 10-inch-square pan.

Make the dough, according to the recipe for Nana's Yeast Dough. Roll the dough out on a lightly floured work surface to fit the prepared pan. Set the dough in the pan, cover with a cloth or transparent wrap and let stand in a warm place for about 1 hour or until doubled in volume.

Heat the oven to 375 degrees. Mix together the sugar and cinnamon. Gently spread the butter over the surface of the raised dough and sprinkle with the sugar-cinnamon mixture. Bake for 25 minutes.

Opposite: Cinnamon Sticky Buns (page 225)
Page following: Scones (page 205)

CINNAMON STICKY BUNS

Makes 12 buns

Dough:
1 package active dry yeast
¼ cup warm (110 degrees) water
1 teaspoon plus 2½ tablespoons sugar
½ cup milk
2 tablespoons unsalted butter
½ teaspoon salt
1 egg yolk
1 teaspoon lemon juice
1½ cups plus 3 tablespoons all-purpose flour
Filling:
¾ cup plus 2 tablespoons brown sugar
½ teaspoon cinnamon
4 tablespoons unsalted butter
¼ cup honey
1 cup coarsely chopped pecans

To make the dough, dissolve the yeast in the warm water. Stir in 1 teaspoon of sugar and let the yeast stand for 5 minutes until it bubbles and foams.

Meanwhile, combine the milk, butter, salt and the remaining sugar in a small saucepan. Bring to a low simmer over moderate heat. Remove from the heat and let cool.

Put the yeast mixture, cooled milk, egg yolk and lemon juice in a mixing bowl and beat until well combined. Beat in 1 1/2 cups of flour, 1/2 cup at a time. Gradually add enough of the remaining flour to make a soft dough. Knead the dough for 8 to 10 minutes, until it is smooth and elastic.

Put the dough in a large, lightly oiled bowl and turn it so that the oiled side is up. Cover with a damp cloth and set in a warm place to rise for about 1 hour, until the dough has doubled in volume.

"My mother wasn't a baker. In fact, she wasn't even a cook. She did many things well, but cooking wasn't one of them. But my best friend, Lonnie, had a mom who just loved to cook. I think that's where I really got my love of good food.

"The first time I saw her make cinnamon sticky buns, I was amazed. I'd never seen anything like that come out of an oven. I thought rolls and bread and cake somehow appeared on bakery shelves or grew in packages.

"At first, she'd make them for me on my birthday or sometimes when I spent the night. I'd ask Lonnie's mom to make them for me so often that finally she decided she'd better show me how. The first few times I tried them, I knew why she wanted me to learn. They are a bit of a project, but they're worth it."—
Cindy Slocum,
Detroit, Michigan

Opposite: Shortbread (page 271)
Page preceding: Peach Cobbler (page 248)

Prepare the filling while the dough rises. Combine 1/2 cup of brown sugar with the cinnamon in a small bowl and set aside. Heat the butter with the remaining sugar and the honey in a small saucepan over low heat, stirring until the sugar is melted.

When the dough has risen, punch it down and turn it out onto a lightly floured work surface. Roll it into a 12-by-16-inch rectangle. Sprinkle the cinnamon-sugar mixture over the dough and roll it up, jelly-roll fashion, starting at one of the long sides. Moisten the edges with water and pinch them together to seal. Cut the roll crosswise into 12 slices.

Spoon half the butter-sugar mixture into the bottom of a 10-inch baking pan. Sprinkle with half the pecans. Put the buns, cut side down, in the pan. Spoon the remaining syrup over the buns and sprinkle with the remaining pecans. Set the buns in a warm place to rise until doubled in volume, about 1 hour.

Heat the oven to 350 degrees. Bake for about 30 minutes or until browned.

Sour Cream Coffee Cake

Serves 8

3 cups sifted all-purpose flour
2 teaspoons baking powder
½ teaspoon baking soda
½ teaspoon salt
½ teaspoon cinnamon
¼ teaspoon ground nutmeg
1 cup packed light brown sugar
8 tablespoons cold unsalted butter
3 large eggs, at room temperature
1 cup sour cream, at room temperature
1 teaspoon vanilla extract

Heat the oven to 350 degrees. Butter an 11-by-7-inch pan.

Sift the flour, baking powder, baking soda, salt, cinnamon and nutmeg into a large bowl. Stir in the brown sugar, making sure there are no lumps. Add the butter, working it in with your fingertips until it resembles coarse meal. Measure out 1 1/2 cups of the mixture and set it aside for the topping.

Combine the eggs, sour cream and vanilla in small bowl. Stir them into the remaining dry ingredients. Pour the batter into the prepared pan and sprinkle the reserved crumbs on top. Bake for 35 to 45 minutes or until a toothpick inserted in the center comes out clean.

"To me, sour cream coffee cake epitomizes old-fashioned, unpretentious baking at its best. Oh, sure, I'm glad that today I can easily buy croissants or brioche or Sachertorte if I'm in the mood, but I rarely find any of those labor-intensive European pastries as soul-satisfying as a good, simple crumb cake, and there's something about sour cream that adds terrific flavor and moistness. Weekday meals are always a rush-rush afffair around our house, but I try whenever possible to whip up a quick coffee cake for late Saturday or Sunday breakfast. It makes me feel as though I'm giving my kids a real homemade treat."— Deborah Miller, Des Moines, Iowa

BUTTERMILK BUCKWHEAT PANCAKES

"The thought of a stack of buckwheat pancakes is enough to bring back a rush of memories of my grandmother, who loved me because I was me. The pancakes were made from batter that had soured just a bit as it stood overnight on the warm top shelf of the black cast-iron stove in my Grandmother Condon's kitchen. The morning feast began with my Grandfather Condon and me bringing my grandmother a handful each of fresh-split kindling and corncobs for the stove. While Grandmother cooked, my grandfather and I 'washed up' (my grandmother's idea). Grandfather didn't like it any more than I did because it was done with cold water in a white enamel bowl resting on a back step. He was a frugal Scot, even with water, so there was always enough left over for me.

"More than six decades later, a serving of buckwheat pancakes awakens memories of grandparents I adored, breakfasts unsurpassed and washings that never got behind the ears."—
Bernard Clayton, Jr., Bloomington, Illinois

Makes about 12 5-inch pancakes

⅓ cup bread crumbs
2 cups scalded milk
½ teaspoon salt
1 package active dry yeast
½ cup warm (105 to 115 degrees) water
1¼ cups buckwheat flour
½ teaspoon baking soda
¼ cup water
1 tablespoon molasses
1 tablespoon oil

Put the bread crumbs in a large mixing bowl, add the scalded milk and soak for 30 minutes. Add the salt. Dissolve the yeast in the warm water and set it aside for 5 to 10 minutes until foamy.

When the breadcrumb mixture has cooled, stir in the yeast and the flour. Cover with a cloth and set in a warm place to rise overnight.

The next morning, dissolve the baking soda in the water and add to the flour mixture, together with the molasses. Stir in the oil until thoroughly mixed.

Heat a lightly oiled griddle or large frying pan over moderate heat. Pour the batter onto the griddle to make 5-inch pancakes and cook them until the edges dry and bubbles appear in the center. Turn and cook on the other side. Continue cooking all the batter this way. Serve the pancakes as soon after they come off the griddle as possible.

French Toast

Serves 2

2 large eggs
½ cup milk, light cream or heavy cream
Salt
4 slices bread, preferably a dense, homemade type
3 tablespoons butter

Heat the oven to 250 degrees.

Beat together the eggs, milk and salt to taste in a large shallow bowl. Dip each slice of bread in the batter and turn until well coated.

Heat 2 tablespoons of butter in a large skillet. When the butter is just beginning to brown, cook 2 slices of the bread over moderate heat until very lightly browned on both sides. Keep the cooked slices warm in the oven while you heat another 1 ounce of butter and cook the remaining bread. Serve warm, with confectioners' sugar, butter and jam.

"Saturdays were a special time to me as a young child. We would turn on the radio for the wide range of children's programming and sit crosslegged in front of the huge Magnavox, a dark wood cabinet that reached to the top of my head. About the time of the show called 'Let's Pretend,' my mother started making breakfast. Best of all were the Saturdays when Mother made us French toast. We would smell the butter browning and we heard the fork beating the eggs and milk together. Mother liked that slightly browned butter to flavor the battered bread that she slipped into the sizzling pan. She turned it over when it was just the right crustiness, heaped it onto a plate she had in the warm oven. She kept the oven door ajar as she added piece after piece until she had a stack high enough for us to dig into."—
Nathalie Dupree,
Atlanta, Georgia.

CHURROS MADRILEÑOS

"Ah! Viejo Madrid de los chulos y el choti—'Old Madrid, city of dancing.' What memories a snapshot can evoke: I see myself strolling hand in hand with Paul—then my fiancé, now my husband of 40 years—on a series of chilly, rainy afternoons in the winter of '49. After visiting the museum we would stroll along the Paseo del Prado looking for a warm place to sit down—and we always found ourselves at the Café Montserrat, a cozy haven of friendly chatter and familiar glances, santuary for poets and bohemians who gave the place a colorful air. I will never forget the exquisite aroma of the hot chocolate, accompanied by the specialty of the house, the cafés famous churros. They would come to the table sweet, crisp and still fairly sizzling from the hot oil, the perfect treat for a wintry day."—
Rosalba de la Carrera, Miami, Florida

Makes about 15 churros

1 cup all-purpose flour
⅛ teaspoon salt
4 tablespoons butter
1 cup water
4 eggs
Vegetable oil, for frying
Superfine or confectioners' sugar

Sift together the flour and salt. Put the butter and water in a saucepan and heat until the butter has melted and the water is boiling. Remove the pan from the heat and stir in the sifted flour mixture all at once. Return the pan to the heat and beat vigorously for 1 to 2 minutes, until the dough pulls away from the sides of the pan and forms a ball. Remove the pan from the heat and add the eggs one at a time, beating well after each addition.

Pour enough oil into a 2 1/2- to 3-quart saucepan to reach a depth of about 2 inches. Heat over high heat until hot but not smoking.

Put the dough into a large pastry bag fitted with a 1/2-inch plain tip. Pipe the dough into the hot oil, cutting off tubes about 6 inches long. Do not overcrowd the pan. Fry the churros until they are crisp and golden brown. Drain on paper towels and dredge with the sugar. Let the oil regain its hot temperature before frying the rest of the dough. Serve warm.

Kropfen Doughnuts

Makes about 45 doughnuts

2 packages active dry yeast
½ teaspoon sugar, for mixing with the yeast
1 cup warm (105 to 115 degrees) water
5 pounds all-purpose flour
1 cup sugar
2 tablespoons salt
4 cups milk
1 cup plus 1 tablespoon butter
8 large eggs
Vegetable oil, for deep-frying
Sifted confectioners' sugar, for dredging

Sprinkle the yeast and 1/2 teaspoon of sugar over the water. Sift the flour, cup of sugar and salt into a large mixing bowl. Pour the milk into a saucepan, add the butter and heat gently until the butter is melted. Cool slightly and beat in the eggs.

Add half the milk mixture to the flour. Add the dissolved yeast and knead until smooth. Add the remaining liquid and knead again until smooth. Lift up the dough, knead again and fold it over. Repeat several times to allow air to enter the dough. Cover the dough with a cloth and set in a warm place to rise for 1 to 1 1/2 hours, until doubled in volume.

Punch down the dough, cover and let it rise again for about 1 hour. Roll out the dough to a thickness of 1/2 inch on a floured work surface. Cut into rounds with a cookie cutter and let stand for 10 minutes.

Pour enough oil into a deep heavy saucepan to reach a depth of about 2 inches. Heat over high heat until hot but not smoking. Fry the doughnuts, a few at a time, until they are golden brown, turning once. Drain on paper towels and dredge with confectioners' sugar.

"Grandma's kitchen came alive each Saturday before Easter. On that eve, the kropfen were created. The milky-white dough rose twice and was lovingly rolled out by Grandma's peaches-and-cream colored hands. Her skin was always silky smooth and she smelled fresh and wonderful.

"The aroma of the dough enticed me to pinch off a piece and nibble when she wasn't looking. I loved to watch her cut out the circular shapes and drop the doughnuts into the hot oil. The kropfen sizzled and danced and soon became golden brown puffs. Their delicate scent wafted through the house and I'm certain it tantalized even the neighbors.

"Best of all, though, was eating the soft, crunchy delicacies and inhaling that scent filled with love and tradition."—
Linda Haner Bauer,
Fairfax Station, Virginia

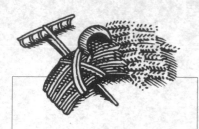

☰ CHEESE BLINTZES ☰

Makes 12 blintzes

Batter:
½ cup milk
½ cup water
2 eggs
¾ cup flour
⅛ teaspoon salt
Filling:
1 cup dry or drained cottage cheese or farmer's cheese
3 ounces cream cheese
1 egg yolk
1 tablespoon sugar
½ teaspoon lemon juice or vanilla extract (optional)
Butter, for frying
Sour cream
Jam

To make the batter, combine the milk, water and eggs in a bowl and whisk until blended. Put the flour and salt in a mixing bowl and gradually whisk in the liquid until the mixture is well blended. Alternatively, put the batter ingredients in a food processor or blender and process until blended. Set the batter aside.

Put the filling ingredients in a bowl and stir until blended. Chill until ready to use.

Heat 1 1/2 teaspoons of butter in a crepe pan or skillet over moderate heat until bubbly. Pour about 2 tablespoons of batter into the pan and tilt until the batter covers the bottom of the pan. Cook the pancake until it is lightly browned on one side. Turn and cook for 15 to 20 seconds more. Remove the pancake from the pan. Cook the remaining batter in the same way, adding more butter as necessary.

"I loved to watch my mother and grandmother make blintzes. My mother mixed the filling in a large wooden bowl, my grandmother beat the batter for the crepe-like shell. While they worked, they talked. If I stayed quiet and barely moved, they sometimes forgot I was there and talked about family secrets.

"But the talking stopped when my grandmother began to fry shells. She swirled the butter in the pan, held it over the flame for a few vital seconds, and flipped it onto a dish. My mother was waiting with an overflowing spoon. With a jerk of her wrist, she filled the crepe and then rolled

Put 1 heaping tablespoon of filling in the bottom third of each pancake. Fold the bottom edge up over the filling. Fold in the sides towards the filling and roll the pancake up. Chill the blintzes until ready to cook.

Heat 2 tablespoons of butter in a skillet. Cook the blintzes seam side down, 3 or 4 at a time, for 2 to 3 minutes until golden brown. Serve with sour cream and jam, passed separately.

it, folding the sides in as she went. Just as my mother moved the blintz to a nearby board, my grandmother flipped the next crepe onto the dish. And so a rhythm would build.

"So the pile of blintzes would grow, for when they ran out of filling, I would get more cheese; and when the shells ran out, I would fetch more eggs. This would go on all day, until the two women were exhausted. Only when the pile of blintzes had become a mountain would they stop—reluctantly."—
Judith Chaves,
North Ferrisburg, Vermont

FRUIT DESSERTS

≋ Apple Brown Betty ≋

Serves 6

1 cup raisins
3 tablespoons brandy
5 to 6 tart cooking apples, peeled, cored
   and cut into ½-inch slices (about 6 cups)
1 tablespoon lemon juice
½ cup all-purpose flour
½ cup sugar
½ teaspoon cinnamon
¼ teaspoon salt
¼ teaspoon ground nutmeg
4 tablespoons butter, chilled and cut into 4 pieces
3 slices firm white bread
1 cup apple cider

Heat the oven to 350 degrees. Butter a deep, 8-inch-square baking dish.

Put the raisins in a small bowl, add the brandy and let soak until most of the liquor is absorbed. Toss the sliced apples with the lemon juice.

Combine the flour, sugar, cinnamon, salt and nutmeg in a food processor fitted with metal blade. Process for 10 seconds. Add the butter and pulse until mixture resembles coarse meal with pea-sized pieces remaining. Remove the mixture from the workbowl. Put the bread in the workbowl and process to coarse crumbs.

Fill the prepared baking dish with half the apples and raisins. Top with half the flour mixture and half the bread crumbs. Add the remaining apples and raisins. Pour the apple cider over the apples. Top with the remaining flour and bread crumbs. Cover the dish with aluminum foil and make a few holes in the top. Bake for 35 minutes. Remove the foil and cook for another 15 minutes, or until the top is golden brown. Serve warm or at room temperature with whipped cream or vanilla ice cream.

"My grandmother had three children, all girls, who lived in the same block in our North Dakota village. She and Grandpa lived in a big Victorian house at the end of the street, a very convenient spot for their grandchildren to stop after school to see what good things Grandma had for us to eat. We were never disappointed. Several times a week she baked bread and cinnamon buns, and at least once a week, cake, fresh pies and cookies. Occasionally, my grandmother would make her special apple brown betty and serve it to us with a glass of cold milk.

"She was a storybook Grandma — short and round and wrinkled ('as an old prune,' she'd say)— dispensing food and love to every child who came through her door."—
Beverly Marchand Barbour, New York, New York

235

CLAFOUTI

Serves 6 to 8

⅔ cup sugar
8 tablespoons unsalted butter
4 eggs
1 cup all-purpose flour
1½ teaspoons vanilla extract
⅛ teaspoon ground nutmeg
2 cups canned or frozen, defrosted sweet cherries, drained
Confectioners' sugar

Heat the oven to 375 degrees. Lightly butter a 9-inch cake pan or deep pie dish.

Beat the sugar with the butter in a large bowl until fluffy and light. Add the eggs one at a time, beating well after each addition. Stir in the flour, vanilla and nutmeg. Fold in the drained cherries.

Pour the batter into the pan and bake for 40 to 50 minutes or until a toothpick inserted in the center comes out clean. Cool the cake on a wire rack. Dust lightly with sifted confectioners' sugar.

"My youngest son was particularly fond of clafouti for dessert. In the summer, during the brief season, I'd make it with fresh cherries, pitting each and every one. Of course it was a lot easier and almost as good with canned or frozen cherries, but I think the sweet equity with fresh made a lot of difference.

"This is a recipe that was passed down to me from friends. There's not a lot of family history behind it but friends are like family to me. We've moved around a lot and this one came with us from Chicago. My next door neighbor, Tillie, gave it to me and I've treasured it all these years. I keep the card she wrote it on, although it's frayed at the edges and the pencil marking is dim. I haven't seen or talked to her in several years now. Time and distance just got in the way. But I feel close to her nevertheless every time I make clafouti." — Candace Taylor, Fort Worth, Texas

APPLE PIE

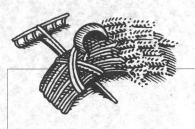

Makes one 9-inch pie

Crust:
2 cups all-purpose flour, sifted
1 teaspoon salt
½ teaspoon ground nutmeg
⅛ teaspoon ground cloves
3 ⅓ tablespoons unsalted butter, chilled and cut into 12 pieces
⅓ cup plus 2 tablespoons solid vegetable shortening
3 to 4 tablespoons iced water
Filling:
5 to 6 large baking apples, such as Rome or Northern Spy,
    cut into ¼-inch-thick slices
2 tablespoons lemon juice
½ teaspoon cinnamon
¼ teaspoon powdered ginger
⅛ teaspoon allspice
¼ cup packed dark brown sugar
2 tablespoons cornstarch
2 tablespoons unsalted butter, melted
½ cup golden raisins
½ cup coarsely chopped walnuts

Put a rack in the center of the oven and heat to 425 degrees.

Combine the flour, salt, nutmeg and cloves in a large bowl and stir to mix. Work the butter into the dry ingredients until the mixture resembles coarse crumbs. Drop teaspoon-sized pieces of shortening into the mixture and work it in until the mixture again resembles coarse crumbs.

Sprinkle the iced water over the mixture, one tablespoon at a time, tossing with a fork or your fingers after each addition until the mixture is just moistened and forms a dough. Lightly mold the dough into a ball, cover with transparent wrap and let sit for 5 minutes.

"The first apples of the season always bring back memories of late summers on Long Island which, then, still had farms and apple orchards. It was a time for holding onto the last days of summer vacation… and a time for the aroma of the first apple pies of the season.

"My great-aunt, short, round and white-haired, usually presided over pie-making. She had come to New York years earlier from Galway, Ireland, and eventually became a successful chef. Now retired, she often appeared at family reunions and coordinated all kitchen feasts and treats. I loved to watch her short, powerful fingers working the pastry and placing apple slices quickly and precisely around the pans. All the cooking activity was accompanied by lively conversation on politics and relatives. To this day, I can still hear the bursts of laughter, all wrapped in the delicious expectation of hot apple pie."—
Kit Mahon,
Camden, New Jersey.

237

Divide the dough in half and roll each half out on a floured work surface or pastry board to an 11-inch circle. Use one of the dough circles to line a 9-inch pie plate. Trim the edges with a sharp knife.

To make the filling, toss the apple slices with the lemon juice in a large bowl. Put the cinnamon, ginger, allspice, brown sugar and cornstarch in a small bowl and stir together. Sprinkle the mixture over the apples and toss together with your hands.

Brush the bottom pie crust with the melted butter. Layer the apple mixture evenly onto the crust, sprinkling the raisins and walnuts between the layers.

Cover the apples with the second circle of dough. Lightly moisten the edge of the top crust with water and press the crusts together to seal. Crimp the edges with the tines of a fork and make 5 or 6 1-inch slits in the top crust to allow steam to escape.

Bake the pie for 15 minutes. Lower the oven temperature to 375 degrees and bake for another 25 to 35 minutes, until the crust is golden brown. Cool the pie slightly on a wire rack.

FRENCH APPLE TART

Makes one 9-inch tart

Pastry:
1¼ cups sifted all-purpose flour
2 tablespoons sugar
⅛ teaspoon salt
6 tablespoons chilled unsalted butter
1 large egg, lightly beaten
Filling:
½ lemon
2 pounds plus 3 medium-size cooking apples, peeled and cored
½ cup white wine
½ cup sugar
4 tablespoons unsalted butter
¼ cup apricot preserves

Sift the flour, sugar and salt into a mixing bowl. Add the butter and work it in with your fingertips or a pastry blender until the mixture resembles coarse meal. Stir in the beaten egg until a dough forms. Wrap the dough in wax paper and chill for 1 hour.

Heat the oven to 375 degrees.

Using a sharp knife or a vegetable peeler, remove the rind of the 1/2 lemon in one strip. Squeeze the lemon, measure 1 tablespoon of the juice and set aside for the glaze. Cut the 2 pounds of apples into quarters and put them in a large saucepan with the white wine, lemon rind, 1/4 cup of the sugar and the butter. Cook over moderate heat until the apples are soft. Remove from the heat, discard the lemon rind and puree the apples in a food processor or blender until smooth. Set them aside to cool.

Roll out the dough on a floured surface to fit a 9-inch tart pan with a removable bottom. Fit the dough into the pan, trim the edges and chill.

"My best friend in college, Marigny, first made French apple tart for me. Although her family is French, I don't think it was a family tradition, so much as her first, very successful, attempt at pastry. She doesn't make it often now— she's an attorney with two kids and a husband— but when she does it's still a hit.

"She deftly slices the apples into even-sized pieces, then artfully arranges them in concentric circles over the filling. It is a work of art, worthy of any professional, right down to the pastry, which is always pretty and, more important, light and flaky.

"I once asked Marigny how in the world she made such a wonderful tart. I didn't insult her, but cooking isn't something she usually spends a lot of time on and this tart is such an exceptional creation. She didn't really have a ready answer except to say that she just loved the smell of this tart baking."— Randi Bishop, Los Angeles, California

Thinly slice the remaining 3 apples. Remove the tart shell from the refrigerator and spread the pureed apple filling evenly into it. Arrange the sliced apples over the filling in concentric circles. Sprinkle with the remaining 1/4 cup of sugar. Bake the tart for 30 to 40 minutes, until the crust is lightly browned.

While the tart is in the oven, prepare the glaze. Put the apricot preserves and the reserved lemon juice in a small saucepan over low heat. Bring to a simmer, stirring constantly. Remove the pan from the heat and strain the glaze. Brush the hot glaze onto the tart as soon as it is taken from the oven.

Amanda Ann's Three-Layer Dried Apple Cake

Filling:
2 to 3 cups dried apple slices
1½ cups sugar
¼ teaspoon cinnamon
⅛ teaspoon ground nutmeg
⅛ teaspoon salt
Cake:
3 cups self-rising flour
1½ cups sugar
3 large eggs, lightly beaten
1 teaspoon vanilla extract
⅔ cup shortening or lard
1 cup milk
Confectioners' sugar (optional)

Put the dried apples in a saucepan and cover with cold water. Bring to the boil and simmer for 4 to 5 minutes or until the apples are tender. Drain off the liquid and mash the apples with a potato masher. Add sugar to taste—about 1/2 cup sugar per cup of apples, or more if you prefer them sweeter. Stir in the cinnamon, nutmeg and salt. Set aside to cool.

Butter and flour 3 8-inch cake pans. Heat the oven to 350 degrees.

Put the flour, sugar, eggs, vanilla and shortening in a mixing bowl. Work the ingredients with your fingers to combine. Gradually add the milk and continue to work until a soft dough forms. Divide the dough into 3 parts and pat into the prepared pans. Bake for 15 minutes or until the layers are lightly browned and a toothpick inserted in the middle comes out clean. Cool the layers on a rack.

"My grandmother, Amanda Ann, widowed for years, spent a lot of time at our house, helping out with the chores. On special occasions, she would take over the kitchen. My special memory is of my father's favorite birthday cake, a plain and simple dried apple cake that she usually made with five layers, although now I make with three. My father always had this cake on his birthday…my mother, Ettie Tart, even baked it for his 96th. The cake had to be made from scratch and, when we were young anyway, began with collecting apples from the trees on our farm. We then peeled, sliced and dried them on sheets of tin in the sun. This was a regular chore in the apple season and meant that plenty of dried apples were stored in a string-tied cloth sack in a dark room, ready for future use. This recipe is as my mother remembers it."—
Carlie Tart, Rocky Mount, North Carolina.

Spread half the cooled apples over the first layer, set the second layer on top and spread with the remaining apples. Top with the third layer and dust with confectioners' sugar, if desired.

Note: To dry apples, peel and core a peck or a bushel of tart apples. Cut into quarters and slice each quarter into 3 to 5 thin slices. Place cotton cloths over large tin trays and spread the apple slices out in a single layer on the trays. Set them in direct sunlight for 3 to 5 days, bringing them in each night and watching for showers. When the apple slices are leathery and dark, they are ready to use, either in baking or as a snack.

≋ BAKED APPLES ≋

Serves 2

3 tablespoons sugar
1 teaspoon cinnamon
¼ teaspoon ground cardamom
¼ teaspoon ground nutmeg
2 baking apples, such as Rome Beauty, cored
3 tablespoons lemon juice
¼ cup water
3 to 4 tablespoons heavy cream

Put a rack in the center of the oven. Heat the oven to 350 degrees.

Stir together the sugar, cinnamon, cardamom and nutmeg in a small bowl.

Peel a 1/2-inch-wide strip from around the top of each apple. Put the apples in a 9-inch glass pie plate or small baking dish. Spoon most of the sugar mixture into the apple cavities and sprinkle the remainder over them. Sprinkle most of the lemon juice into the apple cavities to moisten the sugar, and sprinkle the remainder over them.

Pour the water into the bottom of the dish. Cover tightly with aluminum foil and bake for 25 to 30 minutes, until the apples are tender but still firm. Remove the foil and spoon the syrup from the bottom of the dish over and into the apple cavities. Bake, uncovered, for 10 to 15 minutes more.

Remove the apples from the baking dish and put them in individual serving bowls. Stir the heavy cream into the sugar syrup remaining in the baking dish until well combined. Spoon the cream sauce over the apples and serve them warm.

STRUDEL DOUGH

Makes about 1 pound dough (enough for 1 large strudel)

2 cups unbleached bread flour
¼ teaspoon salt
1 egg
1 tablespoon lemon juice or white vinegar
4 tablespoons vegetable oil or melted butter
1 cup warm water
Extra flour, for pulling the dough
Extra vegetable oil, for pulling dough

"My grandmother in Pennsylvania had the most incredible knack with strudel dough. She could work it and stretch it until just the right instant. It never broke, and was always flaky and beautiful. Her apple strudel, filled with fresh apples, raisins and nuts, was the talk of the town. She was so proud of it, and back then, one of the measures of a woman's worth was her baking skill.

"My grandfather always swelled with pride when she was complimented on her strudel. But he'd always have to complain that she never made it often enough and when she did it disappeared too fast.

"'Too much work,' she'd say. Too many other things that have to be done, then begin ticking off her other chores— washing, ironing, cleaning, milking, sewing. She could go on and on. But when she wanted to, she always managed to find the time to make strudel."—
Connie Williams,
Baltimore, Maryland

Put the flour and salt in a mixing bowl and make a well in the center. Add the egg, lemon juice and oil and beat lightly with a fork. Stir to incorporate the flour, adding the water gradually to make a soft, sticky dough. Beat the dough, lifting and slapping it against the sides of the bowl or on a work surface for about 20 minutes until it is very smooth and elastic. Put the dough in an oiled bowl and brush the top lightly with oil. Cover and set the bowl in a warm place for about 30 minutes.

Cover a large table with a cotton cloth large enough to overhang the sides. Rub flour generously into the cloth, particularly in the center where you will be working the most. Have a bowl of flour at hand while you work.

Put the dough in the center of the cloth and dust heavily with flour. Dip your hands into the flour and pull and roll the dough evenly in all directions until it is as big as a dinner plate. Brush the dough all over with oil.

Dip your hands in flour and insert them, palms down, under the dough. Working from the center out, pull and stretch the dough carefully, moving around the table in a methodical fashion so that you stretch the dough evenly. Work carefully to avoid tearing the dough, but if holes appear, ignore them and try not to make them larger. Continue the process, brushing with oil to keep the dough from drying. When you have finished, the sheet of dough should be tissue-thin, with thick edges. Allow the dough to dry for about 10 minutes. With sharp scissors, snip away the thick edges. Keep the dough covered with a lightly dampened cloth and use as soon as possible.

APPLE STRUDEL

Serves 8

2 pounds cooking apples, peeled and cored
½ cup sugar
⅓ cup raisins
⅓ cup finely chopped walnuts
½ teaspoon cinnamon
1 cup fine bread crumbs
½ pound phyllo dough
1 cup butter, melted
Confectioners' sugar

Heat the oven to 375 degrees. Line two baking sheets with parchment paper.

Slice the apples thin. Put them in a medium-sized bowl together with the sugar, raisins, walnuts and cinnamon. Stir in the bread crumbs.

Unroll the phyllo dough and cover with a slightly dampened cloth. Spread two more damp cloths side by side and place one sheet of dough on each cloth with the widest side facing you. Brush each sheet with the melted butter. Lay another sheet of dough on top of each piece and brush with more melted butter. Repeat this process until all the dough has been used. There should be about 6 layers of dough for each strudel.

Spread half the filling along the top third of one strudel, leaving a 1-inch margin on the left, right and top (long) side. Using the cloth to help you, carefully roll the strudel, starting at the top and rolling it towards you. Repeat this entire process with the second strudel.

Carefully transfer the strudels to the lined baking sheets and tuck the ends underneath. Brush with the remaining melted butter and bake for 25 to 30 minutes, until lightly browned. Remove the strudels from the oven, let cool and sprinkle with sifted confectioners' sugar.

"My mother was a superb baker, but she always left the strudel to her sister, my Aunt Bess, a master strudel maker. She didn't make it often, it took a lot of time. But her ritual fascinated me. She had a white enamel kitchen table and she stretched the strudel on this. I have no idea how it happened to be exactly the right size for this operation, but the dough stretched over the table perfectly.
"First, my aunt took off her wedding ring and then she washed the enamel table. Then she worked the dough with clenched fist so that no fingernails could poke holes through it. My aunt's strudel dough had no imperfections. To this day, I have never figured out how she knew when the dough had reached its maximum stretchability. It almost touched the floor.
"Her strudel was filled with apples, raisins, nuts and cinnamon. My cousins and I could hardly wait for it to cool … you were never allowed to eat hot dough in my aunt's house."—
Marian Burros,
New York, New York.

GRANDMOTHER'S FAMOUS STRUDEL

"My grandmother came to this country several years after World War I. She lived in what was then the Austro-Hungarian Empire but during the war her town was overrun by the Russians. Family folklore tells how, after all the townspeople fled, Grandmother stole back to finish baking the bread for her children. As she rejoined the other evacuees, carrying her precious bread, she heard and felt a tremendous explosion. Looking back, she saw that the bridge—the only exit from town—had been blown up.

"Most of my memories of Grandmother have to do with the kitchen. Her strudel is legendary and still mentioned with reverence by all who tasted it. When she baked, she always sent out boxes of strudel to her children and neighbors. We all lived nearby and benefited often from her generosity. Shortly before she died, Grandmother gave me a lesson in making strudel, together with her recipe, which I now treasure and bake at least once a year."— Gloria Zimmerman, Guilford, Connecticut.

Makes 1 large strudel

4 slices bread, several days old (preferably challah, brioche or firm-textured white bread)
1 navel orange, unpeeled and cut into chunks
½ lemon, unpeeled and cut into chunks
1 cup coarsely chopped walnuts
½ cup sugar
½ cup golden raisins
1 recipe Strudel Dough (see recipe page 243), or
    1 pound purchased phyllo dough
Vegetable oil
Apricot, cherry or raspberry jam

Process the bread in a food processor to make coarse crumbs. Grind the orange and lemon chunks in a meat grinder fitted with the finest blade, or in a food processor—the fruit skins should be finely ground. Combine the bread crumbs, ground orange and lemon, walnuts, sugar and raisins in a large bowl and stir until well mixed.

Heat the oven to 350 degrees. Lightly oil a large baking sheet.

Place the strudel dough on a floured cloth and stretch it as directed in the recipe. If using purchased phyllo dough, spread a sheet out on a floured cloth. Stack 4 pieces of phyllo, brushing each with oil. Using a pastry brush, preferably the feather kind, paint the surface of the strudel dough with vegetable oil. Sprinkle the breadcrumb mixture evenly over the dough, leaving a 2-inch border all round. Spread a strip of jam, about 1/2 inch wide, across the bottom edge of the dough, on top of the crumb mixture.

Using the cloth as an aid, fold 2 sides of the dough over the filling to enclose it. Fold the bottom edge of the dough over to enclose the strip of jam and continue to roll the dough until it is completely rolled.

Carefully transfer the strudel to the prepared baking sheet. Brush the surface of the strudel with vegetable oil and bake for abut 30 minutes, brushing occasionally with more oil, until it is golden brown. Remove from the oven, cool slightly, and cut into 2-inch slices while still warm.

"Strudel… light and fragile strudels, that's what I remember my grandmother baking. I was only three, barely able to see over the edge of the kitchen table. I watched, fascinated, as her nimble fingers lovingly lifted and pulled each fistful of dough across the flour linen tablecloth. Round and round the table she scurried, gently easing the dough until a tissue-thin sheet stretched across the snowy surface. Each week her fillings varied from fragrant fruit, nuts, poppy seeds, and cheese to savory cabbage. Grandma knew my favorite was apple. Though she spoke not a word of English, nor I of Hungarian, the fragrance of her baking strudel and the joy of sharing each fragile warm morsel wrapped us in a love that needed no words."—Darlene Kronschnabel, DePere, Wisconsin

PEACH COBBLER

Serves 6

9 ripe peaches, skins removed, or 3 pounds canned peaches
½ cup plus 1 tablespoon sugar
2 teaspoons lemon juice
1 cup all-purpose flour
1½ teaspoons baking powder
¼ teaspoon salt
¼ cup milk
1 egg

Heat the oven to 400 degrees. Butter a deep 8-inch-square baking dish.

Cut the peaches into 1/2-inch slices. You should have about 4 cups. Put the peaches in a large bowl with 1/2 cup of sugar and the lemon juice. Put the flour, 1 tablespoon sugar, baking powder and salt in the workbowl of a food processor fitted with a metal blade. Process for 10 seconds. Add the milk and egg and process just until the ingredients are moistened. Or, put the dry ingredients in a large bowl and add the milk gradually, stirring to make a cohesive mixture. Add the egg and stir until combined.

Fill the prepared baking dish with the peaches. Using your fingers or a wooden spatula, spread the topping evenly over the fruit. Bake the cobbler for 30 minutes until the crust is lightly browned and the juices are bubbling around the edges. Serve warm with vanilla ice cream or heavy cream.

"My mother baked almost every day and she always did it in a big way. When she made cake, she always made two; when she made pie, she made four. In the summer when the peaches were ripe she made a big cobbler in a roasting pan— sort of 'Texas style,' since we lived in the Rio Grande Valley. Oh, I remember those cobblers. The crust was just right and the just-picked peaches were sweet, juicy and warm."—Florence Dedman, Killingworth, Connecticut

RØDGRØD

Serves 4

1 pound frozen raspberries
1 cup plus 3 tablespoons water
¼ cup sugar
3 tablespoons cornstarch
Superfine sugar for sprinkling
½ cup sliced almonds
½ cup light cream

Combine the frozen berries with 1 cup of water in a medium-sized saucepan over moderate heat. Bring to a simmer. Reduce the heat to low and cook for about 5 minutes until the berries are tender but still whole. Drain the berries in a colander, reserving the cooking juices and transfer them to a serving bowl or individual dishes.

Return the juice to the saucepan over low heat and stir in the sugar. Dissolve the cornstarch in 3 tablespoons of water. Stir the cornstarch mixture into the juice and cook, stirring, for about 5 minutes or until the sugar is dissolved and the sauce thickens.

Pour the sauce over the fruit and sprinkle with superfine sugar. Chill the dessert for at least 2 hours, until it is cold and slightly set.

Heat the oven to 350 degrees.

Spread the almonds on a baking sheet and roast for about 10 minutes, until golden brown. Sprinkle the almonds over the dessert just before serving. Pass the cream separately.

Note: If you can possibly find fresh red currants, adding them to this dish makes the taste incomparable.

"Rødgrød is a wonderful fruit dessert that isn't quite like anything else, although it resembles a pie filling as much as anything. It is light and refreshing, with just a touch of cream. It's Danish in origin, and my father's family has enjoyed it for generations. He liked to remember it as a harbinger of spring, although we always used frozen berries so we could have it any time of the year.

"That is the way we are with traditional foods. Even though technology and transportation have made most foods available almost any time, we still associate certain foods with certain seasons and to have them out of season often spoils their specialness. Raspberries are that way, particularly for me. I know my dad felt the same way."—
Cole Randall,
Reston, Virginia

≋ SUMMER PUDDING ≋

Serves 4 to 6

1 pound fresh raspberries
1 pound blackberries, blueberries, red currants
  or black currants, or a combination of these
¾ cup superfine sugar
10 to 12 slices firm white bread, crusts removed
Whipped cream, for decoration

Lightly butter a deep 2-quart bowl or a charlotte mold. Pick over the berries, discarding any that are brown or musty. Remove any stems. Rinse in a colander under cold running water and drain well. Be careful not to bruise the berries when rinsing and draining them.

Put the fruit and the sugar in a large saucepan over moderate heat. Cook without stirring for 3 to 5 minutes, just until the sugar has melted and the berries begin to yield juice. Remove the pan from the heat.

Cut 1 or more of the bread slices to fit the bottom of the bowl. Line the sides of the bowl with bread slices, making sure they overlap so there are no gaps. Reserve some bread to cover the top of the pudding.

Spoon the fruit mixture into the bowl, reserving the juice left in the saucepan. Cover the fruit with the remaining bread. Take a plate or saucer that just fits inside the rim of the bowl and put it on top of the pudding. Weight with heavy cans or kitchen weights and chill in the refrigerator for at least 8 hours or overnight.

Just before serving, remove the plate and turn the pudding out onto a serving plate. The bread should now be a deep red—if there are any white patches, brush some of the reserved juice over them. Serve the pudding in slices with whipped cream.

KEY LIME PIE

Makes 1 9-inch pie

Crust:
1¾ cups graham cracker crumbs
¼ cup sugar
4 tablespoons unsalted butter, melted
Filling:
4 large egg yolks, at room temperature
14-ounce can sweetened condensed milk
⅔ cup freshly squeezed lime juice
1 teaspoon freshly grated lime zest
½ teaspoon vanilla extract

Heat the oven to 350 degrees.

To make the crust, stir the cracker crumbs with the sugar in a medium-sized bowl. Drizzle the butter over the mixture and toss with a fork or your fingertips until well combined. Press the mixture evenly onto the bottom of a 9-inch pie plate. Bake the crust for 5 to 7 minutes, being careful that the edges do not brown. Cool on a wire rack for 20 minutes and then chill in the refrigerator until ready to fill.

Beat the egg yolks in a medium-sized bowl for 4 to 5 minutes until they are pale yellow and fall in a thick ribbon from the beaters when lifted. Add the condensed milk, lime juice, lime zest and vanilla and beat for 1 1/2 to 2 minutes until well combined.

Using a rubber spatula, spread the filling evenly into the chilled crust. Chill the pie for 4 to 6 hours or overnight, until set.

"Key lime trees grow in lots of backyards in the Florida Keys and my family's was no exception. And so, of course, we made key lime pie using the 'real' thing. You could say it's a matter of pride to native Key Westers, or 'conchs' as we're called, to be able to make the dessert. And, take my word for it, nothing tastes better after a dinner of broiled or grilled fresh-caught fish than a cool, tangy key lime pie." — Nick Lill, Big Pine Key, Florida

≋ BLUEBERRY PIE ≋

Makes one 9-inch pie

Lattice crust:
2 ½ *cups sifted all-purpose flour*
1 *tablespoon sugar*
6 *tablespoons chilled unsalted butter*
6 *tablespoons chilled margarine*
3 to 4 *tablespoons iced water*
Filling:
2 *pints (about 4 cups) fresh blueberries,*
   picked over, washed and drained
2 *teaspoons lemon juice*
½ *cup sugar*
3 *tablespoons cornstarch*
¼ *teaspoon ground nutmeg*
1 *large egg, lightly beaten*

To make the pastry, sift the flour and sugar into a medium-sized bowl. Add the butter and margarine and work into the flour with your fingertips or a pastry blender until the mixture resembles coarse meal. Gradually stir in the water until the dough forms. Wrap the dough in wax paper and chill for 30 minutes.

Put the blueberries and lemon juice in a large bowl. Combine the sugar, cornstarch and nutmeg in a small bowl. Stir the sugar mixture into the blueberries.

Heat the oven to 425 degrees. Roll out half the dough on a lightly floured work surface to fit a 9-inch pie plate. Carefully fit the dough into the pan, trim the edges and chill the pie shell. Roll the remaining dough into a rectangle about 1/8 inch thick. Using a pastry wheel or a sharp knife, cut the dough into 1/2-inch strips.

Spoon the blueberry filling into the chilled shell. Lightly moisten the edges of the shell with water. Lay the dough strips over the top of the filling in a lattice pattern. Tuck the ends under the

bottom crust and flute the edges of the crust. Brush the dough strips with the beaten egg.

Bake the pie for 10 minutes. Lower the oven temperature to 375 degrees and bake the pie for 40 to 50 minutes more, until the crust is lightly browned and the filling is bubbling.

RHUBARB PIE

Makes one 9-inch pie

Lattice crust:
2½ cups sifted all-purpose flour
1 tablespoon sugar
6 tablespoons chilled unsalted butter
6 tablespoons chilled margarine
3 to 4 tablespoons iced water
Filling:
2 pounds rhubarb
1 cup plus 2 teaspoons sugar
⅓ cup all-purpose flour
⅓ cup orange juice
1 egg, lightly beaten

Prepare a lattice crust as for Blueberry Pie (see recipe, page 252).

Heat the oven to 425 degrees.

Remove any green leaves from the rhubarb tops. Cut the rhubarb into 1/2-inch slices. Put them in a large bowl. Combine 1 cup of sugar with the flour and stir into the rhubarb. Add the orange juice and toss until the rhubarb is coated.

"I think one has to be a grown-up to appreciate rhubarb pie. I can remember as a girl, my father getting ecstatic whenever he encountered rhubarb pie on a menu. He would order it before anything else to make sure there would be some left when he was ready for dessert. If rhubarb was available, chocolate meringue wouldn't do. 'Save that for Isabel,' he'd say.
"I'd taste his rhubarb pie, but as a child I didn't appreciate the sweet-tart qualities that so endear rhubarb to the adult palate.
"I've become a believer, however. The first time I made rhubarb pie for my dad, he was astounded. 'But you never liked it,' he exclaimed. I explained that I'd made it just for him. Maybe it was my way of showing him I'd really grown up."—Isabel Butler, Texarkana, Arkansas

253

Spoon the filling into the prepared pie shell. Cover with the lattice top crust and flute the edges. Brush the lattice crust with the beaten egg and sprinkle with the remaining sugar. Bake for 15 minutes. Lower the oven temperature to 375 degrees and baking for 40 to 50 minutes more, until the crust is lightly browned and the filling is bubbly.

≋ LEMON MERINGUE ≋ PIE

Makes one 9-inch pie

Pastry:
1 cup all-purpose flour
¼ teaspoon salt
¼ cup sugar
2 egg yolks
4 tablespoons chilled unsalted butter or margarine, cut into pieces
Filling:
⅓ cup cornstarch
1 cup sugar
⅛ teaspoon salt
1½ cups warm water
2 tablespoons unsalted butter, cut into pieces
3 large egg yolks, lightly beaten
Juice and grated rind of 3 lemons
Topping:
3 large egg whites
¼ teaspoon cream of tartar
½ cup sugar

Heat the oven to 400 degrees.

To make the pastry, sift the flour, sugar and salt into a mixing bowl. Make a well in the center and put the egg yolks in the well. Add the butter. Work all the ingredients with the fingertips until the mixture holds together. Shape the dough into a ball, wrap in wax paper and chill for 1 hour.

Roll the dough out on a lightly floured work surface to a 10- or 11-inch circle. Fit the pastry into a 9-inch pie plate. Trim the edges. Cover the bottom of the pastry shell with aluminum foil. Weight the foil with rice, dried beans or pie weights and bake for 8 minutes.

Take the pastry shell from the oven and discard the foil and weights. Prick the bottom of the shell with a fork, lower the oven temperature to 350 degrees and bake for another 5 minutes.

Put the cornstarch, sugar and salt in a saucepan. Gradually add the water, stirring until the mixture is smooth. Put the pan over moderate heat and cook, stirring, until the mixture starts to boil. Immediately lower the heat and stir for another 2 to 3 minutes. Remove the pan from the heat and stir in the butter.

Put the egg yolks in a bowl and beat briefly. Stir a few spoonfuls of the hot cornstarch mixture into the egg yolks. Add the mixture back to the saucepan and stir to combine. Stir in the lemon juice and rind. Let the mixture cool slightly, stirring occasionally. Pour it into the pastry shell.

Heat the oven to 400 degrees.

Beat the egg whites until frothy. Add the cream of tartar and half the sugar and beat until soft peaks form. Beat in the remaining sugar, 1 tablespoon at a time.

Spread the meringue over the lemon filling while the filling is still warm. Bake just until the meringue is lightly colored, about 10 minutes. Remove the pie from the oven and cool completely on a wire rack.

"My mother-in-law was a wonderful cook and baker and one of her son's favorite desserts was her lemon meringue pie. For the first Thanksgiving dinner we spent together as husband and wife, I called her in Florida for her recipe. Since she was more or less an 'instinctive' cook, the phone call lasted for a long time, as she tried to explain to me exactly how to measure for all the ingredients. Thinking I had it right, I proceeded to prepare the pie but, somehow, something was missing and the whole thing was a disaster. The next time we visited my mother-in-law, I begged her to make the pie and I would watch and write down everything she did. Then I discovered what the difference was— she had never told me to separate the egg yolks and beat the whites with cream of tartar! That was many years ago and I have become very proficient at making lemon meringue pie. Of course, I follow a written recipe."— Frances Kaplan, Brooklyn, New York

≋ BANANA CREAM PIE ≋

Makes one 9-inch pie

Pastry:
1 cup all-purpose flour
¼ cup sugar
2 egg yolks
4 tablespoons chilled unsalted butter or margarine, cut into pieces
Filling:
1 cup heavy cream
1 cup milk
¾ cup sugar
3 egg yolks, lightly beaten
1 teaspoon vanilla extract
2 to 3 firm, ripe bananas
Whipped cream, for decoration

Make the pastry shell following the directions for making the pastry shell for the Lemon Meringue Pie (recipe page 254). When the baked shell is cool, make the filling.

Put the cream, milk and sugar in a saucepan over moderate heat. Stir until the sugar dissolves and the liquid is very hot but not boiling.

Pour about 1/4 cup of the hot liquid into the bowl holding the beaten egg yolks. Stir well and then pour this back into the saucepan with the rest of the hot liquid. Cook over low heat, stirring constantly, for about 10 minutes until the custard is smooth and beginning to thicken. Do not let it boil.

Strain the custard into a bowl and then stir in the vanilla. Lay a piece of transparent wrap or wax paper directly on the surface of the custard to prevent a crust from forming and let it cool to room temperature.

Opposite: Banana Cream Pie (page 256)
Page following: Apple Strudel (page 245)

Slice the bananas and lay them on the bottom of the pie shell. Depending on the size of the bananas you may only need 2 to fill the bottom of the shell. Pour the custard over the bananas and chill the pie until ready to serve. Decorate the top of the chilled pie with sliced bananas and serve with whipped cream.

≋ SWEDISH PANCAKES ≋

Makes 24 pancakes

1 cup all-purpose flour
1 tablespoon sugar
3 large eggs
2 cups milk or half-and-half
5 tablespoons unsalted butter, melted
Blueberry or raspberry preserves or syrup, for serving

Heat the oven to 200 degrees.

Sift the flour and sugar into a mixing bowl. Beat the eggs with the milk or half-and-half. Pour the mixture into the dry ingredients and stir until blended. Stir in 4 tablespoons of the melted butter.

Lightly brush a heavy skillet or griddle with the remaining butter and heat over moderate heat. Drop the batter onto the hot skillet, about a tablespoon at a time. Cook for about one minute or until bubbles start to appear and then turn and cook on the other side. Keep the pancakes warm in the oven while you cook the remaining batter. Serve with blueberry or raspberry preserves or syrup.

"My children were always crazy about pancakes of any kind for breakfast. One special treat was Swedish pancakes, which are some-times served for dessert at dinner, and other times for lunch. In our house, they were for brunch and my boys would beg me for them. I would make a huge batch of them, pour blueberry syrup over them, and watch them disappear. The boys would eat so many that I feared for their health but, being young, they continued to shovel them in and then were able to run outside and play, while my husband and I cleaned up the kitchen and collapsed.

"The recipe was one sent to me by a Swedish college friend and I have always found it easy and 'no fail.'"—
Gillian Cowger,
New Canaan, Connecticut

Opposite: Key Lime Pie (page 251)
Page preceding: Blueberry Pie (page 252)

TRIFLE

Serves 4 to 6

10 ½-inch slices pound cake
¾ cup medium sherry
½ pound fresh or frozen, defrosted raspberries
½ cups sliced almonds
8 canned peach halves, juice reserved
2 bananas, sliced
2 ½ cups milk
4 egg yolks
½ cup sugar
1¼ cups heavy cream
2 tablespoons kirsch

Put 5 slices of the pound cake in the bottom of a large glass bowl, trimming the corners so that they fit neatly. Sprinkle with half the sherry and spread half the raspberries on top. Layer the remaining cake over the raspberries and sprinkle with the remaining sherry. Spread the almonds over the cake and top with the remaining berries.

Arrange the peach halves over the raspberries and sprinkle them with 3 tablespoons of their juice. Top with the sliced bananas.

Pour the milk into a medium-sized pan and bring to the boil. Remove from the heat and set it aside.

Whisk together the egg yolks and sugar in a bowl. Add the slightly cooled milk, whisking to combine. Return the mixture to the pan and cook over low heat for about 10 minutes, stirring constantly, until the custard thickens. When the custard is thick enough to coat the back of a spoon, remove it from the heat, still stirring. Allow it to cool slightly.

Pour the custard over the fruit and cake. Chill the trifle in the refrigerator.

Whisk the cream with the kirsch until soft peaks form. Spread the cream over the top of the trifle, or pipe it in swirls using a pastry bag fitted with a large star tip. Chill the trifle again until ready to serve.

"My mother would make trifle for special occasions such as Christmas or birthdays, as I suppose English housewives did all across the country. Or sometimes it turned up on the table for no reason at all— just as a treat for Sunday afternoon tea. When we were children we used to object to the slightest trace of sherry— it was the custard and cream that appealed to us — but as we grew up, we came to appreciate it. Now I cannot imagine leaving out the sherry, even though my own children protest just as my brothers and I did. They'll learn!"—
Mary Thomson,
Westport, Connecticut

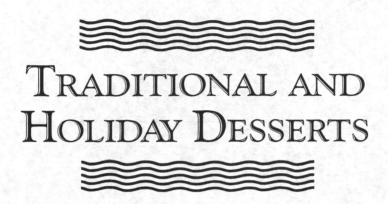

Traditional and Holiday Desserts

≋ Sugar Cookies ≋

Makes about 30 cookies

2 ½ cups all-purpose flour
½ teaspoon salt
1½ teaspoons baking powder
¾ cup unsalted butter, softened
¾ cup sugar
2 large eggs, at room temperature
1½ teaspoons vanilla extract
2 tablespoons lemon juice
Extra sugar for sprinkling

Sift together the flour, salt and baking powder.

Combine the butter and sugar in a large bowl and beat at medium speed for 2 to 3 minutes, until fluffy. Beat in the eggs, vanilla and lemon juice. Beat in the flour mixture at low speed. Form the dough into a ball, wrap tightly in transparent wrap and chill overnight.

Position a rack in the center of the oven. Heat the oven to 350 degrees. Lightly butter two baking sheets.

Divide the dough into two pieces and roll both out to a 1/4-inch thickness on a lightly floured work surface. Cut out the cookies with a 2 1/2-inch round cookie cutter and sprinkle them with the extra sugar.

Put the cookies on the prepared baking sheets and bake for 10 to 12 minutes until they are lightly browned. Transfer them to a wire rack to cool. The cookies will be crisp and crunchy when first baked and will soften up slightly if stored. To store, wrap them loosely in transparent wrap and put in an airtight container.

Granny Lou's
Molasses Cookies

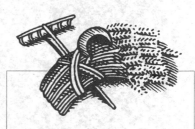

Makes 4 dozen cookies

8 tablespoons unsalted butter, softened
1½ cups sugar
1 large egg
1 cup light molasses
1 teaspoon vanilla extract
3 cups all-purpose flour
½ teaspoon baking soda
2 teaspoons baking powder
½ teaspoon salt
½ teaspoon freshly grated nutmeg
1 teaspoon cinnamon
2 teaspoons powdered ginger
1 cup buttermilk
½ cup red currant jelly

Cream the butter with the sugar in a mixing bowl. Beat in the egg and the molasses until well combined. Stir in the vanilla.

Sift the flour with the baking soda, baking powder, salt, nutmeg, cinnamon and ginger in another bowl. Stir with a whisk to distribute the spices evenly through the flour.

Add the flour mixture to the molasses mixture, alternating with the buttermilk, beating after each addition. Beat briefly until all the ingredients are well mixed. Chill the mixture for at least 3 hours, or overnight.

Heat the oven to 375 degrees. Butter a baking sheet.

Divide the dough into thirds. Roll out one portion 1/4 inch thick on a generously floured work surface, leaving the remaining dough in the refrigerator. Cut the rolled dough into circles with a 2 1/2-inch cookie cutter. Put the circles on the buttered

"I cannot see or smell a molasses cookie without thinking of my great-grand-mother, Granny Lou. Although I was small when I visited her, her house bloomed with the smells of unforget-table spices and freshly baked cookies. Granny Lou would wait for us in the sun room, seated on her her blue silk tufted rocking chair. We always went into the house through the kitchen and it became a tradition to reach into the tightly sealed cookie tin near the door to grab one of her special molasses cookies. These cookies had a target-like eye of red currant jelly in the middle. I always ate the soft cookie around the edge, saving the jelly for the last bite. I thought they should have more jelly, but years later when I tried making them myself with more jelly, I discovered that the extra jelly merely left a hole in the cookie. These same cookies continue to live on in our family to be made on special occasions."—
Thayer Wine,
Holladay, Tennessee

baking sheet and drop 1/2 teaspoon red currant jelly onto the center of each cookie. Or you may drop the soft dough onto the baking sheets by tablespoonfuls. Bake for 10 to 12 minutes. Cool for 2 minutes on the baking sheet, before transferring to a rack to cool completely. Repeat with the remaining portions of dough. Store the cookies in an airtight tin, or freeze them.

"My grandmother had many grandchildren and we all visited her big, rambling house very often. She always had a big cookie jar filled to the top with her homemade cookies—chocolate chip, sugar cookies with colored sprinkles, pinwheel cookies, and (my favorite) molasses cookies. She would put the jar on the big wooden kitchen table in the middle of the room and a large pitcher of cold milk and tall glasses and we would all help ourselves to a special mid-afternoon snack. She always said the same thing, 'Don't spoil your supper.' Of course, we all ate until we were bursting and the table and floor were littered with cookie crumbs. I can still hear the laughter in that kitchen and I can still see my grandmother smiling lovingly at her 'mob.'"— Sarah Davenport, Topeka, Kansas

≋ Nommie's Rogelach ≋

Makes 32 cookies

Filling:
4 ounces pecans
8 ounces (about 1 cup) dried currants
½ cup sugar
1 tablespoon cinnamon
Dough:
2 8-ounce packages cream cheese
2 cups all-purpose flour
1 cup unsalted butter, softened
2 tablespoons sugar
12-ounce jar apricot preserves

Chop the pecans in a food processor fitted with a metal blade until finely ground. Take care not to overprocess as the nuts may turn to paste. Combine the ground pecans, currants, sugar and cinnamon in a small bowl and set aside.

Combine all the ingredients for the dough in the workbowl of the food processor fitted with a metal blade. Process until the dough holds together in a ball. Turn the dough out on a lightly floured work surface and divide it into 4 pieces. Dust each piece with a little flour, shaking off the excess. Roll each piece of dough between 2 sheets of wax paper into a 9- or 10-inch circle. Chill the circles for at least 1 hour.

Heat the oven to 375 degrees and butter 2 baking sheets.

Spread each circle with preserves, making sure to cover the dough completely. Divide the filling among the 4 circles, spreading it evenly over the preserves. With a small, sharp knife, cut each circle into 8 wedges. Roll each wedge into a cone, beginning with the wide end and ending at the point. Arrange the cookies on the baking sheets and chill for 10 minutes. Bake for 20 to 25 minutes, until golden brown. Cool the cookies on wire racks and store in an airtight container.

"Whenever my mother came to visit us after I was grown, she immediately took over the kitchen. My two young sons and I were expected to stand and wait for her famous rogelach to come out of the oven. The boys were told that the cookies were just for them and they, of course, gobbled them up as good grandchildren would.

"The whole town loved my mother's rogelach, yet not too long ago my sons, now 30 and 28 years old, were reminiscing between themselves. 'Did you like Nommie's cookies?' Steven asked John. 'No, but I didn't want to hurt her feelings,' John replied. 'Me too!' Steven concurred.

"Nevertheless, I still get requests for her recipe and I think for good reason."—
Pat Miller,
Englewood, Colorado

263

# LEBKUCHEN

"At Christmastime, my
mother would make
lebkuchen. She prepared the
dough at home and then
brought it to the bakery in
town to be baked. At that
time in Germany, shortly
after the War, not many
people had ovens that they
could bake in and so the baker
assigned each person a time
slot and she could bring in her
desserts for him to bake.
Family recipes for holiday
treats were well-guarded
secrets and because the
women were good-naturedly
jealous of each other, every
year they accused the baker of
mixing up their doughs and
giving a rival family another
family's lebkuchen."—
Marla Hermann,
Canton, Ohio

Makes about 3 dozen

3 cups all-purpose flour
½ teaspoon baking powder
1 teaspoon baking soda
½ teaspoon salt
8 tablespoons unsalted butter, softened
½ cup packed brown sugar
1 large egg, at room temperature, lightly beaten
1 tablespoon lemon juice
1 teaspoon cinnamon
½ teaspoon ground cardamom
½ teaspoon ground cloves
¾ teaspoon ground nutmeg
⅛ teaspoon powdered ginger
½ cup finely chopped citron
½ cup honey
Confectioners' sugar

Position a rack in the center of the oven. Heat the oven
to 350 degrees. Butter a baking sheet.

Sift the flour, baking powder, baking soda and salt into a
medium-sized bowl. Put the butter and sugar in a large bowl and beat
at medium speed for 1 to 2 minutes, until fluffy. Beat in the egg,
lemon juice, spices and citron.

Heat the honey in a small saucepan over moderately low
heat until it is just warm and slightly thinned. Beat the honey into
the butter mixture until well blended. Stir the flour mixture, 1/4 cup
at a time, into the butter mixture. Knead thoroughly until the mixture is well combined. Divide the dough into thirds.

Roll one piece of dough to a 1/4-inch thickness on a
floured work surface, using a floured rolling pin and sprinkling the
dough with flour as necessary. Cut out the dough with a 2 1/2-inch

round cookie cutter. Roll and cut the remaining dough in the same way.

Put the cookies on the prepared baking sheet. Bake for 10 to 13 minutes until lightly browned. Remove from the oven and cool on wire racks. Sift confectioners' sugar over the cooled cookies and store them in an airtight container with a cut-up apple to add flavor and moisture. The cookies will keep for several weeks but the apple should be replaced from time to time.

HAMENTASCHEN

Makes about 3 dozen

2 ½ cups all-purpose flour
2 teaspoons baking powder
1 teaspoon salt
½ cup sugar
Grated rind of 1 orange
8 tablespoons butter
1 egg, lightly beaten
¼ cup orange juice
Filling:
½ cup milk
⅓ cup sugar
1 cup poppy seeds
2 tablespoons butter
2 ounces (about ⅓ cup) chocolate chips
½ cup raisins
½ cup almonds
¼ teaspoon cinnamon

"When we were young, Purim meant dressing up in costumes as Queen Esther, brave Mordecai, or King Ahasuerus. Of course, no one wanted to be the evil Haman! My mother and my aunt would spend hours before Purim making the costumes for me and my cousins to wear. Then we would all parade around the neighborhood, proudly showing them off to everyone.

"One of the treats we always had during Purim was hamentaschen— wonderful sweet, triangular pastries made to look like Haman's Hat. Some had prune fillings, some had poppy seed fillings, and some were made with raisins and other fruit, but they were always delicious."
— Joan Rothman, Philadelphia, Pennsylvania

Combine the flour, baking powder, salt, sugar and orange rind in a mixing bowl. Add the butter and work it in with your fingertips until the mixture resembles coarse meal. Stir in the egg and orange juice until the dough forms a ball.

Flatten the ball of dough slightly, wrap in transparent wrap and chill for at least 30 minutes.

To make the filling, combine the milk and sugar in a saucepan and bring to the boil. Add the poppy seeds and stir constantly for 3 to 4 minutes, until the seeds expand. Remove the pan from the heat. Add the butter, chocolate chips, raisins, almonds and cinnamon and stir until the butter has melted. Let the mixture cool.

Heat the oven to 400 degrees.

Put the dough between two floured pieces of wax paper and roll it out to a 1/4-inch thickness, sprinkling the dough with more flour as necessary to prevent the dough from sticking.

Cut the dough into rounds using a 2 1/2-inch cookie cutter. Put a teaspoonful of filling in the center of each round. Pinch the sides of the dough up to enclose the filling, forming a triangle shape. Put the cookies on an ungreased baking sheet and cook for 10 to 15 minutes, until golden brown. Remove them from the oven and cool on a wire rack.

Hungarian Nut Crescents

Makes 50 to 60

Dough:
½ pound (1 cup) butter
½ pound (1 cup) shortening
6¼ cups flour
1 package active dry yeast
2 cups sour cream
3 large egg yolks
Salt
Filling:
½ pound ground walnuts
1¼ cups sugar, plus extra for sprinkling
¼ teaspoon cinnamon
1 teaspoon vanilla extract
3 large egg whites
Egg wash:
1 large egg yolk
Water

"This recipe is a legacy from my Hungarian grandmother and links my children to their Old World heritage in a most positive way. No one can eat just one of these rich little crescents."—
Bunny Polmer,
Washington, D.C.

Cut the butter and shortening into the flour until the mixture is crumbly. Stir the yeast into the sour cream. Add the egg yolks and salt to the cream, stirring until well combined. Add the sour cream mixture to the flour and stir until a smooth dough forms. Shape the dough into a large ball. Cover with transparent wrap and chill overnight.

To make the filling, combine the nuts with the sugar and cinnamon. Beat the egg whites with the vanilla until stiff peaks form and fold into the nut mixture.

Sprinkle a work surface with sugar. Divide the chilled dough into 6 portions. Work with 1 portion at a time, returning the remaining portions to the refrigerator. Roll 1 portion of the dough

out on the sugared work surface to a thickness of 1/8 inch. Sprinkle with more sugar. Cut the dough into 2-by-2-inch squares. Spread some of the nut filling along one side of the square and roll up. Bend slightly to form a crescent and place, seam side down, on a buttered baking sheet. Repeat until all the dough is used.

To make the egg wash, beat the egg yolk with a few drops of water. Brush the crescents with the egg wash and bake for 15 to 20 minutes.

≋ BIRDS IN THE NEST ≋

Makes about 35

1 cup brown sugar
½ pound (1 cup) butter or shortening
2 large eggs, separated
2 tablespoons water
2 cups all-purpose flour
1 teaspoon vanilla extract
Salt
½ cup ground nuts
Grape or currant jelly, or the flavor of your choice

Heat the oven to 350 degrees.

Beat the sugar with the butter or shortening until creamy. Stir in the egg yolks, water, flour, vanilla and salt. Form the mixture into a ball. Break pieces of the dough off with your fingers or a teaspoon to form walnut-sized balls.

Dip the balls in the unbeaten egg whites and then roll them in the ground nuts. Place the balls on a baking sheet. Slightly flatten each one to make a disk and press a fingertip lightly in the center to form a shallow well. Fill the well with a small amount of your favorite jelly. Bake the cookies for 20 minutes.

BROWNIES

Makes 24 brownies

1½ *cups sifted all-purpose flour*
½ *teaspoon baking soda*
1½ *cups sugar*
5½ *tablespoons unsalted butter*
¼ *cup water*
6 *ounces semisweet chocolate, coarsely chopped*
3 *ounces unsweetened chocolate, coarsely chopped*
2 *teaspoons vanilla extract*
4 *large eggs, at room temperature*
1 *cup coarsely chopped walnuts*

Position a rack in the center of the oven. Heat the oven to 325 degrees.

Sift the flour and baking soda into a small bowl.

Combine the sugar, butter and water in a large saucepan over moderately low heat and bring to a simmer. Remove the pan from the heat. Stir in both kinds of chocolate and the vanilla. Set the mixture aside to cool until lukewarm.

Meanwhile, lightly butter a 13-by-9-inch pan.

When the chocolate mixture is lukewarm, beat in the eggs one at a time with a wooden spoon. Stir in the sifted flour mixture and the walnuts. Pour the mixture into the lined pan and bake for 30 to 35 minutes, until a toothpick inserted in the center comes out with moist crumbs. Set the brownies on a wire rack and cool to room temperature before cutting and removing them from the pan.

"My Auntie Lee loved chocolate. Whenever I visited her she had either just baked brownies (the soft, fudgy kind) or was planning something we could bake together. I remember one time in particular when we decided to make chocolate sauce (probably to spoon over the brownies and ice cream) but instead we ate all the sauce right out of the pan without ever spooning it on anything. For some reason, this is one of my favorite memories and I would like to do the same thing with my niece."—
Debbie Sykes,
Palo Alto, California

ALFAJORES

"As with most holidays everywhere, Easter is a time of wonderful food in Peru, where I grew up. Throughout South America, Easter is celebrated around the table, with all your relatives present. When it came to celebrating a holiday, my mother and grandmother would actually collaborate. Natural enemies at heart, they would form this wonderful alliance for the sole objective of creating a magnificent feast! And no Easter was complete without the wonderful crispy egg pastry called alfajores. It is impossible to eat just one, and I never did–even when I was on my best behavior!"—Felipe Rojas-Lombardi, New York, New York

Makes 8 to 10 4½-inch pastries

3 ¼ cups all-purpose flour
½ teaspoon baking powder
5 tablespoons lard, melted
20 egg yolks
3 tablespoons Pisco
5 4-ounce cans condensed milk (8½ cups) or 2 quarts fresh milk
4-inch stick cinnamon
2 cups sugar (if using fresh milk)
Confectioners' sugar, for sprinkling

Heat the oven to 375 degrees. Line a baking sheet with parchment paper.

Sift 3 cups of the flour and the baking powder into a bowl and set aside. Heat the lard in a small saucepan. Beat the egg yolks in a mixing bowl. Gradually beat in the the melted lard and the Pisco. Stir in the sifted flour mixture and mix well to form a smooth dough.

Turn the dough out onto a floured surface and roll to a thickness of about 1/8 inch. Cut the dough into 4-inch circles, using a cookie cutter or an inverted glass. Place the circles on the baking sheet, prick with the tines of a fork and bake for 15 to 20 minutes or until just golden. Remove the pastries from the oven and cool on a rack.

If you are using condensed milk, put it in an enameled saucepan. Add the cinnamon stick and bring to the boil, stirring. Reduce the heat to very low and simmer for 2 1/2 hours, stirring with a wooden spoon every 10 to 15 minutes. When ready, the milk should be the consistency of pudding and leave a track on the bottom of the pan. Remove from the heat and stir with a wooden spoon for a few minutes, until smooth and light in color. Set aside to cool.

If using fresh milk, combine the milk, sugar and cinnamon stick in an enameled saucepan and bring to the boil, stirring. Simmer over very low heat for 4 1/2 hours, stirring every 5 minutes for the first 2 1/2 hours and continuously for the remaining 2 hours. When the milk has a thick, pudding-like consistency, remove it from the heat and beat with a wooden spoon for a few minutes until smooth and light in color.

To assemble the alfajores, put 2 tablespoons of the cooled milk pudding in the center of a pastry, on its flat side. Place a second pastry, flat side down, on top. Sprinkle with confectioners' sugar and serve.

 ## SHORTBREAD

Makes 16 triangles

1 cup all-purpose flour
1 cup rice flour or fine semolina
12 tablespoons unsalted butter, cut into 12 pieces
½ cup sugar
1 tablespoon superfine sugar, for dusting

Heat the oven to 300 degrees.

Put the flours in a large bowl. Add the butter and work it in with your fingertips until the mixture resembles coarse meal. Alternatively, put the flour in a food processor, add the butter and pulse 4 or 5 times. Stir in the sugar.

Divide the mixture between two 9-inch round cake tins, pressing it down with your fingers and the back of your hand until it is even. Prick all over with a fork and score each round lightly into 8 triangular wedges.

"I remember the first time I tasted shortbread. My mother made some in preparation for a visit from her own mother. I took one little nibble and made a discovery that happens now and again with eating: This was my kind of food—as much as salty black olives, chicken cooked with fruit and soft bread pudding. I have always liked contrasts and the marriage of buttery richness and flaky tenderness in the shortbread was almost too good to be true."— Mary McNeely, Philadelphia, Pennsylvania

Bake the shortbread for 35 to 40 minutes. Dust with the superfine sugar. Cut through the wedges while the shortbread is still slightly warm.

ＧＩＮＧＥＲＢＲＥＡＤ

Makes 16 squares

8 tablespoons unsalted butter
1 cup molasses
½ cup sour cream
2 eggs
1 ¾ cups all-purpose flour
1 teaspoon baking powder
½ teaspoon baking soda
½ teaspoon salt
2 ½ teaspoons powdered ginger

Heat the oven to 350 degrees. Butter a 9-inch-square baking pan.

Beat the butter with the molasses until the mixture is creamy and the color lightens slightly. Stir in the sour cream and beat in the eggs, one at a time.

Sift together the flour, baking powder, baking soda, salt and ginger. Stir the dry ingredients into the butter mixture and mix well.

Pour the mixture into the prepared pan and bake in the center of the oven for 30 minutes or until a toothpick inserted in the center comes out clean. Cool the gingerbread for 5 minutes in the pan before turning out onto a wire rack to cool completely. Cut into squares when cool.

Opposite: Trifle (page 258)
Page following: Baklava (page 287)

≋ Vanilla Ice Cream ≋

Makes 1½ quarts

2 cups chilled heavy cream
2 cups chilled whole milk
1 cup sugar
2 teaspoons vanilla extract

Chill the canister of the ice cream freezer before making the ice cream.

Mix the cream, milk and sugar in the cold canister. Stir with a wooden or metal spoon until the sugar dissolves. Stir in the vanilla. Set the canister in the freezer and make the ice cream according to the manufacturer's instructions.

Chocolate Ice Cream

Makes about 1½ quarts

2 ounces unsweetened chocolate
¾ cup sugar
⅛ teaspoon salt
1 cup whole milk
1 cup heavy cream
1 teaspoon vanilla extract

Melt the chocolate, sugar and salt in the top of a double boiler over hot, not simmering, water. Stir until the chocolate melts and the sugar and salt dissolve.

Heat the milk and cream in a saucepan over moderate heat. Do not let the liquid boil or even form bubbles around the side of the pan. Pour the hot milk mixture and the melted chocolate into

"Judging by the number of reminiscences I've seen about it in print, homemade ice cream must be the most nostalgic food in the world. But every time I read someone else's recollections of aching arms and slurping the freshly made ice cream from the dasher, I think of my Grandma Jo— that's Josephine Wilhelmina— and her all-too-infrequent summertime impulses to haul out the ice cream maker. She would always enlist our 'elbow grease' ('we' being two young granddaughters with limitless appetites but undeveloped forearm muscles). We'd start zealously, cranking as fast as we could, until we practically collapsed with exhaustion; the ice cream would get harder and harder to churn, but Grandma did not allow a moment's rest until it was just right. Finally, when we knew she was ready to relent anyway, we would melodramatically beg for mercy and she'd let us dig into the icy canister. The flavor choices? Chocolate or vanilla— but who needed anything more?"— Eileen Yeager, Port St. Lucie, Florida

Opposite: Summer Pudding (page 250)
Page preceding: Lemon Meringue Pie (page 254)

the canister of an ice cream freezer. Stir in the vanilla extract. Chill for 2 to 3 hours or longer until very cold. Freeze in the ice cream freezer according to the manufacturer's instructions.

STRAWBERRY ICE CREAM

Makes 1½ pints

1 pint fresh strawberries
¾ cup sugar
1 cup chilled heavy cream
1 cup chilled whole milk
1½ teaspoons vanilla extract

Chill the canister of an ice cream freezer.

Wash and hull the strawberries. Mash half of the berries with a fork, put them in a bowl and sprinkle them with 2 to 3 tablespoons of sugar. Slice the remaining berries and put them in a bowl with 2 to 3 tablespoons of sugar. Chill both bowls of berries.

Pour the milk and cream into the cold canister and add the remaining sugar. Stir with a wooden or metal spoon until the sugar dissolves. Stir in the vanilla and the crushed berries. Freeze according to the manufacturer's instructions. When the ice cream is nearly frozen but is still soft, lift the canister from the freezer. If you are using a freezer that requires salt, be sure to wipe the outside of the canister well before lifting off the lid. Add the sliced berries to the partially frozen ice cream, pushing them gently with a wooden spoon into the ice cream. Return the canister to the freezer and continue freezing.

FRUITED BREAD PUDDING

Serves 4 to 6

4 to 4½ cups 1-inch firm white bread cubes
2 large eggs, at room temperature
1½ cups half-and-half
⅓ cup packed brown sugar
¼ teaspoon cinnamon
¼ teaspoon ground nutmeg
1 teaspoon vanilla extract
1 cup mashed ripe banana (about 2 medium-size bananas)
1½ cups coarsely chopped tart apples

Position a rack in the center of the oven and heat to 350 degrees. Butter a 1 1/2-quart soufflé dish.

Put the bread cubes in a large bowl.

Combine the eggs, half-and-half, sugar, cinnamon, nutmeg and vanilla in another bowl and beat at low speed for 1 to 1 1/2 minutes. Beat in the bananas and stir in the apples. Pour the mixture over the bread cubes and toss together with your hands or a large spoon.

Scrape the mixture into the prepared dish and sprinkle the top with additional brown sugar, if desired. Bake for 40 to 45 minutes, until puffed and golden brown. Remove from the oven and set on a wire rack. Let stand for 10 minutes before serving.

"My whole family is mad for bread puddings— in fact, I'm not sure I've ever met anyone who isn't, though everyone seems to have an unshakable opinion as to just how it should be made. My mother usually whipped up a simple version— usually with white bread, sometimes with wholewheat bread, and always with nutmeg sprinkled on the top. But sometimes she'd see fit to make her special fruit pudding, and then we knew one of three things had to be true: she was in an exceptionally good mood, we'd been uncommonly well-behaved, or someone special was coming to dinner. I inherited most of Mom's favorite recipes, and the only complaint I've ever had about her bread puddings from my own family is that I don't make it often enough."—
Edna Nelson,
Howard Beach, New York

ZABAGLIONE

Serves 4

4 large egg yolks, at room temperature
4 tablespoons sugar
3 tablespoons Marsala wine

Put the egg yolks in a bowl. Gradually beat in the sugar at medium speed. Increase to high speed and continue beating for 2 to 3 minutes, until the mixture is pale yellow and leaves a thick ribbon when the beaters are lifted.

Stir in the wine, using a wire whisk. Hold the bowl over a pan of hot, not simmering, water and beat the custard with the wire whisk for 2 to 3 minutes, until it thickens and becomes frothy. Serve warm or chilled, over fresh fruit or ladyfingers.

"When my grandmother was living with us she made zabaglione all the time. She'd take an egg yolk, add the sugar and Marsala and put it in a little ceramic cup— such as a demitasse cup— and then set the cup in boiling water. That was it, and she often gave this simple dessert to me when I came home from school. I still remember the wonderful winey taste, how sweet and delicious the zabaglione tasted, and how safe and good it felt to be home from school and with my grandmother."— Bianca Etkin, Queens, New York

CHOCOLATE PUDDING

Serves 4

1½ cups milk
½ cup heavy cream
¾ cup sugar
3 tablespoons cornstarch
⅛ teaspoon salt
4 tablespoons unsweetened cocoa powder
1 teaspoon vanilla extract

Pour 1 1/4 cups of the milk and the heavy cream into a large saucepan. Add the sugar and heat over moderately high heat, stirring, until the sugar dissolves and the milk is just simmering.

"Chocolate pudding has to be one of the quintessential comfort foods. The packaged stuff is edible if you're desperate, but folks who've never had homemade really have no idea what they're missing. My mom didn't like the skin on the top, so she would always lay a sheet of waxed paper on the pudding— unless I was there to stop her, because the skin is my favorite part."— Robert Foley, Duluth, Minnesota

Put the remaining 1/4 cup of milk in a small bowl with the cornstarch, salt and cocoa. Whisk or stir until it forms a smooth, thick paste. Pour about 1/2 cup of the hot milk mixture into the bowl and stir well to mix. Add this mixture to the hot milk remaining in the saucepan. Stir over moderate heat for 2 minutes until the pudding thickens. Remove from the heat and stir in the vanilla.

Immediately spoon the pudding into individual pudding cups, parfait glasses or a single serving bowl. Let cool almost to room temperature and then chill for 2 to 3 hours. Lay a piece of wax paper or transparent wrap directly on top of the pudding before chilling to prevent a skin from forming on the top.

RICE PUDDING

"My mother nearly always made rice pudding on Mondays, to serve as a hot dessert after cold roast meat. The way she made it, it was always creamy, without being too thick, with a nice golden brown skin on the top. My father was especially fond of the skin and always got the lion's share. We didn't mind too much; the rest of the pudding was pretty good, too."— Mary Thomson, Westport, Connecticut

Serves 4

1 cup short-grain rice
1 quart milk
½ cup plus 1 tablespoon brown sugar
2 tablespoons butter
1 teaspoon grated lemon rind
½ teaspoon ground nutmeg

Heat the oven to 325 degrees. Butter a 2-quart flat-bottomed baking dish.

Combine the rice and the milk in a saucepan and bring to the boil. Simmer for 5 minutes, stirring constantly. Remove from the heat.

Stir in 1/2 cup of the brown sugar, the butter and grated lemon peel. Pour the mixture into the baking dish and sprinkle with the nutmeg and remaining 1 tablespoon of brown sugar. Bake for 50 minutes.

FLAN

Serves 8

1½ *cups sugar*
6 *eggs*
2 ¼ *cups milk*
1 *teaspoon vanilla extract*
¼ *teaspoon salt*

Heat the oven to 325 degrees. Lightly butter 8 custard cups.

Put 3/4 cup of the sugar in a small pan, add 1 teaspoon of water and stir over moderate heat until dissolved. Bring to the boil and simmer, still stirring, for 3 minutes. Divide the syrup equally between the 8 custard cups.

Beat the remaining 3/4 cup of sugar with the eggs in a large bowl. Beat in the milk, vanilla and salt. Pour the custard into the cups. Put the cups in a roasting pan and pour in enough hot water to reach halfway up the sides of the cups.

Bake the custards for 1 hour or until a toothpick inserted in the center comes out clean. Remove the cups from the roasting pan and let cool slightly. Place them on a baking sheet and chill for 3 hours. Loosen the sides with a knife and invert the cups onto individual serving dishes, allowing the syrup to run down the sides of the custard and into the dish.

"My first trip to Europe many years ago, was on a French ship. One of the desserts served often on that trip was flan and I developed such a taste for it that I continued to order it when we landed in France and throughout the rest of the visit. Upon returning to the U.S., I asked everyone I kenw for a good recipe for it, and was finally rewarded when my neighbor wrote to her French cousins and obtained a typical French flan recipe. I made it for years for my family and now my grandchildren request it whenever they stay at my home."— Pam Padula, *Troy, New York*

KUGEL

Serves 4 to 6

2 eggs
⅔ cup sugar
2 medium-size apples, peeled and grated
2 tablespoons lemon juice
½ pound medium-wide cooked egg noodles
⅓ cup golden raisins
½ cup chopped walnuts
4 tablespoons butter, melted
¼ teaspoon ground nutmeg

Heat the oven to 350 degrees. Butter a 9-by-9-by-2-inch baking dish.

Beat the eggs with the sugar in a large bowl. Add the grated apples and lemon juice and mix well. Stir in the noodles, raisins, walnuts, melted butter and nutmeg.

Pour the mixture into the baking dish and bake for 1 hour, until the top is golden brown.

"There are many different types of kugel and many different family recipes. My mother made her kugel with sour cream, eggs, sugar, vanilla, crushed pinapple, raisins, apple, and cornflake crumbs. The result was so delectable we would have eaten it for dessert.

"I still use my mother's recipe and whenever I serve it on special holidays, my sister and I remember how our mother was so delighted to see her family's obvious enjoyment and appreciation of the wonderful dish she had prepared with such love."—
Sylvia Weinstein,
Ft. Lauderdale, Florida

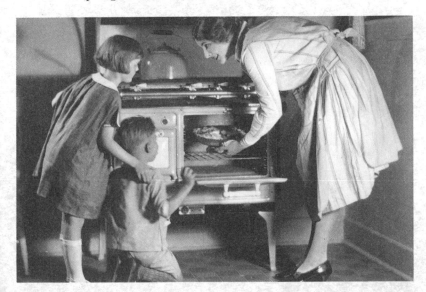

PLUM PUDDING

Serves 6 to 8

"My mother made her own plum pudding, which, by the way, is also known as Christmas pudding in England. She made it several weeks in advance, always in the same, off-white pottery pudding bowl with a rim. She said making it this far ahead gave it plenty of time to get moist and rich before December 25. While she made it, we all took a turn at stirring the pudding batter, and made a wish as we did so. My mother put a few silver threepenny bits (saved from years earlier) into the pudding. If your serving had a threepenny bit in it, it was supposed to be good luck. But of course you couldn't keep the coin. You had to give it back for next year's pudding. Still, getting one caused much excitement."—
Mary Thomson,
Westport, Connecticut

1 cup shredded beef suet
1½ cups currants
1½ cups golden raisins
½ cup candied mixed fruit peel, chopped
1 cup slivered almonds
2 cups brown sugar
Rind of 1 orange, grated
2 cups fresh bread crumbs
1¼ cups all-purpose flour
¼ teaspoon ground nutmeg
¼ teaspoon cinnamon
⅛ teaspoon ground cloves
⅛ teaspoon powdered ginger
1 medium-size cooking apple, peeled, cored and chopped
4 eggs
⅔ cups dark beer
½ cup brandy
½ cup orange juice
5 tablespoons brandy

Combine the suet, fruit and dry ingredients in a large mixing bowl. Lightly beat the eggs with the beer, 1/2 cup of brandy and the orange juice. Pour into the fruit mixture and mix well.

Pour the mixture into 1 large or 2 small heatproof pudding basins or molds. Cover with a double layer of buttered aluminum foil, pleated in the middle to allow the mixture to rise. Press the foil down well around the edges to seal. Tie a piece of string around the rim of the bowl and across the top to make a handle.

Put the pudding bowl into a pan and carefully add enough water to come two-thirds of the way up the side of the bowl. Bring the water to the boil and cover the saucepan tightly. Lower the heat and steam the pudding for 6 hours, adding more boiling water as necessary.

Remove the pudding bowl from the pan and let cool. When cool, remove the foil and replace with a fresh piece, tying it with string as before. Store the pudding in a cool, dry place.

Before serving, steam the pudding as before for 2 hours. When the pudding is ready, heat the 5 tablespoons of brandy in a small saucepan. Turn the pudding out onto a serving dish, pour the hot brandy over it and set it alight. Serve the pudding with Hard Sauce (see below).

HARD SAUCE

Makes about ¾ cup

8 tablespoons unsalted butter
¾ cup sugar
4 tablespoons brandy

Beat the butter until it is pale and creamy. Gradually beat in the sugar. Slowly add the brandy, beating until it is well incorporated.

Pack the sauce into a dish, cover tightly with transparent wrap and chill in the refrigerator until ready to serve. Serve with plum pudding or mincemeat pie.

"When we were children we all got together at my grand-parents for Christmas Day dinner. There was always plum pudding, mincemeat pie and usually pumpkin pie for dessert, but our favorite part of dessert by far was the sweet, buttery hard sauce. The cut glass bowl my grandmother used to serve it in inevitably ended up on the 'children's table,' a couple of card tables squeezed into the dining room for the noisy set. Our favorite uncle (very much a grown-up) endeared himself to us even more by sitting at our table a few times while we were young and I remember the year my older brother dared him to eat the entire bowl of hard sauce. My uncle did it–just gobbled up the whole bowl, much to the dismay of the adults at the more sedate table across the room! We still talk about that 30 years later; it's become a family legend."—
Mary McNeely,
Philadelphia, Pennsylvania

FLOATING ISLAND

Serves 4

3 eggs, separated
2/3 cup sugar
4 cups milk
1 teaspoon vanilla extract
1/4 teaspoon cream of tartar

"Back in Texas my mother made desserts in big batches. When she made custard, it was in a huge soup pot, and as often as not, the custard was used to make floating island. Nothing fancy about this dessert, just sweetened, whipped egg whites, poached a little in hot milk and set to float on a smooth sea of custard. But it sure was good and is still one of my favorites."—
Florence Dedman,
Killingworth, Connecticut

Put the egg yolks in the top of a double boiler over hot but not boiling water. Add 1/3 cup of the sugar, 2 cups of the milk and the vanilla. Whisk until well combined. Stir with the wire whisk until the custard thickens enough to coat the back of a wooden spoon, about 15 minutes.

Pour the custard into a serving bowl, cover the surface with transparent wrap to prevent a skin from forming and cool completely.

Meanwhile, make the meringue "islands." Put the egg whites in a large grease-free bowl. Add the cream of tartar and the remaining 1/3 cup of sugar and beat until stiff peaks form. Put the remaining 2 cups of milk in a saucepan and bring to a gentle simmer. Drop rounded tablespoons of meringue into the hot milk, a few at a time, and poach for about 4 minutes, turning once. Using a slotted spoon, lift the meringues out carefully and drain on paper towels. Repeat until all the meringues are poached.

Pile the meringues on top of the custard and chill before serving.

≋ Boston Cream Pie ≋

Makes one 9-inch pie

6 large eggs, at room temperature
¾ cup plus 2 tablespoons sugar
1 teaspoon vanilla extract
1½ cups sifted all-purpose flour
¼ teaspoon salt
4 tablespoons unsalted butter, melted
1½ cups heavy cream
6 ounces semisweet chocolate, chopped

Put a rack in the center of the oven and heat the oven to 350 degrees. Lightly butter and flour two 9-inch round pans.

Combine the eggs and 3/4 cup of the sugar in a large heatproof bowl. Put the bowl over a pan of hot, not simmering, water. Stir with a wire whisk until the sugar is dissolved and the mixture is hot to the touch (110 degrees on a candy thermometer). Remove the bowl from the heat and beat with an electric mixer for 5 to 7 minutes until the mixture is cool and has tripled in volume. It should be very light, fluffy and lemon-colored.

Beat the vanilla into the egg mixture. Combine the flour and salt and sift over the egg mixture, folding in the flour with a rubber spatula. Gently drizzle in the butter and stir just until blended.

Pour the batter into the prepared pans. Bake for 25 to 30 minutes, until a toothpick inserted in the middle of the cakes comes out clean and the top springs back when lightly pressed. Cool the cakes on wire racks for 10 minutes. Remove them from the pans and cool completely on racks.

Heat 3/4 cup of cream in a small saucepan until it starts to simmer. Remove the pan from the heat and stir in the chopped chocolate until it is melted and smooth. Set aside to cool to room temperature.

"I think most people make Boston Cream Pie with a custard filling, but my family has always been partial to Aunt Adelaide's version— as she says, 'There must be a reason why they don't call it "Boston Custard Pie."' Her Boston Cream Pie practically levitates off the plate. The layers are really an airy genoise rather than plain yellow cake, and the filling is lightly sweetened whipped cream. The whole is swathed in a stupendous semisweet chocolate glaze. If Adelaide never made another decent thing, her culinary talents would still be revered in our clan for this one triumphant cake."— Joan Shank, San Jose, California

Beat the remaining 3/4 cup of cream with the remaining 2 tablespoons of sugar until soft peaks form. Put one cake layer on a serving plate and spread with the whipped cream. Put the second cake layer on top. Gently pour the chocolate glaze over the top of the cake, allowing some to drizzle down the sides.

GRANDMA SEARLES' CUSTARD PIE

Makes one 9-inch pie

Pastry:
1 cup sifted all-purpose flour
1 teaspoon salt
5 tablespoons lard, cut into pieces
5 tablespoons butter, cut into pieces
5 tablespoons water
Filling:
6 large eggs
1 cup sugar
2 cups milk
Nutmeg, for sprinkling

Sift the flour and salt into a mixing bowl. Add the lard and butter and work in with your fingertips or a pastry blender until the mixture resembles coarse crumbs. Gradually stir in the water until the dough holds together. Wrap the dough in transparent wrap and chill for 15 to 20 minutes.

Heat the oven to 450 degrees.

Roll the pastry out on a lightly floured work surface, using a floured pin. Line a 9-inch deep pie plate with the pastry. Trim and flute the edges.

Beat together the eggs, sugar and milk, and pour into the pie shell. Sprinkle generously with nutmeg. Bake the pie for 10 minutes. Lower the heat to 350 degrees and bake for 30 to 45 minutes more or until the custard has set. Serve the pie cold.

PHYLLO DOUGH

Makes 1 pound

2 cups unbleached bread flour
½ teaspoon salt
¾ cup warm water
2 tablespoons vegetable oil
Cornstarch, for rolling
Extra flour, for rolling
Extra oil, for rolling

Put the flour and salt in a large mixing bowl. Add the water slowly, beating constantly until the mixture is smooth. Knead the mixture in the bowl or on a work surface until it forms a soft, sticky dough. If you are kneading the dough on a work surface, use a scraper to help keep the dough together.

Add the oil to the dough by teaspoonfuls, kneading until each addition is absorbed before adding more. Continue kneading vigorously for about 20 minutes until the dough is smooth and shiny. Put the dough in an oiled bowl, cover and allow to rest for at least 2 hours before using.

"My maternal grandmother was 'keeper of the kitchen' and what a kitchen it was! She baked and cooked, while my step-grandfather had a wonderful smokehouse from which flowed sausage, whole baby pigs and lambs rotissed to a succulent turn. There also were hams and all manner of smoked, dried and freshly grilled foods. From my grandmother's pots and pans came stews that I have never found the match of and from her oven came the lightest, thinnest, most tender phyllo creations I've tasted, made from phyllo freshly pulled on large round tables draped in fresh white linen. There is a magic moment with phyllo when it is perfect for filling and rolling. Too soon, and the dough is too wet and the filling will glue the layers together; too late and the phyllo will be dry.

"My grandmother had her phyllo dough down to a science and she was such an expert that the phyllo was never too dry or too wet. She would hum happily as she

285

Cover a large table with a cotton cloth large enough to overhang the sides. Rub the cloth generously with cornstarch, particularly in the center where you will be working the most. Have a bowl of flour at hand while you work.

Put the dough in the center of the cloth and dust heavily with cornstarch. Dip your hands into the cornstarch and pull and roll the dough evenly in all directions into a thin round.

Dip your fists in flour and place palms down under the dough. Working from the center out, pull and stretch the dough carefully, moving around the table in a methodical fashion to stretch the dough evenly. Work carefully to avoid tearing the dough, but if holes appear, ignore them and try not to make them larger. Continue the process, brushing with oil to keep the dough from drying. When you are finished, the sheet of dough will be tissue-thin, with thick edges. Allow the dough to dry for about 20 minutes. With sharp scissors, snip away the thick edges. With a sharp knife, cut the dough into 12-by-16-inch sheets. Stack the sheets on a cookie sheet, dusting each layer with cornstarch.

The dough may be used immediately, or it can be stored, tightly wrapped, in the refrigerator for up to a week, or in the freezer for up to 3 weeks.

 # BAKLAVA

Makes about 50 pieces

1½ cups butter, melted
1½ cups coarsely chopped almonds
1½ cups coarsely chopped walnuts
2 teaspoons cinnamon
½ teaspoon ground cloves
1 pound phyllo pastry, about 25 sheets
1½ cups sugar
1 cup honey
¾ cup water

Heat the oven to 350 degrees. Brush a 13-by-9-inch pan with some of the melted butter.

Combine the nuts, cinnamon and cloves in a bowl.

Put one sheet of phyllo in the bottom of the buttered pan with the excess pastry hanging over the edge of the pan. Brush with melted butter. Repeat with 7 more sheets of phyllo, brushing each with melted butter.

Sprinkle one third of the nut mixture over the pastry. Layer four more phyllo sheets on top, brushing each with melted butter. Sprinkle another third of the nut mixture on top and cover with four more phyllo sheets, again brushing each with melted butter. Sprinkle the remaining nut mixture on top and cover with the remaining 8 sheets of phyllo, brushing with melted butter as before. Fold all the overhanging edges up onto the seventh phyllo sheet before topping with the final sheet. Trim the excess pastry from the top sheet with a sharp knife and brush the top with the remaining butter. Using a sharp knife, make diagonal cuts about 1 1/2 inches apart across the entire pastry and then back again to form diamond shapes, cutting through all the pastry layers.

Bake for 1 hour. Turn the oven off and leave the pan in the oven for another 30 minutes.

"When I was in college, one of my closest friends was Christina, a Greek exchange student. It was she who first introduced me to the joys of Greek cuisine— especially moussaka and baklava. Her mother would send her packages from Athens containing all sorts of wondrous things, but I waited especially for the baklava. Ah, the sweet honey and flaky phyllo pastry and the nuts and cinnamon! Christina would invite a few of us to her room in our dorm and we would feast long into the night. I have lost touch with Christina over the years, but I have never lost my taste for baklava."—
Joanne Doheny,
Pittsfield, Massachusetts

Meanwhile, prepare the syrup. Combine the sugar, honey and water in a saucepan over moderate heat, stirring until the sugar is dissolved. Increase the heat and bring to the boil, stirring constantly. Lower the heat to moderate again and simmer for 5 minutes. Remove from the heat.

As soon as the baklava is removed from the oven, pour the warm syrup over it, allowing it to penetrate through all the layers. Cut through the baklava again to separate the diamonds. Cool completely before serving.

CHEESECAKE

Serves 12

1 cup graham cracker crumbs
4 tablespoons butter, melted
1½ pounds cream cheese, softened
1 cup sugar
3 large eggs, at room temperature
1 teaspoon vanilla extract
½ teaspoon almond extract
1½ cups sour cream, at room temperature

Heat the oven to 350 degrees. Lightly butter a 9-inch springform pan.

Combine the graham cracker crumbs and the melted butter in a small bowl. Press the mixture evenly onto the bottom of the springform pan.

Put the cream cheese in a large bowl and beat until smooth. Beat in the sugar and the eggs, scraping the sides of the bowl frequently. Beat in the vanilla and almond extracts and sour cream.

Opposite: Flan (page 278)
Page following: Coconut Cake (page 292)

Pour the mixture into the graham cracker crust and bake for 55 to 60 minutes, until the cheesecake is puffed and firm to the touch. Remove the cheesecake from the oven and run a thin knife around the edge to loosen it from the pan. Let cool completely and chill for several hours or overnight before serving.

"My mother's sister, Aunt Connie, has always made the best cheesecake around. No family occasion is complete without 'Aunt Connie's Cheesecake.' My children, who normally are partial to chocolate brownies and cake, have developed such a passion for this cheesecake that they have requested it for every birthday and graduation celebration for years. She is very gracious about sharing her recipe and I have made it for them many times, paying strict attention to Aunt Connie's directions to be sure to put in enough cream cheese and sour cream to make it rich. Although my children always praise my cheesecake politely, I think they prefer Aunt Connie's, maybe because hers was the original."— Maureen Lowe, Pittsfield, Massachusetts

Opposite: Plum Pudding (page 280)
Page preceding: Boston Cream Pie (page 283)

289

≋ DEVIL'S FOOD CAKE ≋

Makes one 8-inch layer cake

Cake:
1¼ cups packed brown sugar
⅓ cup cocoa powder
½ cup milk
2¼ cups sifted cake flour
1 teaspoon baking soda
½ teaspoon salt
8 tablespoons unsalted butter, softened
2 teaspoons vanilla extract
3 large eggs, at room temperature
½ cup buttermilk, at room temperature
Frosting:
8 tablespoons unsalted butter, softened
3 cups confectioners' sugar
4 tablespoons heavy cream
3 ounces unsweetened chocolate, melted and cooled
1 teaspoon vanilla extract

Heat the oven to 350 degrees. Lightly butter and flour two 8-inch round pans.

Combine 1/4 cup of the brown sugar with the cocoa and milk in a small saucepan over low heat. Stir constantly until the mixture is smooth. Remove from the heat and let cool.

Sift the flour, baking soda and salt into a medium-sized bowl. Beat the butter with the remaining 1/2 cup of brown sugar in a large bowl until the mixture is light and fluffy. Stir in the vanilla. Beat in the eggs, one at a time. Stir in the cooled cocoa mixture. Gradually stir in the sifted dry ingredients, alternating with the buttermilk.

Pour the batter into the prepared pans and bake for 25 to 30 minutes, until a toothpick inserted in the center comes out clean. Let the cake cool in the pans for about 5 minutes and then turn the layers out onto wire racks to cool completely.

To make the frosting, put the butter in a medium-sized bowl and beat with an electric mixer for 1 to 2 minutes, until fluffy. Reduce the speed and add the confectioners' sugar, a cup at a time. Once the sugar is well incorporated, slowly add the cream, chocolate and vanilla extract and beat until the frosting is light and fluffy.

When the cake is cooled, frost the top of one layer and place the second layer on top of it. Frost the top and sides of the cake.

 # POUND CAKE

Makes one large tube cake

1 cup unsalted butter, softened
1 cup sugar
1 teaspoon finely grated lemon rind
1 teaspoon vanilla extract
5 large eggs
2 ¼ cups sifted cake flour
½ teaspoon salt

Position a rack in the center of the oven. Heat the oven to 350 degrees. Lightly butter a 6-cup fluted tube pan. Dust with flour and tap out the excess.

Beat the butter in a large bowl until creamy. Gradually add the sugar and continue beating for 4 to 5 minutes, until the mixture is very pale, light and fluffy. Beat in the lemon rind and vanilla. Add the eggs one at a time, beating well after each addition. Stir in the flour and salt.

Scrape the batter into the prepared pan and bake for 55 to 60 minutes, until a toothpick inserted in the center comes out clean. Cool the pan on a wire rack for 10 minutes. Invert the cake onto a wire rack and remove the pan. Leave the cake on the rack to cool completely.

*"My mother loved to bake and I have warm childhood memories of coming home from school and smelling something good in the oven. Very often, it was pound cake. Mother would give me a big slice with a glass of cold milk or a cup of hot chocolate (if the weather was cold or rainy) and I would enjoy every mouthful. My friends from school all enjoyed coming to our house after school, and they looked forward to their 'snack' with me. They all envied me for having a mother who baked almost every day and they were right— she was very special and her baking showed the love she had for her family."—
Deanna Lombardo,
Rye, New York*

Coconut Cake

Makes one 9-inch layer cake

3 cups cake flour
2 teaspoons baking powder
1/4 teaspoon salt
1½ cups sugar
1 cup butter, at room temperature
1 teaspoon vanilla extract
4 eggs
Frosting:
2 egg whites
1½ cups sugar
½ cup water
2 teaspoons light corn syrup
1 teaspoon vanilla extract
¾ cup shredded sweetened coconut

"Though I grew up outside of Chicago, our next door neighbors were transplanted Alabamans who, in three decades, never got used to city life or to the North in particular. Mabel was a dyed-in-the-wool Southern cook who turned up her nose contemptuously at Chicago staples like pizza and keilbasa, preferring to ply her husband Clayton with the foods they had known in their youth. She was a particularly avid baker who curned out chess pies and pecan tarts and blackberry jam cakes at a furious clip, always offering a slice or two across the back fence because 'Clayton and I can't finish it all by ourselves' (although, judging by her girth, she did make a consid-erable dent in her wares). Since my childhood sweet tooth knew no bounds, her coconut cake was a dream come true."—
Dorothy Wallach,
Evanston, Illinois

Heat the oven to 375 degrees. Butter two 9-inch round pans and line them with wax paper.

Sift the flour onto a sheet of wax paper with the baking powder and the salt.

Put the sugar and butter in a large bowl and beat until light and fluffy. Combine the vanilla and eggs in a smaller bowl and beat lightly. Gradually add the eggs to the butter mixture, beating well after each addition. Gently stir in the sifted flour mixture.

Scrape the batter into the prepared pans and bake in the center of the oven for 30 minutes or until a toothpick inserted in the middle of one layer comes out clean. Cool the layers in their pans on a wire rack for 5 minutes. Turn out onto the rack and cool completely.

To make the frosting, combine the egg whites, sugar, water and corn syrup in the top of a double boiler over simmering water. Beat vigorously with an electric or rotary beater for about 7 minutes or until stiff peaks form. Remove from the heat and beat in the vanilla and 1/2 cup of the coconut.

Put the remaining coconut in a dry 8-inch skillet and toast over moderate heat, stirring constantly, until golden brown. Remove the coconut to a plate to cool.

Spread one third of the frosting over one of the cooled cake layers and top with the second layer. Spread the remaining frosting over the top and sides of the cake. Sprinkle the toasted coconut on top.

ANGEL FOOD CAKE

Makes one 10-inch tube cake

1½ cups egg whites (11 to 12 large eggs)
1 teaspoon cream of tartar
1 teaspoon salt
1¼ cup sugar, sifted
1 teaspoon vanilla extract
1 cup flour, sifted twice

Heat the oven to 375 degrees.

Beat the egg whites with the cream of tartar and salt with an electric mixer on high speed until foamy. Continue beating, adding the 1 cup of the sugar a tablespoon or two at a time until the egg whites form stiff peaks. Gently fold in the vanilla.

Sprinkle the remaining sugar and the flour over the top of the egg whites and fold them into the batter using a rubber spatula. Cut cleanly with the side of the spatula as you fold the dry ingredients into the egg whites–do not slap them with the side of the spatula. Mix

only until the flour and sugar are combined. Be careful not to overfold.

Pour the batter into an unbuttered 10-inch tube pan. Bake for 30 to 35 minutes until the crust is lightly browned. The top of the cake will be cracked. Invert the tube pan on a funnel or bottle and let the cake cool completely in the pan before removing it.

Sunshine Cake

Makes one 10-inch tube cake

7 large eggs, separated
1¼ cups sugar
1 teaspoon vanilla extract
¼ teaspoon salt
1 teaspoon cream of tartar
¾ cup cake flour, sifted 4 times

Heat the oven to 325 degrees.

Beat the egg yolks until thick and light. Gradually beat in the sugar and the vanilla extract and continue beating until the batter is very smooth.

Add the salt to the egg whites and beat them until foamy. Add the cream of tartar and continue beating until stiff but not dry. Fold the whites into the yolk mixture. Gradually fold in the flour. Do not overmix.

Pour the batter into a 10-inch tube pan. Bake for 55 minutes. Increase the heat to 350 degrees and bake for 10 minutes more, or until a toothpick inserted in the cake comes out clean. Cool in the pan for 10 minutes. Turn out onto a rack to cool completely.

Chocolate Cake

Makes one 8-inch layer cake

2¼ cups sifted cake flour
¾ teaspoon baking soda
¼ teaspoon baking powder
½ teaspoon salt
4 ounces unsweetened chocolate
½ cup water
8 tablespoons unsalted butter, softened
1¼ cups sugar
2 teaspoons vanilla extract
2 large eggs, at room temperature
⅔ cup milk
Frosting:
1 cup heavy cream
⅔ pound semisweet chocolate, chopped
4 tablespoons unsalted butter, chilled

Position a rack in the center of the oven. Heat the oven to 350 degrees. Lightly butter and flour two 8-inch cake layer pans.

Sift together the flour, baking soda, baking powder and salt in a medium-sized bowl. Put the chocolate and water in the top of a double boiler over hot, not simmering, water. Stir until the chocolate is melted and the mixture is smooth. Remove from the heat and let cool completely.

Beat the butter in a large bowl until creamy. Gradually add the sugar and continue beating for 3 to 5 minutes, until the mixture is light and fluffy. Beat in the vanilla and the eggs. Stir in the melted chocolate. Stir in the flour mixture, a third at a time, alternating with the milk.

Pour the batter into the prepared pans and bake for 25 to 30 minutes, until a toothpick inserted in the center of the cake comes out clean. Cool the cakes in their pans on wire racks for 10 minutes.

"When I was a girl just everyone baked cakes. I remember a sort of spice cake with caramel icing and blackberry jam that always made an appearance at family gatherings, but just as clearly I remember delicious, sweet chocolate cake. I rarely make the spice cake anymore, but I still follow one of my mother's recipes for chocolate cake. Passed down just as it was, it's become one of my children's favorites, too."— Hildreth Rosendahl, Newtown, Connecticut

Remove them from the pans and cool completely.

For the frosting, put the cream in a medium-sized saucepan and bring to the boil. Stir in the chopped chocolate. When it is melted, stir in the butter, a tablespoon at a time, waiting until each piece is incorporated before adding the next.

When the cake has cooled completely, spread the top of one layer with the frosting and put the other layer on top of it. Spread the remaining frosting on the sides and top of the cake.

 # SPONGE CAKE

Makes one 10-inch tube cake

1 cup cake flour
½ teaspoon salt
1 cup sugar
1 teaspoon baking powder
1 tablespoon water
1 tablespoon lemon juice
1 tablespoon grated lemon rind
6 large eggs, at room temperature, separated
Confectioners' sugar

Position a rack in the center of the oven. Heat the oven to 350 degrees.

Sift the cake flour, salt, 1/3 cup of the sugar and the baking powder into a small bowl. Combine the water, lemon juice and lemon rind in another bowl.

Beat the egg yolks in a medium-sized bowl for 7 to 8 minutes until they are pale yellow and thick enough to leave a

ribbon when the beaters are lifted. Gradually add 1/3 cup sugar to the egg yolks, alternating with the lemon juice-water mixture beating well after each addition, using a rubber spatula, fold the sifted flour mixture into the egg yolks about 1 tablespoon at a time. Do not overmix.

Beat the egg whites in a large bowl until they are foamy. Gradually add the remaining 1/3 cup sugar and continue beating until the whites form stiff, shiny peaks. Gently fold the egg yolk mixture into the beaten egg whites.

Pour the batter into an unbuttered 10-inch tube pan. Bake for 30 to 35 minutes, until the top is slightly rounded and golden brown, and a toothpick inserted in the center of the cake comes out clean. Remove the cake from the oven and cool completely in the pan on a wire rack. Sprinkle with sifted confectioners' sugar before serving, if desired.

 FRUIT CAKE

Makes one 9-inch loaf cake

1 cup dark raisins
1 cup golden raisins
1 cup muscat raisins
7½ ounces glacé cherries, halved
1¼ cups brandy
2½ cups self-rising flour
1 teaspoon cinnamon
⅛ teaspoon mace
1 cup unsalted butter, softened
½ cup plus 2 tablespoons granulated sugar
4 large eggs, at room temperature
1 cup coarsely chopped walnuts
5 walnut halves (optional)

"Christmas was a mysteriously secretive time when I was a child, as I suppose it is for every child, if she's lucky. The screened porch between the kitchen and the dining room kept the dining room cool during the cold months of winter and so all the wonderful food my mother made in the weeks before Christmas went in that room— and we children had to stay out. She made fruit cake every year without fail, which I remember she baked in a big old washtub. It sat in the dining room most of the fall, just getting better and better. Besides fruit cake, we always had cookies, fudge and sea-foam candy at Christmas— all very special, and rarely seen in our Kentucky kitchen other times of the year."— Hildreth Rosendahl, Newtown, Connecticut

Combine the raisins and cherries in a shallow baking dish. Add 3/4 cup of the brandy, cover with transparent wrap and leave to soak for 8 hours or overnight.

Butter the bottom and sides of a 9-by-5 1/2-by-2 1/2-inch loaf pan. Line the bottom with wax paper. Heat the oven to 350 degrees.

Combine the flour, cinnamon and mace in a medium-sized bowl. Put the butter in a large mixing bowl and beat until creamy. Gradually beat in the sugar. Add the eggs one at a time, beating well after each addition. Stir in the flour mixture just until it is incorporated. Using a rubber spatula, fold in the dried fruit mixture and the chopped nuts.

Scrape the batter into the prepared pan, Smooth the top and, if desired, put the walnut halves in a row on the top. Bake for 1 hour. Lower the oven temperature to 300 degrees and bake for 40 to 50 minutes more, until a toothpick inserted in the center of the cake comes out clean. The cake should be dark golden brown with very dark edges.

Put the cake on a wire rack, still in its pan. Spoon 1/4 cup of the remaining brandy evenly over the cake while it is still hot. Allow it to sit for 30 minutes and then spoon the remaining brandy over the top. Allow to sit for a further 30 minutes.

Run a sharp knife around the edges of the cake and remove it from the pan to another wire rack. Allow the cake to cool completely and then wrap it tightly in aluminum foil. Store the cake in a cool place. If you plan to store it for several weeks or longer, put it in a tin or wrap it in a couple layers of foil. Unwrap the cake every two or three weeks and pour about a 1/4 cup of brandy over the top.

MINCEMEAT PIE

Makes one 8-inch pie

Mincemeat:
1 pound apples, peeled, cored and finely chopped
1½ cups seedless raisins
1½ cups currants
½ pound shredded beef suet
½ cup mixed candied citrus peel
Grated rind of 1 orange
Grated rind of 1 lemon
1½ cups brown sugar
1 cup slivered almonds, chopped
½ teaspoon cinnamon
½ teaspoon ground nutmeg
½ teaspoon allspice
3 tablespoons brandy or whiskey
Pastry:
2 cups all-purpose flour
1 tablespoon sugar
12 tablespoons butter, cut into 12 pieces
1 egg yolk
2 to 3 tablespoons cold water
1 egg yolk beaten with 1 tablespoon water, for glaze

Combine all the mincemeat ingredients in a large bowl and mix well. Cover and allow to sit for at least 1 hour.

Sift the flour and sugar into a mixing bowl. Work the butter into the dry ingredients with your fingertips until the mixture resembles coarse bread crumbs. Combine the egg yolk and the water in a small bowl and whisk lightly. Gradually add the liquid to the flour mixture, mixing with a fork until a dough forms. Wrap the dough in transparent wrap and chill for 10 to 15 minutes.

Roll out two-thirds of the dough on a lightly floured work surface and line an 8-inch pie plate with it. Cover with transparent wrap and chill for another 10 minutes.

"When I was growing up in England, my grandmother made big batches of individual mincemeat pies and brought them out whenever company stopped by. She told us that every pie you ate represented a day of happiness in the new year— so my brother and I, who lived just down the road from my grandmother, ate as many of the little pies as we possibly could manage."— Betty Jerome, Bronx, New York

Heat the oven to 350 degrees.

Spoon half the mincemeat into the lined pie plate. Reserve the remaining mincemeat for later use. Roll the remaining pastry and cut it into 1/2-inch-wide strips. Brush the edges of the pie crust with water to moisten and lay the strips across in a lattice pattern, pressing the ends lightly so they adhere to the edges. Brush the pastry with the egg yolk glaze and bake for 35 to 40 minutes, until the pastry is golden.

PUMPKIN PIE

Makes one 9-inch pie

Pastry:
1 cup all-purpose flour
½ teaspoon salt
¼ teaspoon ground cloves
⅓ cup plus 1 tablespoon solid vegetable shortening
2 to 3 tablespoons iced water
Filling:
½ cup heavy cream
½ cup evaporated milk
½ cup sugar
½ cup brown sugar
1½ teaspoons cinnamon
½ teaspoon powdered ginger
¼ teaspoon ground cloves
½ teaspoon salt
2 large eggs, at room temperature
2 cups (1 pound) mashed pumpkin
3 tablespoons Marsala wine

Position a rack in the center of the oven. Heat the oven to 350 degrees.

Sift the flour, 1/2 teaspoon of salt and 1/4 teaspoon of ground cloves into a large bowl. Work the shortening into the flour mixture using your fingertips or a pastry blender, until it is the texture of raw oatmeal. Sprinkle the water over the mixture and toss lightly. Press the dough into a ball and let it sit for 5 minutes.

Put the dough between two sheets of wax paper on a floured work surface and roll it into a 10-inch circle. Gently ease the dough into a 9-inch pie plate and crimp the edges. Prick the bottom of the pie shell 3 to 4 times with a fork.

Combine the cream and evaporated milk in a small saucepan and heat over moderate heat, stirring occasionally, until the mixture begins to bubble around the edge of the pan. Remove from the heat and let cool until lukewarm, 5 to 8 minutes.

Combine the sugars, cinnamon and ginger with the 1/4 teaspoon of cloves and 1/2 teaspoon of salt in a small bowl. Put the eggs in a large bowl and beat at low speed for 1 to 1/2 minutes, until foamy. Gradually beat in the sugar mixture and continue beating on medium speed for 1 1/2 to 2 minutes until the mixture is thick and smooth. Beat in the pumpkin. Beat in the cream mixture on low speed (if a skin has formed on the cream, remove it first). Continue beating for 1 1/2 to 2 minutes, until all the ingredients are well combined. Beat in the Marsala.

Pour the pie filling into the shell and bake for 50 to 60 minutes until the filling is set and the crust is golden brown. Cool the pie on a wire rack.

"What is fall without pumpkin pie? What is Thanksgiving without turkey and pumpkin pie? For some reason, my memories of my childhood in New England center around food, and one of my fondest memories is the trip to the pumpkin farm with my father in the cold, crisp fall air to choose the pumpkin for my Halloween jack o'lantern and the right pumpkins for Mother's pie. We would trudge home, cold and rosy-cheeked, and proudly present the pumpkins to Mother for her approval, and then wait impatiently for the spicy, delectable smells of the pie baking to fill the house. We were never disappointed in the pie— it was always worth waiting for."—
Henry Goodhouse,
Hanover, New Hampshire

TSOUREKI
(GREEK EASTER BREAD)

Makes one 12-inch round braided loaf or two 16-inch braided loaves

2 packages active dry yeast
1 cup milk, scalded and cooled to lukewarm
3 large eggs
¾ cup sugar
8 tablespoons unsalted butter, melted and cooled
1 teaspoon mahlepi, crushed (optional)
1 teaspoon salt
1 teaspoon vanilla extract
½ teaspoon anise extract
5 to 6 cups all-purpose flour
Glaze:
1 egg
2 teaspoons milk or cream
Sesame seeds
2 to 4 hard-cooked red Easter eggs (see note)

Dissolve the yeast in the warm milk in a small bowl. Beat the eggs with the sugar in a large mixing bowl. Pour in the butter, mahlepi, if using, salt, yeast mixture, vanilla and anise and mix well. Gradually beat in 5 cups of the flour.

Turn the dough onto a lightly floured surface and work in enough of the remaining flour to form a soft, not sticky, dough. Knead the dough for 10 minutes, until it is smooth and elastic. Put the dough into a buttered bowl, turning so that it is buttered all over. Cover the bowl and place it in a warm, draft-free place for about 1 1/2 hours, until the dough has doubled in size.

Punch down the dough, transfer it to a lightly floured surface and knead briefly before dividing into the required portions. For 1 large, round loaf, divide the dough into 3 equal portions. Roll each portion into a 30-inch rope. Braid the 3 ropes together, seal the

ends and form into a circle. Gently lay the circle in a buttered 12-by-2 1/3-inch round pan. Press 4 red eggs into the braid, equally spaced.

Prepare the glaze by combining the egg with the milk or cream. Brush the dough with the glaze, cover, and set in a warm place for 1 to 1 1/2 hours, until doubled in size. Brush with more glaze and sprinkle with sesame seeds.

For 2 braided loaves, divide the dough in half. Divide each half into 3 equal pieces. Roll each piece into a 14-inch rope, making the rope thicker in the center and tapering at the ends. Braid the first 3 ropes together and seal the ends. Repeat with the remaining 3 ropes. Gently lay each braid on a buttered baking sheet. Press a red egg into the top of each braid. Prepare the glaze by combining the egg with the milk or cream. Brush each loaf with glaze, cover, and set in a warm place for about 1 hour, until doubled in size. Brush with more glaze and sprinkle with sesame seeds.

Heat the oven to 375 degrees. Bake the large, round loaf for 45 to 55 minutes, the smaller braided loaves for 35 minutes, or until a toothpick inserted in the center comes out clean. Remove the loaves from the pans and cool on a rack.

Note: Red Easter egg dye may be purchased at Greek food markets. Follow the package instructions for deep red-colored eggs.

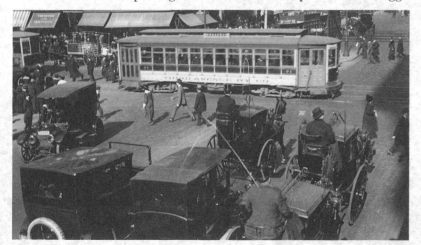

"Winters in Cleveland were always cold and biting when I was a kid. As the first winds kicked up their fury and brought with them snow wet and wild off the lake, Mother would begin holiday baking. She would bake and bake, day after day, often on, through and beyond Christmas. For weeks, she would fill our home with the smells of Greek delicacies and pastries: baklava, kadaife *and* kourabiedes. *Out of the oven would march, in endless procession, crumbly, easy-to-munch treats, layered with phyllo dough, honey and nuts. Best of all, I remember Mother's* tsourekias, *Greek breads which were soft to chew, filled with a subtle sweetness that no matter how hard I try, I cannot to this day duplicate. Mother would knead the dough with her chubby fists, place mountains of it in huge, white, speckled iron pots which she set on radiators to rise…*

"The next morning, I would stuff as many tsourekias *as I could in the pockets of my peacoat. While I was munching on them, I never once felt the chill of the wind blowing through my bones."—* Stephen Michaelides, Cleveland, Ohio

PRESERVES, PICKLES AND CONDIMENTS

Opposite: Rogelach (page 263)
Page following: Hamentaschen (page 265)

Kosher Dill Pickles

Makes 6 quarts

6 pounds (½ peck) 3- to 4-inch pickling cucumbers
1½ quarts water
¼ cup kosher salt
2 cups cider vinegar
¾ teaspoon alum or cream of tartar
1 bunch fresh dill, including seeds
    (if the dill has no seeds, use 1 teaspoon of dill seeds)
6 cloves garlic

Wash six 1-quart jars with soapy water and rinse well. Put the jars in a large saucepan, cover with water and bring to the boil. Boil for 20 minutes, turn off the heat and leave the jars in the water while you make the pickles. Wash, rinse and sterilize the lids in the same way, using a separate pan. Drain the jars and lids before using, so they are dry but still hot.

Scrub the cucumbers thoroughly with a vegetable brush.

Combine the water, salt, vinegar and alum in a large saucepan and bring to the boil.

Pack the cucumbers into the hot, sterilized jars, dividing the fresh dill stalks and seeds evenly among the jars. Split each garlic clove in half and add two halves to each jar. Pour the boiling brine over the cucumbers, leaving a 1/2-inch space at the top. Wipe the rims clean and seal with the sterilized lids. Let the pickles stand for 4 to 6 weeks before opening them. Alternatively, the filled jars may be processed in a water bath following the instructions of a reliable canning manual.

"Every year just before Passover, my parents would take me down to the Lower East Side in New York to choose the fish for gefülte fish, the Passover wine for the Seder, and matzos. For me, the best part of the excursion was the stop at the pickle store, where I was allowed to pick out the largest, juiciest pickle from the huge barrel standing out in front of the store. Then I would munch on the pickle as we walked along the bustling street, dripping the juice down my dress. The wonderful smells and the spicy taste of the pickle were all worth the mess I made!"— Carole Cohen, Merrick, New York

Opposite: Kosher Dill Pickles (page 305)
Page preceding: Marmalade (page 314)

PEPPER RELISH

Makes 3 pints

2 large red peppers, coarsely chopped
2 large green peppers, coarsely chopped
2 large yellow peppers, coarsely chopped
1 onion, coarsely chopped
1 cup cider vinegar
1 cup white vinegar
1½ teaspoons salt
1 cup sugar
3 hot dried pequin peppers
   or 1 teaspoon hot pepper flakes (optional)
1 tablespoon mixed whole pickling spices

Wash three 1-pint jars with soapy water and rinse well. Put the jars in a large saucepan, cover with water and bring to the boil. Boil for 20 minutes, turn off the heat and leave the jars in the water while you make the relish. Wash, rinse and sterilize the lids in the same way, using a separate pan. Drain the jars and lids just before using, so they are dry but still hot.

Put the peppers and onion in a bowl. Cover with boiling water, let stand for 5 minutes and drain in a colander.

Combine the remaining ingredients in a large saucepan and bring to the boil. Add the peppers and onion, lower the heat and simmer for 25 minutes.

Ladle the mixture into the hot, sterilized jars leaving a 1/2-inch space at the top. Wipe the rims clean and seal with the sterilized lids. Alternatively, the filled jars may be processed in a water bath following the instructions of a reliable canning manual.

"This relish was one of many summer canning rituals for my grandmother. And it was a year round delight for the rest of us. This sweet-hot relish can do wonders for cold meat or poultry, scrambled eggs, cream cheese, black-eyed peas or just about anything you put it on. There was always a jar handy for my grandfather at every meal. He loved the stuff. I even saw him put it on green beans, which he otherwise hated.

"Sometimes my grandmother added a few more dried pequins than usual. She said she liked the added punch. My family has always had a hot palate, maybe that's where it came from. But be careful if you try it. Pequins are hot little devils and they'll take the roof off your mouth if you aren't careful."—
Mary Jane Poole,
Roswell, New Mexico

PICCALILLI

Makes 6 pints

1 pound green beans, cut into 1-inch pieces
1 large cauliflower, cut into small florets
½ pound small white onions, peeled
2 medium-size onions, chopped
3 cloves garlic, sliced
4 cups malt vinegar
2 medium-size cucumbers, peeled,
    seeded and cut into 1/2-inch pieces (about 2 cups)
½ cup brown sugar
3 tablespoons pickling spice
5 tablespoons dry mustard
4 tablespoons all-purpose flour
1½ tablespoons turmeric
1 cup sugar
1 tablespoon salt
½ tablespoon pepper

Wash six 1-pint or three 1-quart jars with soapy water and rinse well. Put the jars in a large saucepan, cover with water and bring to the boil. Boil for 20 minutes, turn off the heat and leave the jars in the water while you make the piccalilli. Wash, rinse and sterilize the lids in the same way, using a separate pan. Drain the jars and lids before using, so they are dry but still hot.

Combine the beans, cauliflower, onions, garlic and vinegar in a large saucepan. Bring to the boil over moderate heat, stirring constantly. Add the cucumbers and brown sugar and simmer for 5 minutes.

Put the pickling spice, mustard, flour, turmeric and sugar in a medium-sized bowl and mix well. Gradually spoon about 1 cup of the simmering vinegar into the dry ingredients, stirring constantly to prevent lumping. Stir in a second cup of vinegar and pour the mixture back into the saucepan. Simmer for 3 minutes, stirring occasionally. Stir in the salt and pepper.

"When I was a kid we lived in north New Jersey and often spent summer weekends down at the shore. On the way home we would usually stop at a farm stand and pick up a peck of tomatoes, a couple of melons, some of that fabulous corn on the cob for which New Jersey can't be beat, and whatever other irrisistible summertime produce they were featuring that day. On one of these weekends my mother would take along her piccalilli recipe and buy vegetables to order for it; she seemed to have a genius for picking the hottest weekend of the year, because by the time we got home and the canning jars had been boiling for awhile the kitchen resembled nothing so much as a Turkish bath. But no matter— a double or triple batch of piccalilli would last us most of the remaining year, and it made something special out of many a routine supper."—
Allan Litvak,
San Diego, California

Spoon the solids into the hot, sterilized jars. Pour the liquid into the jars, leaving a 1/2-inch space at the top. Wipe the rims clean and seal with the sterilized lids. Alternatively, the filled jars may be processed in a water bath following the instructions of a reliable canning manual. When cool, store the piccalilli in a cool place for at least 2 months before serving.

≋ PICKLED BEETS ≋

Makes 5 pints

4 ½ pounds (10 cups) beets, cooked, peeled
   and sliced or quartered, cooking water reserved
2 cups cider vinegar
1 cup white vinegar
¾ cup sugar
5 bay leaves
20 black peppercorns
10 cloves
1 onion, chopped

Wash five 1-pint jars with soapy water and rinse well. Put the jars in a large saucepan, cover with water and bring to the boil. Boil for 20 minutes, turn off the heat and leave the jars in the water while you make the beets. Wash, rinse and sterilize the lids in the same way, using a separate pan. Drain the jars and lids before using, so they are dry but still hot.

Combine 1 cup of the beet cooking water with the vinegars, sugar, bay leaves, peppercorns and cloves. Bring to the boil.

Pack the hot, sterilized jars with the beets. Divide the chopped onion among the jars. Pour the boiling liquid over the beets, leaving a 1/2-inch space at the top, dividing the spices equally among the jars. Wipe the rims clean and seal with the sterilized lids. Alternatively, the filled jars may be processed in a water bath following the instructions of a reliable canning manual.

"Pickling was always something my dad like to do. It was a hobby for him. He loved his little garden plot in the city and started his plantings in the spring with the state fair in mind.

"Although he won ribbons for many different foods, he won more for his beets than anything else. They were always a deep garnet color, perfect in size and texture. He became somewhat a legend for his beets, in fact. Now, I know that one recipe for pickled beets is about the same as the other, but there was just something he did that made them as good as they could be.

"I asked him his secret once, and frankly he couldn't tell me. I don't think he was holding anything back. It's just something he said he enjoyed doing and was good at. Maybe that was his secret." — Amy Ver Hass, Kansas City, Kansas

Green Tomato Mincemeat

Makes 10 pints

6 pounds green tomatoes
2 pounds tart apples
2 cups raisins
4 cups packed brown sugar
2 cups strong coffee
Juice and grated rind of 1 lemon
2 teaspoons grated orange rind
½ cup red wine
1 teaspoon salt
1 teaspoon ground nutmeg
1 teaspoon ground allspice

Core and quarter the tomatoes and apples. Put them in a food processor with the raisins and process briefly until coarsely chopped. Combine these with the rest of the ingredients in a large saucepan. Bring to the boil and simmer for 2 hours, uncovered, stirring frequently.

Meanwhile, wash 10 1-pint jars in soapy water and rinse well. Put the jars in a large saucepan, cover with water and bring to the boil. Boil for 20 minutes, turn off the heat and leave the jars in the water while you finish simmering the mincemeat. Wash, rinse and sterilize the lids in the same way, using a separate pan. Drain the jars and lids just before using, so that they are still hot.

At the end of the simmering time, pack the mincemeat into the hot jars, leaving a 1/2-inch space at the top. Wipe the rims clean and seal with the sterilized lids. Alternatively, the filled jars may be processed in a water bath following the instructions of a reliable canning manual.

"My most vivid and sentimental memories of my early days in the kitchen were with my Dutch grandmother Koster during the holidays. The family would arrive early at her ranch and, while most of the relatives played games or took walks, I felt honored that Grandma let me help her prepare the feast. The kitchen was small and not all the grandchildren were allowed to help, so I paid rapt attention to the lessons and felt immensely proud that this 'master chef' chose me to take part.

"Among my favorites were the accompaniments to the traditional holiday fare, such as brandied, spiced figs made with figs from Grandma's own trees and green tomato mincemeat, which used the end-of-season tomatoes. To this day, I always feel more comfortable in the kitchen than in the dining room."—
Vicki Sebastiani,
Sonoma, California

GREEN TOMATO PICKLES

Makes 2 quarts

3 pounds green tomatoes, washed and thinly sliced
2 onions, thinly sliced
3 green peppers, thinly sliced
6 tablespoons salt
5 cups sugar
3 cups cider vinegar
3 teaspoons mustard seeds
3 teaspoons whole cloves
3 teaspoons black peppercorns
3 teaspoons allspice berries
2 teaspoons celery seeds (optional)
2½ teaspoons cinnamon

Combine the tomatoes, onions and peppers in a large bowl. Cover with salt and let stand for 8 to 12 hours.

Wash four 1-pint or two 1-quart jars with soapy water and rinse well. Put the jars in a large saucepan, cover with water and bring to the boil. Boil for 20 minutes, turn off the heat and leave the jars in the water while you finish making the pickles. Wash, rinse and sterilize the lids in the same way, using a separate pan. Drain the jars and lids before using, so they are dry but still hot.

Drain the tomatoes, onions and peppers and rinse thoroughly under cold running water. Combine the sugar, vinegar and spices in a large saucepan and bring to the boil. Add the tomatoes, onions and peppers, return to the boil and simmer for about 20 minutes or until the tomatoes are transparent.

Pack the mixture into the hot, sterilized jars, dividing the spices evenly between the jars and leaving a 1/2-inch space at the top of each jar. Wipe the rims clean and seal with the sterilized lids.

Alternatively, the filled jars may be processed in a water bath following the instructions of a reliable canning manual.

To make a relish, chop the tomatoes, onion and peppers coarsely rather than slicing them, and prepare in the same way.

MANGO CHUTNEY

Makes about 2 cups

1 firm, ripe mango, peeled and chopped
1 teaspoon finely chopped ginger
1 scallion, thinly sliced
2 tablespoons lime juice
2 teaspoons sugar
1 tablespoon finely chopped fresh mint

Combine the chopped mango with the ginger, scallion, lime juice and sugar. Toss gently and let sit for 15 minutes. Sprinkle with mint and toss just before serving. The chutney may be stored in the refrigerator for up to 5 days.

*"My grandparents, who had grown up and raised their children in the Bronx, retired to Florida back when that was a fairly unusual thing to do. They bought a stucco bungalow within walking distance of the Gulf and proceeded to run amok growing mangos, papayas, Key limes and every other kind of tropical exotic they could get their hands on; some of my earliest gastromic memories are of devouring home-grown mangoes, the juice running down my arms, and of stirring up the creamy filling for Key Lime pies. Though Grandma was pretty much a meat-and-potatoes cook, she was forced to get creative in order to find uses for her backyard bounty. I don't know where she discovered her recipe for mango chutney, but it made a hit with the family and she often served it as a relish with the Sunday roast. Where she got the ginger I haven't a clue— but then Grandma could be pretty resourceful."—
Sarah Lefton,
Poughkeepsie, New York*

HAKUSAI NO TSUKEMONO
(HOT PICKLED CABBAGE)

Makes 2 quarts

3 pounds Chinese cabbage
3 to 4 teaspoons salt
3 to 4 small hot red peppers (togarashi), or more to taste
Soy sauce, for serving

Remove any discolored or bruised leaves from the cabbage and set them aside. Wash the cabbage and cut lengthwise into 2-inch wedges. Sprinkle the wedges with half the salt and layer with the peppers in a 2-gallon crock. Cover the cabbage with the reserved leaves, sprinkle with the remaining salt and lay a clean plate on top. Put weights (food cans or a gallon jug filled with water) totaling about 10 pounds on the plate, cover with a clean cloth and leave the cabbage to drain for about 8 hours.

When the cabbage has given off enough moisture to cover the plate, reduce the weight to about 5 pounds (if you are using the jug filled with water, pour off half the water) and allow the cabbage to cure in the brine for up to 24 hours longer. At this point, refrigerate the pickles in their brine. They may be kept for at least 2 weeks, during which time they will continue to ferment.

Just before serving the pickles, rinse them under cold water and gently squeeze out the excess moisture. Cut the wedges into 1-inch pieces and serve sprinkled with soy sauce.

≋ Red Currant Jelly ≋

Makes about 4 pints

4 quarts ripe red currants
Sugar

Wash and drain the currants. Put them in a large, heavy saucepan over low heat, crushing the bottom layer to prevent burning. Cook the currants, uncovered, until they begin to soften and yield liquid. Increase the heat to moderate and continue to cook until the currants are soft and colorless. Drain the fruit overnight through a wet, wrung-out jelly bag.

Wash four 1-pint jars with soapy water and rinse well. Put the jars in a large saucepan, cover with water and bring to the boil. Boil for 20 minutes, turn off the heat and leave the jars in the water while you finish making the jelly. Wash, rinse and sterilize the lids in the same way, using a separate pan. Drain the jars and lids before using, so they are dry but still hot.

Measure the fruit juice and pour it into a stainless steel or enamel pan. Add 1 cup sugar for every cup of juice. Do not cook more than 4 cups of juice at a time. Bring to the boil, stirring until the sugar dissolves. Simmer for 10 to 15 minutes or until a jelly thermometer registers 220 degrees. Skim the surface and pour into the hot, sterilized jars, leaving a 1/2-inch space. Wipe the rims clean and seal with the sterilized lids. The filled jars may also be processed in a water bath following the instructions of a reliable canning manual.

"My mother is an unstoppable gardener. But, despite her reluctance to stop gardening long enough to make jelly, she was forced to reconsider when her currant bushes on Martha's Vineyard overflowed. She used a large, wide copper pot, knowing how boiling jelly tends to roil and expand unbelievably, boiling over and making a mess on the stove unless the pot is really ample. First, she cooked the fruit over low heat until the color was almost entirely drawn out. Having no jelly bag, she improvised with a large strainer and an old damask napkin. She let the juice drip through the strainer and the napkin and then poured the juice back into the pot to be boiled and skimmed, and boiled again. Only then did she begin testing for jelling. With a cold spoon, she spooned up a small amount of jelly, let it cool a little and then dripped it from the side of the spoon until the syrup was thick enough for two drops to join and fall as a single large drop. When this occurred the jelly was poured into ready-sterilized glasses."—
Elizabeth S. Schneider,
New York, New York

MARMALADE

Makes 5 pints

2½ pounds oranges (bitter, if you can find them)
10 cups water
8 cups sugar

Using a vegetable peeler, carefully peel off the colored part of the orange rind, making sure you do not include any of the white pith. Cut the rind into julienne strips.

Squeeze the juice from the oranges into a large saucepan, reserving the pulp and seeds. Put the remaining orange flesh, together with the pulp and seeds, on a piece of muslin or a triple thickness of cheesecloth and tie tightly with string to make a small bag. Add this to the pan of orange juice along with the water and the julienned peel. Bring to the boil and skim the surface. Lower the heat and simmer gently, uncovered, for 2 hours.

Wash five 1-pint jars with soapy water and rinse well. Put the jars in a large saucepan, cover with water and bring to the boil. Boil for 20 minutes, turn off the heat and leave the jars in the water while you finish making the marmalade. Wash, rinse and sterilize the lids in the same way, using a separate pan. Drain the jars and lids before using, so they are dry but still hot.

Transfer the bag of orange pulp to a plate. Add the sugar to the pan and stir over low heat until completely dissolved. Squeeze all the juice from the muslin bag into the pan. Bring to the boil and cook, uncovered, for 20 minutes.

Spoon a little of the marmalade onto a saucer, chill in the refrigerator and then gently push the edge of the marmalade with your finger. If the skin crinkles, the marmalade is ready. If not, continue boiling for another 5 minutes and repeat the test, boiling the marmalade until the chilled spoonful sets. Alternatively, test the marmalade with a jelly thermometer— it should register 220 degrees.

"When I was little, the great event that followed Christmas was marmalade-making time, when for a couple of late January weeks the Cambridge greengrocers' shops were filled with crates of bitter Seville oranges.

"The local housewives, my mother among them, took turns hiring Eaden Lilley's orange slicing machine— a glorified meat grinder that screwed onto the kitchen table. As we cranked its knife handle, wafer-thin orange slices fell in a golden torrent into our huge enamel bread bin, there to be covered with water and left to steep overnight.

"The real fun came the next day: pouring mountains of preserving sugar out of their big blue-paper bags into the wide pan set on the cooker top and engulfing them with floods of orange mixture. Standing on a chair beside the cooker, I stirred away with my wooden spoon until the mountains became sediments and finally dissolved into the steaming Seville sea.

"I also served as tester and consumer of countless samples of the thickening tawny syrup, and took pride in neatly

Pour the marmalade into the hot, sterilized jars, leaving a 1/2-inch space at the top. Wipe the rims clean and seal with the sterilized lids. Alternatively, the filled jars may be processed in a water bath following the instructions of a reliable canning manual.

APPLE BUTTER

Makes 3 pints

5 pounds apples, peeled, cored and sliced
2 cups apple cider
½ cup packed brown sugar
2 teaspoons cinnamon
½ teaspoon ground nutmeg

Combine the apples and cider in a large saucepan. Cook over moderate heat until the apples are very soft. Cool slightly and puree in a food processor or food mill.

Return the apple puree to the saucepan. Add the sugar and spices. Cook, stirring occasionally, over low heat for 2 to 3 hours, until the mixture is dark brown and very thick.

Meanwhile, wash six 1/2-pint jars with soapy water and rinse well. Put the jars in a large saucepan, cover with water and bring to the boil. Boil for 20 minutes, turn off the heat and leave the jars in the water while you finish the apple butter. Wash, rinse and sterilize the lids in the same way, using a separate pan. Drain the jars and lids before using, so they are dry but still hot

Ladle the hot butter into the prepared jars, leaving a 1/2-inch space at the top. Wipe the rims clean and seal with the sterilized lids. Alternatively, the filled jars may be processed in a water bath following the instructions of a reliable canning manual.

sealing cellophane tops on the ranks of filled jars.

"But the best part of all was the fragrant, bittersweet scent that filled our house in that distant, special time; thinking of it, I can smell it still."— Jean Atcheson, Princeton Junction, New Jersey

"The first time I ever ate apple butter was at summer camp in the Berkshires. I was a very nervous first-year camper and the huge 'mess hall' (dining-room) at the camp, with all the children singing, yelling, or stamping their feet, terrified me. The meal was alien to me too— typical New England fare— I was from Long Island. My bunkmate, also a first-year camper, whispered to me to try the apple butter, served in a small, white pottery bowl. I followed her lead and smeared some on a big slab of bread. The texture and taste were surprisingly good and I reached for more, smiling at my new friends and beginning to enjoy myself. I still love apple butter and now I have beautiful memories of my summers at camp."—
Rose Schimmel,
Orlando, Florida

≋ STRAWBERRY JAM ≋

Makes 2 pints

2 quarts (8 cups) strawberries, washed and hulled
4 cups sugar

Lightly crush half the berries and put them, together with the whole berries, in a large saucepan. Add the sugar and bring to a simmer over moderate heat without stirring until a syrup forms. Simmer, stirring occasionally, for 1 to 2 hours or until a jelly thermometer registers 220 degrees.

Wash four 1/2-pint jars with soapy water and rinse well. Put the jars in a large saucepan, cover with water and bring to the boil. Boil for 20 minutes, turn off the heat and leave the jars in the water while you finish making the jam. Wash, rinse and sterilize the lids in the same way, using a separate pan. Drain the jars and lids before using, so they are dry but still hot.

Remove the jam from the heat and skim any foam from the surface. Ladle the jam into the hot, sterilized jars, leaving a 1/2-inch space at the top. Wipe the rims clean and seal with the sterilized lids. Alternatively, the filled jars may be processed in a water bath, following the instructions of a reliable canning manual. Let the jars cool undisturbed before storing.

Index

Illustrations

 Conversion Tables

The cup and spoon measures given in the book are U.S. Customary (cup = 235 mL; 1 tablespoon = 15 mL). Use these tables when working with British Imperial or Metric kitchen utensils.

LIQUID MEASURES

The Imperial pint is larger than the U.S. pint; therefore note the following when measuring liquid ingredients.

U.S.	IMPERIAL
1 cup = 8 fluid ounces	1 cup = 10 fluid ounces
½ cup = 4 fluid ounces	½ cup = 5 fluid ounces
1 tablespoon = ¾ fluid ounce	1 tablespoon = 1 fluid ounce

U.S. MEASURE	METRIC*	IMPERIAL*
1 quart (4 cups)	950 mL	1½ pints + 4 tablespoons
1 pint (2 cups)	450 mL	¾ pint
1 cup	236 mL	¼ pint + 6 tablespoons
1 tablespoon	15 mL	1 + tablespoon
1 teaspoon	5 mL	1 teaspoon

*Note that exact quantities are not always given. Differences are more crucial when dealing with larger quantities. For teaspoon and tablespoon measures, simply use scant or generous quantities; or for more accurate conversions rely upon metric.

SOLID MEASURES

Outside the U.S., cooks measure more items by weight. Here are approximate equivalents for basic items in this book.*

	U.S. CUSTOMARY	METRIC	IMPERIAL
Beans (dried, raw)	1 cup	225g	8 ounces
Butter	1 cup	225g	8 ounces
	½ cup	115g	4 ounces
	¼ cup	60g	2 ounces
	1 tablespoon	15g	½ ounce
Cheese (grated)	1 cup	115g	4 ounces
Coconut (shredded)	½ cup	60g	2 ounces
Fruit (chopped)	1 cup	225g	8 ounces
Herbs (chopped)	¼ cup	7g	¼ ounce
Mushrooms (chopped)	1 cup	70g	2½ ounces
Nut Meats (chopped)	1 cup	115g	4 ounces
Pasta (dried, raw)	1 cup	225g	8 ounces
Peas (shelled)	1 cup	225g	8 ounces
Raisins (and other)	1 cup	175g	6 ounces
Rice (uncooked)	1 cup	225g	8 ounces
(cooked)	3 cups	225g	8 ounces
Spinach (cooked)	½ cups	285g	10 ounces
Vegetables (chopped)	1 cup	115g	4 ounces

*To avoid awkward measurements, some conversions are not exact.

DRY MEASURES

The following items are measured by weight outside of the U.S.. These items are variable, especially flour, depending on individual variety of flour and moisture. American cup measurements on following items, are loosely packed, flour is measured directly from package (presifted).

	U.S. CUSTOMARY	METRIC	IMPERIAL
Flour (all-purpose)	1 cup	150g	5 ounces
	½ cup	70g	2½ ounces
Cornmeal	1 cup	175g	6 ounces
Sugar (granulated)	1 cup	190g	6½ ounces
	½ cup	85g	3 ounces
	¼ cup	40g	1¾ ounces
(powdered)	1 cup	80g	2⅔ ounces
	½ cup	40g	1⅓ ounces
	¼ cup	20g	¾ ounces
(brown)	1 cup	160g	5⅓ ounces
	½ cup	80g	2⅔ ounces
	¼ cup	40g	1⅓ ounces

Oven Temperatures

Gas Mark	1/4	2	4	6	8
Fahrenheit	225°	300°	350°	400°	450°
Celsius	110°	150°	180°	200°	230°